Honda XR250/400 Owners Workshop Manual

by Alan Ahlstrand and John H Haynes

Member of the Guild of Motoring Writers

Models covered:
XR250L, 1991 through 1996
XR250R, 1986 through 2004
XR400R, 1996 through 2004

(2219 - 3S4)

AB

Haynes Publishing
Sparkford Nr Yeovil
Somerset BA22 7JJ England

Haynes North America, Inc
859 Lawrence Drive
Newbury Park
California 91320 USA
www.haynes.com

Acknowledgments

Our thanks to G.P. Sports, Santa Clara, California, for providing the XR250L and XR400R used in these photographs, to Honda of Milpitas, Milpitas, California, for providing the XR250R and to Thousand Oaks Honda for supplying the bike for the cover photo. Our thanks also to Chris Campbell, service manager at G.P. Sports, and Pete Sirett, service manager at Honda of Milpitas, for arranging the facilities and fitting the mechanical work into their shops' busy schedules. Craig Wardner at G.P. Sports and Bruce Farley at Honda of Milpitas, the technicians who did the mechanical work, deserve special mention both for their extensive knowledge and for their ability to explain things.

A book in the Haynes Owners Workshop Manual Series

Printed in Malaysia

ISBN-13: 978-1-62092-096-1
ISBN-10: 1-62092-096-4

Library of Congress Control Number: 2014936083

We take great pride in the accuracy of information given in this manual, but motorcycle manufacturers make alterations and design changes during the production run of a particular motorcycle of which they do not inform us. No liability can be accepted by the authors or publishers for loss, damage or injury caused by any errors in, or omissions from, the information given.

Contents

1997 Honda XR250R

About this manual

Its purpose

The purpose of this manual is to help you get the best value from your motorcycle. It can do so in several ways. It can help you decide what work must be done, even if you choose to have it done by a dealer service department or a repair shop; it provides information and procedures for routine maintenance and servicing; and it offers diagnostic and repair procedures to follow when trouble occurs.

We hope you use the manual to tackle the work yourself. For many simpler jobs, doing it yourself may be quicker than arranging an appointment to get the vehicle into a shop and making the trips to leave it and pick it up. More importantly, a lot of money can be saved by avoiding the expense the shop must pass on to you to cover its labor and overhead costs. An added benefit is the sense of satisfaction and accomplishment that you feel after doing the job yourself.

Using the manual

The manual is divided into Chapters. Each Chapter is divided into numbered Sections, which are headed in bold type between horizontal lines. Each Section consists of consecutively numbered paragraphs or steps.

At the beginning of each numbered Section you will be referred to any illustrations which apply to the procedures in that Section. The reference numbers used in illustration captions pinpoint the pertinent Section and the Step within that Section. That is, illustration 3.2 means the illustration refers to Section 3 and Step (or paragraph) 2 within that Section.

Procedures, once described in the text, are not normally repeated. When it's necessary to refer to another Chapter, the reference will be given as Chapter and Section number. Cross references given without use of the word 'Chapter' apply to Sections and/or paragraphs in the same Chapter. For example, 'see Section 8' means in the same Chapter.

References to the left or right side of the vehicle assume you are sitting on the seat, facing forward.

Motorcycle manufacturers continually make changes to specifications and recommendations, and these, when notified, are incorporated into our manuals at the earliest opportunity.

Even though we have prepared this manual with extreme care, neither the publisher nor the authors can accept responsibility for any errors in, or omissions from, the information given.

NOTE

A **Note** provides information necessary to properly complete a procedure or information which will make the procedure easier to understand.

CAUTION

A **Caution** provides a special procedure or special steps which must be taken while completing the procedure where the Caution is found. Not heeding a Caution can result in damage to the assembly being worked on.

WARNING

A **Warning** provides a special procedure or special steps which must be taken while completing the procedure where the Warning is found. Not heeding a Warning can result in personal injury.

Introduction to the Honda XR250/400

The XR250R and its street-legal version, the XR250L, are highly popular and successful middleweight trail bikes. The XR400R, with its light weight and larger engine, has been enthusiastically received.

The engine on all models is an air-cooled single with an overhead camshaft, employing Honda's Radial Four-Valve Combustion (RFVC) valve arrangement. Power is transmitted through a six-speed transmission on 250 models and a five-speed on 400s. All models use a wet multi-plate clutch and chain final drive.

Fuel is delivered to the cylinder by a slide-type carburetor.

The front suspension consists of telescopic forks mounted in upper and lower triple clamps. The rear suspension on all models uses a single shock absorber/coil spring unit and Honda's Pro-Link progressive rising rate suspension linkage. A disc brake is used at the front on all models. Early models used a drum brake at the rear; later models use a disc brake.

Identification numbers

The frame serial number is stamped into the front of the frame **(see illustration)** and printed on a label affixed to the frame. The engine number is stamped into the left side of the crankcase **(see illustration)**. Both of these numbers should be recorded and kept in a safe place so they can be furnished to law enforcement officials in the event of a theft.

The frame serial number, engine serial number and carburetor identification number should also be kept in a handy place (such as with your driver's license) so they are always available when purchasing or ordering parts for your machine.

The models covered by this manual are as follows:

XR250L, 1991 through 1996
XR250R, 1986 through 2004
XR400R, 1996 through 2004

Identifying models and years

XR250L

Engine code	MD17E
Initial frame number	
1991 (except California)	MD220*MK000003
1991 (California)	MD221*MK000004
1992 (except California)	MD220*NM100005
1992 (California)	MD221*NM100002
1993 (except California)	MD220*PM200004
1993 (California)	MD221*PM000002
1994 (except California)	MD220*RM300001
1994 (California)	MD221*RM300001
1995 (except California)	MD220*SM400001
1995 (California)	MD221*SM400001
1996 (except California)	MD220*TM500001
1996 (California)	MD221*TM500001

XR250R

Engine code	
1986 through 1995	ME06E
1996 on	ME08E
Initial frame number	
1986	ME060*GK200014
1987	ME060*HK300002
1988	ME060*JK400001
1989	ME060*KK500001
1990	ME060*LK600003
1991	ME060*MK700001
1992	ME060*NM800004
1993	ME060*PM900001
1994	ME060*RM000001
1995	Not available
1996	ME080*TM800001
1997	ME080*VM000001
1998	
Non-California	ME080*WK300001 to 300522 or WM100001 to 100877
California	ME081*WM100001 to 100182 or WK300001 to 300044
1999	
Non-California	ME080*XK400001 on
California	ME081*XK400001 on
2000	
Non-California	ME080*XK500001 on
California	ME081*XK500001 on
2001	
Non-California	ME080*1K600001 on
California	ME081*1K600001 on
2002	
Non-California	JH2ME080*27K00001
California	JH2ME081*27K00001
2003	
Non-California	JH2ME080*3M800001
California	JH2ME081*3M800001

The frame serial number is located at the front of the frame

The engine serial number is located on the left side of the crankcase

2004	
Non-California	JH2ME080*4K900001
California	JH2ME081*4K900001

XR400R

Engine code	NE03E
Initial frame number	
1996	NE030*TM000001
1997	JH2NE303*VM
1998	
Non-California	NE030*WK300001 on or WM200001 to 200158
California	NE031* WK300001 on or WM200001 to 200158
1999	
Non-California	NE030*XK400001 on
California	NE031*XK400001 on
2000	
Non-California	NE030*XK500001 on
California	NE031*XK500001 on
2001	
Non-California	NE030*1K600001 on
California	NE031*1K600001 on
2002	
Non-California	JHN2E030*27K00001
California	JHN2E031*27K00001
2003	
Non-California	JHN2E030*3M800001
California	JHN2E031*3M800001
2004	
Non-California	JH2NE030*4M900001
California	JH2NE031*4M900001

General specifications

Bore
    XR250L, XR250R .... 73.0 mm (2.87 inches)
    XR400R .... 85.0 mm (3.35 inches)
Stroke
    XR250L, XR250R .... 59.5 mm (2.34 inches)
    XR400R .... 70.0 mm (2.76 inches)
Compression ratio
    XR250L, XR400R .... 9.3 to 1
    XR250R .... 10.2 to 1
Wheelbase
    XR250L .... 1430 mm (56.3 inches)
    XR250R
        1986 through 1991 .... 1424 mm (56.1 inches)
        1992 through 1995 .... 1415 mm (55.7 inches)
        1996 on .... 1400 mm (55.1 inches)
    XR400R .... 1425 mm (56.1 inches)
Overall length
    XR250L .... 2160 mm (85.0 inches)
    XR250R
        1986 through 1991 .... 2100 mm (82.7 inches)
        1992 through 1995 .... 2110 mm (83.1 inches)
        1996 on .... 2120 mm (83.5 inches)
    XR400R .... 2130 mm (83.9 inches)
Overall width
    XR250L .... 860 mm (33.9 inches)
    XR250R
        1986 through 1991 .... 910 mm (35.8 inches)
        1992 through 1995 .... 900 mm (35.4 inches)
        1996 on .... 830 mm (32.7 inches)
    XR400R .... 840 mm (33.1 inches)
Overall height
    XR250L .... 1220 mm (48.0 inches)
    XR250R
        1986 through 1991 .... 1226 mm (48.3 inches)
        1992 through 1995 .... 1220 mm (48.0 inches)
        1996 on .... 1225 mm (48.2 inches)
    XR400R .... 1240 mm (48.8 inches)
Seat height
    XR250L .... 885 mm (34.8 inches)
    XR250R
        1986 through 1995 .... 925 mm (36.4 inches)
        1996 on .... 915 mm (36.0 inches)
    XR400R .... 930 mm (36.6 inches)
Ground clearance
    XR250L .... 285 mm (11.2 inches)
    XR250R
        1986 through 1991 .... 326 mm (12.8 inches)
        1992 through 1995 .... 325 mm (12.8 inches)
        1996 on .... 305 mm (12.0 inches)
    XR400R .... 310 mm (12.2 inches)
Dry weight
    XR250L
        1991 and 1992 .... 118 kg (260.1 lbs)
        1993 through 1996 .... 122.6 kg (269.7 lbs)
    XR250R
        1986 through 1991 .... 108.6 kg (239.4 lbs)
        1992 through 1995 .... 108 kg (238.1 lbs)
        1996 on .... 104 kg (229.3 lbs)
    XR400R .... 116.5 kg (276 lbs)

Buying parts

Once you have found all the identification numbers, record them for reference when buying parts. Since the manufacturers change specifications, parts and vendors (companies that manufacture various components on the machine), providing the ID numbers is the only way to be reasonably sure that you are buying the correct parts.

Whenever possible, take the worn part to the dealer so direct comparison with the new component can be made. Along the trail from the manufacturer to the parts shelf, there are numerous places that the part can end up with the wrong number or be listed incorrectly.

The two places to purchase new parts for your motorcycle - the accessory store and the franchised dealer - differ in the type of parts they carry. While dealers can obtain virtually every part for your motor-cycle, the accessory dealer is usually limited to normal high wear items such as shock absorbers, tune-up parts, various engine gaskets, cables, chains, brake parts, etc. Rarely will an accessory outlet have major suspension components, cylinders, transmission gears, or cases.

Used parts can be obtained for roughly half the price of new ones, but you can't always be sure of what you're getting. Once again, take your worn part to the wrecking yard (breaker) for direct comparison.

Whether buying new, used or rebuilt parts, the best course is to deal directly with someone who specializes in parts for your particular make.

Maintenance techniques, tools and working facilities

Basic maintenance techniques

There are a number of techniques involved in maintenance and repair that will be referred to throughout this manual. Application of these techniques will enable the amateur mechanic to be more efficient, better organized and capable of performing the various tasks properly, which will ensure that the repair job is thorough and complete.

Fastening systems

Fasteners, basically, are nuts, bolts and screws used to hold two or more parts together. There are a few things to keep in mind when working with fasteners. Almost all of them use a locking device of some type (either a lock washer, locknut, locking tab or thread adhesive). All threaded fasteners should be clean, straight, have undamaged threads and undamaged corners on the hex head where the wrench fits. Develop the habit of replacing all damaged nuts and bolts with new ones.

Rusted nuts and bolts should be treated with a penetrating oil to ease removal and prevent breakage. Some mechanics use turpentine in a spout type oil can, which works quite well. After applying the rust penetrant, let it -work for a few minutes before trying to loosen the nut or bolt. Badly rusted fasteners may have to be chiseled off or removed with a special nut breaker, available at tool stores.

If a bolt or stud breaks off in an assembly, it can be drilled out and removed with a special tool called an E-Z out (or screw extractor). Most dealer service departments and motorcycle repair shops can perform this task, as well as others (such as the repair of threaded holes that have been stripped out).

Flat washers and lock washers, when removed from an assembly, should always be replaced exactly as removed. Replace any damaged washers with new ones. Always use a flat washer between a lock washer and any soft metal surface (such as aluminum), thin sheet metal or plastic. Special locknuts can only be used once or twice before they lose their locking ability and must be replaced.

Tightening sequences and procedures

When threaded fasteners are tightened, they are often tightened to a specific torque value (torque is basically a twisting force). Over-tightening the fastener can weaken it and cause it to break, while under-tightening can cause it to eventually come loose. Each bolt, depending on the material it's made of, the diameter of its shank and the material it is threaded into, has a specific torque value, which is noted in the Specifications. Be sure to follow the torque recommendations closely.

Fasteners laid out in a pattern (i.e. cylinder head bolts, engine case bolts, etc.) must be loosened or tightened in a sequence to avoid warping the component. Initially, the bolts/nuts should go on finger tight only. Next, they should be tightened one full turn each, in a criss-cross or diagonal pattern. After each one has been tightened one full turn, return to the first one tightened and tighten them all one half turn, following the same pattern. Finally, tighten each of them one quarter turn at a time until each fastener has been tightened to the proper torque. To loosen and remove the fasteners the procedure would be reversed.

Disassembly sequence

Component disassembly should be done with care and purpose to help ensure that the parts go back together properly during reassembly. Always keep track of the sequence in which parts are removed. Take note of special characteristics or marks on parts that can be installed more than one way (such as a grooved thrust washer on a shaft). It's a good idea to lay the disassembled parts out on a clean surface in the order that they were removed. It may also be helpful to make sketches or take instant photos of components before removal.

When removing fasteners from a component, keep track of their locations. Sometimes threading a bolt back in a part, or putting the washers and nut back on a stud, can prevent mix-ups later. If nuts and bolts can't be returned to their original locations, they should be kept in a compartmented box or a series of small boxes. A cupcake or muffin tin is ideal for this purpose, since each cavity can hold the bolts and nuts from a particular area (i.e. engine case bolts, valve cover bolts, engine mount bolts, etc.). A pan of this type is especially helpful when working on assemblies with very small parts (such as the carburetors and the valve train). The cavities can be marked with paint or tape to identify the contents.

Whenever wiring looms, harnesses or connectors are separated, it's a good idea to identify the two halves with numbered pieces of masking tape so they can be easily reconnected.

Gasket sealing surfaces

Throughout any motorcycle, gaskets are used to seal the mating surfaces between components and keep lubricants, fluids, vacuum or pressure contained in an assembly.

Many times these gaskets are coated with a liquid or paste type gasket sealing compound before assembly. Age, heat and pressure can sometimes cause the two parts to stick together so tightly that they are very difficult to separate. In most cases, the part can be loosened by striking it with a soft-faced hammer near the mating surfaces. A regular hammer can be used if a block of wood is placed between the hammer and the part. Do not hammer on cast parts or parts that could be easily damaged. With any particularly stubborn part, always recheck to make sure that every fastener has been removed.

Spark plug gap adjusting tool

Feeler gauge set

Control cable pressure luber

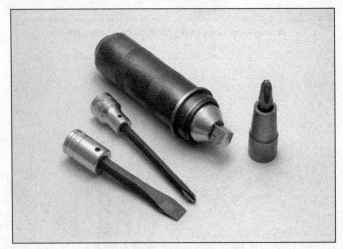

Hand impact screwdriver and bits

Avoid using a screwdriver or bar to pry apart components, as they can easily mar the gasket sealing surfaces of the parts (which must remain smooth). If prying is absolutely necessary, use a piece of wood, but keep in mind that extra clean-up will be necessary if the wood splinters.

After the parts are separated, the old gasket must be carefully scraped off and the gasket surfaces cleaned. Stubborn gasket material can be soaked with a gasket remover (available in aerosol cans) to soften it so it can be easily scraped off. A scraper can be fashioned from a piece of copper tubing by flattening and sharpening one end. Copper is recommended because it is usually softer than the surfaces to be scraped, which reduces the chance of gouging the part. Some gaskets can be removed with a wire brush, but regardless of the method used, the mating surfaces must be left clean and smooth. If for some reason the gasket surface is gouged, then a gasket sealer thick enough to fill scratches will have to be used during reassembly of the components. For most applications, a non-drying (or semi-drying) gasket sealer is best.

Hose removal tips

Hose removal precautions closely parallel gasket removal precautions. Avoid scratching or gouging the surface that the hose mates against or the connection may leak. Because of various chemical reactions, the rubber in hoses can bond itself to the metal spigot that the hose fits over. To remove a hose, first loosen the hose clamps that secure it to the spigot. Then, with slip joint pliers, grab the hose at the clamp and rotate it around the spigot. Work it back and forth until it is completely free, then pull it off (silicone or other lubricants will ease removal if they can be applied between the hose and the outside of the spigot). Apply the same lubricant to the inside of the hose and the outside of the spigot to simplify installation.

If a hose clamp is broken or damaged, do not reuse it. Also, do not reuse hoses that are cracked, split or torn.

Tools

A selection of good tools is a basic requirement for anyone who plans to maintain and repair a motorcycle. For the owner who has few tools, if any, the initial investment might seem high, but when compared to the spiraling costs of routine maintenance and repair, it is a wise one.

To help the owner decide which tools are needed to perform the tasks detailed in this manual, the following tool lists are offered: *Maintenance and minor repair, Repair and overhaul* and *Special*. The newcomer to practical mechanics should start off with the *Maintenance and minor repair* tool kit, which is adequate for the simpler jobs. Then, as confidence and experience grow, the owner can tackle more difficult tasks, buying additional tools as they are needed. Eventually the basic kit will be built into the *Repair and overhaul* tool set. Over a period of time, the experienced do-it-yourselfer will assemble a tool set complete enough for most repair and overhaul procedures and will add tools from the *Special* category when it is felt that the expense is justified by the frequency of use.

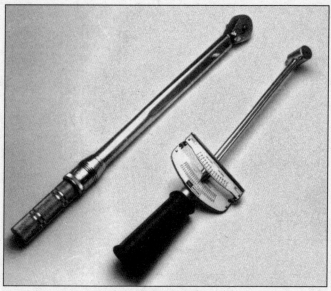

Torque wrenches (left - click; right - beam type)

Snap-ring pliers (top - external; bottom - internal)

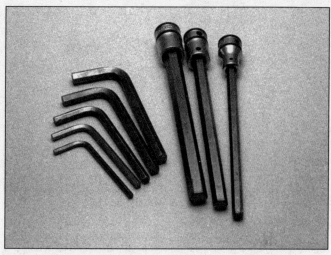

Allen wrenches (left), and Allen head sockets (right)

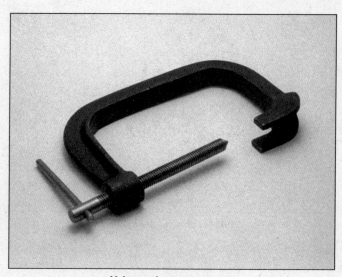

Valve spring compressor

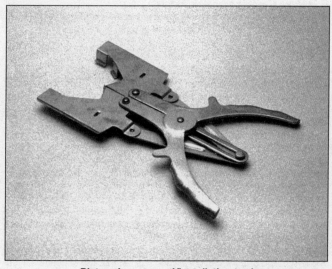

Piston ring removal/installation tool

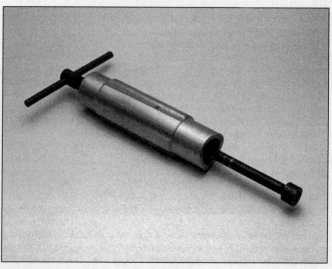

Piston pin puller

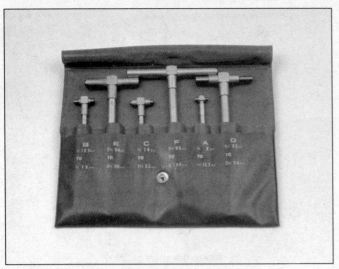

Telescoping gauges

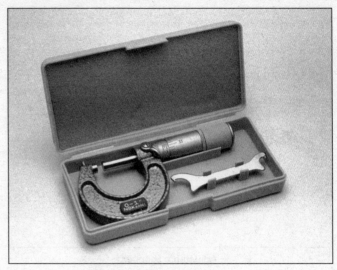

0-to-1 inch micrometer

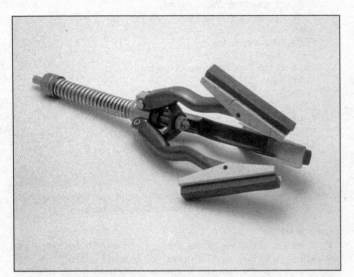

Cylinder surfacing hone

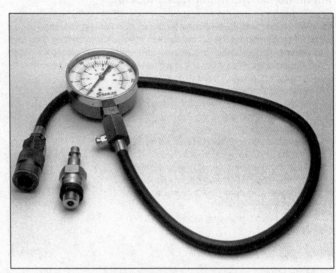

Cylinder compression gauge

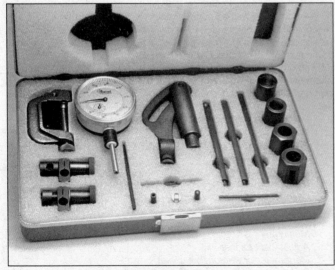

Dial indicator set

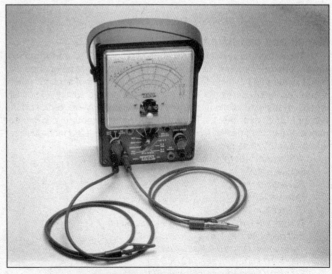

Multimeter (volt/ohm/ammeter)

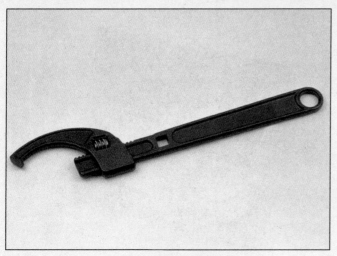

Adjustable spanner

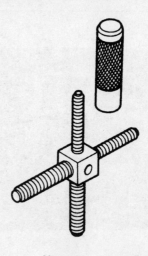

Alternator rotor puller

Maintenance and minor repair tool kit

The tools in this list should be considered the minimum required for performance of routine maintenance, servicing and minor repair work. We recommend the purchase of combination wrenches (box end and open end combined in one wrench); while more expensive than open-ended ones, they offer the advantages of both types of wrench.

Combination wrench set (6 mm to 22 mm)
Adjustable wrench - 8 in
Spark plug socket (with rubber insert)
Spark plug gap adjusting tool
Feeler gauge set
Standard screwdriver (5/16 in x 6 in)
Phillips screwdriver (No. 2 x 6 in)
Allen (hex) wrench set (4 mm to 12 mm)
Combination (slip-joint) pliers - 6 in
Hacksaw and assortment of blades
Tire pressure gauge
Control cable pressure luber
Grease gun
Oil can
Fine emery cloth
Wire brush
Hand impact screwdriver and bits
Funnel (medium size)
Safety goggles
Drain pan
Work light with extension cord

Repair and overhaul tool set

These tools are essential for anyone who plans to perform major repairs and are intended to supplement those in the Maintenance and minor repair tool kit. Included is a comprehensive set of sockets which, though expensive, are invaluable because of their versatility (especially when various extensions and drives are available). We recommend the 3/8 inch drive over the 1/2 inch drive for general motorcycle maintenance and repair (ideally, the mechanic would have a 3/8 inch drive set and a 1/2 inch drive set).

Alternator rotor removal tool
Socket set(s)
Reversible ratchet
Extension - 6 in
Universal joint
Torque wrench (same size drive as sockets)
Ball pein hammer - 8 oz
Soft-faced hammer (plastic/rubber)
Standard screwdriver (1/4 in x 6 in)
Standard screwdriver (stubby - 5/16 in)

Phillips screwdriver (No. 3 x 8 in)
Phillips screwdriver (stubby - No. 2)
Pliers - locking
Pliers - lineman's
Pliers - needle nose
Pliers - snap-ring (internal and external)
Cold chisel - 1/2 in
Scriber
Scraper (made from flattened copper tubing)
Center punch
Pin punches (1/16, 1/8, 3/16 in)
Steel rule/straightedge - 12 in
Pin-type spanner wrench
A selection of files
Wire brush (large)

Note: *Another tool which is often useful is an electric drill with a chuck capacity of 3/8 inch (and a set of good quality drill bits).*

Special tools

The tools in this list include those which are not used regularly, are expensive to buy, or which need to be used in accordance with their manufacturer's instructions. Unless these tools will be used frequently, it is not very economical to purchase many of them. A consideration would be to split the cost and use between yourself and a friend or friends (i.e. members of a motorcycle club).

This list primarily contains tools and instruments widely available to the public, as well as some special tools produced by the vehicle manufacturer for distribution to dealer service departments. As a result, references to the manufacturer's special tools are occasionally included in the text of this manual. Generally, an alternative method of doing the job without the special tool is offered. However, sometimes there is no alternative to their use. Where this is the case, and the tool can't be purchased or borrowed, the work should be turned over to the dealer service department or a motorcycle repair shop.

Paddock stand (for models not fitted with a centerstand)
Valve spring compressor
Piston ring removal and installation tool
Piston pin puller
Telescoping gauges
Micrometer(s) and/or dial/Vernier calipers
Cylinder surfacing hone
Cylinder compression gauge
Dial indicator set
Multimeter
Adjustable spanner
Manometer or vacuum gauge set
Small air compressor with blow gun and tire chuck

Buying tools

For the do-it-yourselfer who is just starting to get involved in motorcycle maintenance and repair, there are a number of options available when purchasing tools. If maintenance and minor repair is the extent of the work to be done, the purchase of individual tools is satisfactory. If, on the other hand, extensive work is planned, it would be a good idea to purchase a modest tool set from one of the large retail chain stores. A set can usually be bought at a substantial savings over the individual tool prices (and they often come with a tool box). As additional tools are needed, add-on sets, individual tools and a larger tool box can be purchased to expand the tool selection. Building a tool set gradually allows the cost of the tools to be spread over a longer period of time and gives the mechanic the freedom to choose only those tools that will actually be used.

Tool stores and motorcycle dealers will often be the only source of some of the special tools that are needed, but regardless of where tools are bought, try to avoid cheap ones (especially when buying screwdrivers and sockets) because they won't last very long. There are plenty of tools around at reasonable prices, but always aim to purchase items which meet the relevant national safety standards. The expense involved in replacing cheap tools will eventually be greater than the initial cost of quality tools.

It is obviously not possible to cover the subject of tools fully here. For those who wish to learn more about tools and their use, there is a book entitled *Motorcycle Workshop Practice Manual* (Book no. 1454) available from the publishers of this manual. It also provides an introduction to basic workshop practice which will be of interest to a home mechanic working on any type of motorcycle.

Care and maintenance of tools

Good tools are expensive, so it makes sense to treat them with respect. Keep them clean and in usable condition and store them properly when not in use. Always wipe off any dirt, grease or metal chips before putting them away. Never leave tools lying around in the work area.

Some tools, such as screwdrivers, pliers, wrenches and sockets, can be hung on a panel mounted on the garage or workshop wall, while others should be kept in a tool box or tray. Measuring instruments, gauges, meters, etc. must be carefully stored where they can't be damaged by weather or impact from other tools.

When tools are used with care and stored properly, they will last a very long time. Even with the best of care, tools will wear out if used frequently. When a tool is damaged or worn out, replace it; subsequent jobs will be safer and more enjoyable if you do.

Working facilities

Not to be overlooked when discussing tools is the workshop. If anything more than routine maintenance is to be carried out, some sort of suitable work area is essential.

It is understood, and appreciated, that many home mechanics do not have a good workshop or garage available and end up removing an engine or doing major repairs outside (it is recommended, however, that the overhaul or repair be completed under the cover of a roof).

A clean, flat workbench or table of comfortable working height is an absolute necessity. The workbench should be equipped with a vise that has a jaw opening of at least four inches.

As mentioned previously, some clean, dry storage space is also required for tools, as well as the lubricants, fluids, cleaning solvents, etc. which soon become necessary.

Sometimes waste oil and fluids, drained from the engine or cooling system during normal maintenance or repairs, present a disposal problem. To avoid pouring them on the ground or into a sewage system, simply pour the used fluids into large containers, seal them with caps and take them to an authorized disposal site or service station. Plastic jugs (such as old antifreeze containers) are ideal for this purpose.

Always keep a supply of old newspapers and clean rags available. Old towels are excellent for mopping up spills. Many mechanics use rolls of paper towels for most work because they are readily available and disposable. To help keep the area under the motorcycle clean, a large cardboard box can be cut open and flattened to protect the garage or shop floor.

Whenever working over a painted surface (such as the fuel tank) cover it with an old blanket or bedspread to protect the finish.

Safety first

Regardless of how enthusiastic you may be about getting on with the job at hand, take the time to ensure that your safety is not jeopardized. A moment's lack of attention can result in an accident, as can failure to observe certain simple safety precautions. The possibility of an accident will always exist, and the following points should not be considered a comprehensive list of all dangers. Rather, they are intended to make you aware of the risks and to encourage a safety conscious approach to all work you carry out on your vehicle.

Essential DOs and DON'Ts

DON'T rely on a jack when working under the motorcycle. Always use a workstand to support the weight of the motorcycle and place it under the recommended lift or support points.

DON'T attempt to loosen extremely tight fasteners while the motorcycle is on a jack or stand - it may fall.

DON'T start the engine without first making sure that the transmission is in Neutral.

DON'T remove the radiator cap from a hot cooling system - let it cool or cover it with a cloth and release the pressure gradually.

DON'T attempt to drain the engine oil until you are sure it has cooled to the point that it will not burn you.

DON'T touch any part of the engine or exhaust system until it has cooled sufficiently to avoid burns.

DON'T siphon toxic liquids such as gasoline, antifreeze and brake fluid by mouth, or allow them to remain on your skin.

DON'T inhale brake lining dust - it is potentially hazardous (see *Asbestos* below).

DON'T allow spilled oil or grease to remain on the floor - wipe it up before someone slips on it.

DON'T use loose fitting wrenches or other tools which may slip and cause injury.

DON'T push on wrenches when loosening or tightening nuts or bolts. Always try to pull the wrench toward you. If the situation calls for pushing the wrench away, push with an open hand to avoid scraped knuckles if the wrench should slip.

DON'T attempt to lift a heavy component alone - get someone to help you.

DON'T rush or take unsafe shortcuts to finish a job.

DON'T allow children or animals in the work area while you are working on the motorcycle.

DO wear eye protection when using power tools such as a drill, sander, bench grinder, etc.

DO keep loose clothing and long hair well out of the way of moving parts.

DO make sure that any jack, lift or stand used has a safe working load rating adequate for the job.

DO get someone to check on you periodically when working alone on a vehicle.

DO carry out work in a logical sequence and make sure that everything is correctly assembled and tightened.

DO keep chemicals and fluids tightly capped and out of the reach of children and pets.

DO remember that your vehicle's safety affects that of yourself and others. If in doubt on any point, get professional advice.

Asbestos

Certain friction, insulating, sealing, and other products - such as brake linings, brake bands, clutch linings, torque converters, gaskets, etc. - may contain asbestos or other hazardous friction material. Extreme care must be taken to avoid inhalation of dust from such products, since it is hazardous to health. If in doubt, assume that they do contain asbestos.

Fire

Remember at all times that gasoline is highly flammable. Never smoke or have any kind of open flame around when working on a vehicle. But the risk does not end there. A spark caused by an electrical short circuit, by two metal surfaces contacting each other, or even by static electricity built up in your body under certain conditions, can ignite gasoline vapors, which in a confined space are highly explosive. Do not, under any circumstances, use gasoline for cleaning parts. Use an approved safety solvent.

On models so equipped, always disconnect the battery ground (-) cable at the battery before working on any part of the fuel system or electrical system. Never risk spilling fuel on a hot engine or exhaust component. It is strongly recommended that a fire extinguisher suitable for use on fuel and electrical fires be kept handy in the garage or workshop at all times. Never try to extinguish a fuel or electrical fire with water.

Fumes

Certain fumes are highly toxic and can quickly cause unconsciousness and even death if inhaled to any extent. Gasoline vapor falls into this category, as do the vapors from some cleaning solvents. Any draining or pouring of such volatile fluids should be done in a well ventilated area.

When using cleaning fluids and solvents, read the instructions on the container carefully. Never use materials from unmarked containers.

Never run the engine in an enclosed space, such as a garage. Exhaust fumes contain carbon monoxide, which is extremely poisonous. If you need to run the engine, always do so in the open air, or at least have the rear of the vehicle outside the work area.

The battery

Never create a spark or allow a bare light bulb near a battery. They normally give off a certain amount of hydrogen gas, which is highly explosive.

Always disconnect the battery ground (-) cable at the battery before working on the fuel or electrical systems.

If possible, loosen the filler caps or cover when charging the battery from an external source (this does not apply to sealed or maintenance-free batteries). Do not charge at an excessive rate or the battery may burst.

Take care when adding water to a non maintenance-free battery and when carrying a battery. The electrolyte, even when diluted, is very corrosive and should not be allowed to contact clothing or skin.

Always wear eye protection when cleaning the battery to prevent the caustic deposits from entering your eyes.

Household current

When using an electric power tool, inspection light, etc., which operates on household current, always make sure that the tool is correctly connected to its plug and that, where necessary, it is properly grounded. Do not use such items in damp conditions and, again, do not create a spark or apply excessive heat in the vicinity of fuel or fuel vapor.

Secondary ignition system voltage

A severe electric shock can result from touching certain parts of the ignition system (such as the spark plug wires) when the engine is running or being cranked, particularly if components are damp or the insulation is defective. In the case of an electronic ignition system, the secondary system voltage is much higher and could prove fatal.

Hydrofluoric acid

This extremely corrosive acid is formed when certain types of synthetic rubber, found in some O-rings, oil seals, fuel hoses, etc. are exposed to temperatures above 750-degrees F (400-degrees C). The rubber changes into a charred or sticky substance containing the acid. Once formed, the acid remains dangerous for years. If it gets onto the skin, it may be necessary to amputate the limb concerned.

When dealing with a vehicle which has suffered a fire, or with components salvaged from such a vehicle, wear protective gloves and discard them after use.

Motorcycle chemicals and lubricants

A number of chemicals and lubricants are available for use in motorcycle maintenance and repair. They include a wide variety of products ranging from cleaning solvents and degreasers to lubricants and protective sprays for rubber, plastic and vinyl.

Contact point/spark plug cleaner is a solvent used to clean oily film and dirt from points, grime from electrical connectors and oil deposits from spark plugs. It is oil free and leaves no residue. It can also be used to remove gum and varnish from carburetor jets and other orifices.

Carburetor cleaner is similar to contact point/spark plug cleaner but it usually has a stronger solvent and may leave a slight oily reside. It is not recommended for cleaning electrical components or connections.

Brake system cleaner is used to remove grease or brake fluid from brake system components (where clean surfaces are absolutely necessary and petroleum-based solvents cannot be used); it also leaves no residue.

Silicone-based lubricants are used to protect rubber parts such as hoses and grommets, and are used as lubricants for hinges and locks.

Multi-purpose grease is an all purpose lubricant used wherever grease is more practical than a liquid lubricant such as oil. Some multi-purpose grease is colored white and specially formulated to be more resistant to water than ordinary grease.

Gear oil (sometimes called gear lube) is a specially designed oil used in transmissions and final drive units, a s well as other areas where high friction, high temperature lubrication is required. It is available in a number of viscosities (weights) for various applications.

Motor oil, of course, is the lubricant specially formulated for use in the engine. It normally contains a wide variety of additives to prevent corrosion and reduce foaming and wear. Motor oil comes in various weights (viscosity ratings) of from 5 to 80. The recommended weight of the oil depends on the seasonal temperature and the demands on the engine. Light oil is used in cold climates and under light load conditions; heavy oil is used in hot climates and where high loads are encountered. Multi-viscosity oils are designed to have characteristics of both light and heavy oils and are available in a number of weights from 5W-20 to 20W-50.

Gas (petrol) additives perform several functions, depending on their chemical makeup. They usually contain solvents that help dissolve gum and varnish that build up on carburetor and intake parts. They also serve to break down carbon deposits that form on the inside surfaces of the combustion chambers. Some additives contain upper cylinder lubricants for valves and piston rings.

Brake fluid is a specially formulated hydraulic fluid that can withstand the heat and pressure encountered in brake systems. Care must be taken that this fluid does not come in contact with painted surfaces or plastics. An opened container should always be resealed to prevent contamination by water or dirt.

Chain lubricants are formulated especially for use on motorcycle final drive chains. A good chain lube should adhere well and have good penetrating qualities to be effective as a lubricant inside the chain and on the side plates, pins and rollers. Most chain lubes are either the foaming type or quick drying type and are usually marketed as sprays.

Degreasers are heavy duty solvents used to remove grease and grime that may accumulate on engine and frame components. They can be sprayed or brushed on and, depending on the type, are rinsed with either water or solvent.

Solvents are used alone or in combination with degreasers to clean parts and assemblies during repair and overhaul. The home mechanic should use only solvents that are non-flammable and that do not produce irritating fumes.

Gasket sealing compounds may be used in conjunction with gaskets, to improve their sealing capabilities, or alone, to seal metal-to-metal joints. Many gasket sealers can withstand extreme heat, some are impervious to gasoline and lubricants, while others are capable of filling and sealing large cavities. Depending on the intended use, gasket sealers either dry hard or stay relatively soft and pliable. They are usually applied by hand, with a brush, or are sprayed on the gasket sealing surfaces.

Thread cement is an adhesive locking compound that prevents threaded fasteners from loosening because of vibration. It is available in a variety of types for different applications.

Moisture dispersants are usually sprays that can be used to dry out electrical components such as the fuse block and wiring connectors. Some types can also be used as treatment for rubber and as a lubricant for hinges, cables and locks.

Waxes and polishes are used to help protect painted and plated surfaces from the weather. Different types of paint may require the use of different types of wax polish. Some polishes utilize a chemical or abrasive cleaner to help remove the top layer of oxidized (dull) paint on older vehicles. In recent years, many non-wax polishes (that contain a wide variety of chemicals such as polymers and silicones) have been introduced. These non-wax polishes are usually easier to apply and last longer than conventional waxes and polishes.

Troubleshooting

Contents

Engine doesn't start or is difficult to start

1   Kickstarter moves but engine won't start

1   Engine kill switch Off.
2   Wiring open or shorted. Check all wiring connections and harnesses to make sure that they are dry, tight and not corroded. Also check for broken or frayed wires that can cause a short to ground (see wiring diagram, Chapter 8).
3   Engine kill switch defective. Check for wet, dirty or corroded contacts. Clean or replace the switch as necessary (Chapter 4).

2   Kickstarter moves but engine does not turn over

1   Kickstarter mechanism damaged. Inspect and repair or replace (Chapter 2).
2   Damaged kickstarter pinion gears. Inspect and replace the damaged parts (Chapter 2).

3   Kickstarter won't turn engine over (seized)

Seized engine caused by one or more internally damaged components. Failure due to wear, abuse or lack of lubrication. Damage can include seized valves, rocker arms, camshaft, piston, crankshaft, connecting rod bearings, or transmission gears or bearings. Refer to Chapter 2 for engine disassembly.

4   No fuel flow

1   No fuel in tank.
2   Tank cap air vent obstructed. Usually caused by dirt or water. Remove it and clean the cap vent hole.
3   Clogged strainer in fuel tap. Remove and clean the strainer (Chapter 1).
4   Fuel line clogged. Pull the fuel line loose and carefully blow through it.
5   Inlet needle valve clogged. A very bad batch of fuel with an unusual additive may have been used, or some other foreign material has entered the tank. Many times after a machine has been stored for many months without running, the fuel turns to a varnish-like liquid and forms deposits on the inlet needle valve and jets. The carburetor should be removed and overhauled if draining the float chamber does not solve the problem.

5   Engine flooded

1   Float level too high. Check as described in Chapter 3 and replace the float if necessary.
2   Inlet needle valve worn or stuck open. A piece of dirt, rust or other debris can cause the inlet needle to seat improperly, causing excess fuel to be admitted to the float bowl. In this case, the float chamber should be cleaned and the needle and seat inspected. If the needle and seat are worn, then the leaking will persist and the parts should be replaced with new ones (Chapter 3).
3   Starting technique incorrect. Under normal circumstances (i.e., if all the carburetor functions are sound) the machine should start with little or no throttle. When the engine is cold, the choke should be operated and the engine started without opening the throttle. When the engine is at operating temperature, only a very slight amount of throttle should be necessary. If the engine is flooded, turn the fuel tap off and hold the throttle open while cranking the engine. This will allow additional air to reach the cylinder. Remember to turn the fuel tap back on after the engine starts.

6   No spark or weak spark

1   Spark plug dirty, defective or worn out. Locate reason for fouled plug using spark plug condition chart and follow the plug maintenance procedures in Chapter 1.
2   Spark plug cap or secondary wiring faulty. Check condition. Replace either or both components if cracks or deterioration are evident (Chapter 4).
3   Spark plug cap not making good contact. Make sure that the plug cap fits snugly over the plug end.
4   Defective alternator (see Chapter 4).
5   Defective CDI unit (see Chapter 4).
6   Ignition coil defective. Check the coil, referring to Chapter 4.
7   Kill switch shorted. This is usually caused by water, corrosion, damage or excessive wear. The kill switch can be disassembled and cleaned with electrical contact cleaner. If cleaning does not help, replace the switch (Chapter 8).
8   Wiring shorted or broken between:
a)   *CDI unit and engine kill switch*
b)   *CDI unit and ignition coil*
c)   *CDI unit and alternator*
d)   *Ignition coil and plug*
     Make sure that all wiring connections are clean, dry and tight. Look for chafed and broken wires (Chapter 4).

7   Compression low

1   Spark plug loose. Remove the plug and inspect the threads. Reinstall and tighten to the specified torque (Chapter 1).
2   Cylinder head not sufficiently tightened down. If the cylinder head is suspected of being loose, then there's a chance that the gasket or head is damaged if the problem has persisted for any length of time. The head nuts and bolts should be tightened to the proper torque in the correct sequence (Chapter 2).
3   Improper valve clearance. This means that the valve is not closing completely and compression pressure is leaking past the valve. Check and adjust the valve clearances (Chapter 1).
4   Cylinder and/or piston worn. Excessive wear will cause compression pressure to leak past the rings. This is usually accompanied by worn rings as well. A top end overhaul is necessary (Chapter 2).
5   Piston rings worn, weak, broken, or sticking. Broken or sticking piston rings usually indicate a lubrication or carburetion problem that causes seizures or excess carbon deposits to form on the pistons and rings. Top end overhaul is necessary (Chapter 2).
6   Piston ring-to-groove clearance excessive. This is caused by excessive wear of the piston ring lands. Piston replacement is necessary (Chapter 2).
7   Cylinder head gasket damaged. If the head is allowed to become loose, or if excessive carbon build-up on a piston crown and combustion chamber causes extremely high compression, the head gasket may leak. Retorquing the head is not always sufficient to restore the seal, so gasket replacement is necessary (Chapter 2).
8   Cylinder head warped. This is caused by overheating or improperly tightened head nuts and bolts. Machine shop resurfacing or head replacement is necessary (Chapter 2).
9   Valve spring broken or weak. Caused by component failure or wear; the spring(s) must be replaced (Chapter 2).
10   Valve not seating properly. This is caused by a bent valve (from over-revving or improper valve adjustment), burned valve or seat (improper carburetion) or an accumulation of carbon deposits on the seat (from carburetion or lubrication problems). The valves must be cleaned and/or replaced and the seats serviced if possible (Chapter 2).

8   Stalls after starting

1   Improper choke action. Make sure the choke lever is getting a full

stroke and staying in the out position.
2   Ignition malfunction. See Chapter 4.
3   Carburetor malfunction. See Chapter 3.
4   Fuel contaminated. The fuel can be contaminated with either dirt or water, or can change chemically if the machine is allowed to sit for several months or more. Drain the tank and float bowl and refill with fresh fuel (Chapter 3).
5   Intake air leak. Check for loose carburetor-to-intake joint connections or loose carburetor top (Chapter 3).
6   Engine idle speed incorrect. Turn throttle stop screw until the engine idles at the specified rpm (Chapter 1).

9   Rough idle

1   Ignition malfunction. See Chapter 4.
2   Idle speed incorrect. See Chapter 1.
3   Carburetor malfunction. See Chapter 3.
4   Idle fuel/air mixture incorrect. See Chapter 3.
5   Fuel contaminated. The fuel can be contaminated with either dirt or water, or can change chemically if the machine is allowed to sit for several months or more. Drain the tank and float bowls (Chapter 3).
6   Intake air leak. Check for loose carburetor-to-intake joint connections, loose or missing vacuum gauge access port cap or hose, or loose carburetor top (Chapter 3).
7   Air cleaner clogged. Service or replace air cleaner element (Chapter 1).

Poor running at low speed

10   Spark weak

1   Spark plug fouled, defective or worn out. Refer to Chapter 1 for spark plug maintenance.
2   Spark plug cap or secondary wiring defective. Refer to Chapters 1 and 4 for details on the ignition system.
3   Spark plug cap not making contact.
4   Incorrect spark plug. Wrong type, heat range or cap configuration. Check and install correct plug listed in Chapter 1. A cold plug or one with a recessed firing electrode will not operate at low speeds without fouling.
5   CDI unit defective. See Chapter 4.
6   Alternator defective. See Chapter 4.
7   Ignition coil defective. See Chapter 4.

11   Fuel/air mixture incorrect

1   Pilot screw out of adjustment (Chapter 3).
2   Pilot jet or air passage clogged. Remove and overhaul the carburetor (Chapter 3).
3   Air bleed holes clogged. Remove carburetor and blow out all passages (Chapter 3).
4   Air cleaner clogged, poorly sealed or missing.
5   Air cleaner-to-carburetor boot poorly sealed. Look for cracks, holes or loose clamps and replace or repair defective parts.
6   Float level too high or too low. Check and replace the float if necessary (Chapter 3).
7   Fuel tank air vent obstructed. Make sure that the air vent passage in the filler cap is open.
8   Carburetor intake joint loose. Check for cracks, breaks, tears or loose clamps or bolts. Repair or replace the rubber boot and its O-ring.

12   Compression low

1   Spark plug loose. Remove the plug and inspect the threads. Rein-

stall and tighten to the specified torque (Chapter 1).
2   Cylinder head not sufficiently tightened down. If the cylinder head is suspected of being loose, then there's a chance that the gasket and head are damaged if the problem has persisted for any length of time. The head nuts should be tightened to the proper torque in the correct sequence (Chapter 2).
3   Improper valve clearance. This means that the valve is not closing completely and compression pressure is leaking past the valve. Check and adjust the valve clearances (Chapter 1).
4   Cylinder and/or piston worn. Excessive wear will cause compression pressure to leak past the rings. This is usually accompanied by worn rings as well. A top end overhaul is necessary (Chapter 2).
5   Piston rings worn, weak, broken, or sticking. Broken or sticking piston rings usually indicate a lubrication or carburetion problem that causes excess carbon deposits or seizures to form on the piston and rings. Top end overhaul is necessary (Chapter 2).
6   Piston ring-to-groove clearance excessive. This is caused by excessive wear of the piston ring lands. Piston replacement is necessary (Chapter 2).
7   Cylinder head gasket damaged. If the head is allowed to become loose, or if excessive carbon build-up on the piston crown and combustion chamber causes extremely high compression, the head gasket may leak. Retorquing the head is not always sufficient to restore the seal, so gasket replacement is necessary (Chapter 2).
8   Cylinder head warped. This is caused by overheating or improperly tightened head nuts and bolts. Machine shop resurfacing or head replacement is necessary (Chapter 2).
9   Valve spring broken or weak. Caused by component failure or wear; the spring(s) must be replaced (Chapter 2).
10 Valve not seating properly. This is caused by a bent valve (from over-revving or improper valve adjustment), burned valve or seat (improper carburetion) or an accumulation of carbon deposits on the seat (from carburetion, lubrication problems). The valves must be cleaned and/or replaced and the seats serviced if possible (Chapter 2).

13   Poor acceleration

1   Carburetor leaking or dirty. Overhaul the carburetor (Chapter 3).
2   Timing not advancing. The CDI units may be defective. If so, they must be replaced with new ones, as they can't be repaired.
3   Engine oil viscosity too high. Using a heavier oil than that recommended in Chapter 1 can damage the oil pump or lubrication system and cause drag on the engine.
4   Brakes dragging. Usually caused by a sticking caliper piston (disc brakes) or brake cam (drum brakes), by a warped disc or drum or by a bent axle. Repair as necessary (Chapter 6).

Poor running or no power at high speed

14   Firing incorrect

1   Air cleaner restricted. Clean or replace element (Chapter 1).
2   Spark plug fouled, defective or worn out. See Chapter 1 for spark plug maintenance.
3   Spark plug cap or secondary wiring defective. See Chapters 1 and 4 for details of the ignition system.
4   Spark plug cap not in good contact. See Chapter 4.
5   Incorrect spark plug. Wrong type, heat range or cap configuration. Check and install correct plugs listed in Chapter 1. A cold plug or one with a recessed firing electrode will not operate at low speeds without fouling.
6   CDI unit defective. See Chapter 4.
7   Ignition coil defective. See Chapter 4.

15   Fuel/air mixture incorrect

1   Pilot screw out of adjustment. See Chapter 3 for adjustment

procedures.

2   Main jet clogged. Dirt, water or other contaminants can clog the main jets. Clean the fuel tap strainer, the float bowl area, and the jets and carburetor orifices (Chapter 3).

3   Main jet wrong size. The standard jetting is for sea level atmospheric pressure and oxygen content. See Chapter 3 for high altitude adjustments.

4   Throttle shaft-to-carburetor body clearance excessive. Refer to Chapter 3 for inspection and part replacement procedures.

5   Air bleed holes clogged. Remove and overhaul carburetor (Chapter 3).

6   Air cleaner clogged, poorly sealed, or missing.

7   Air cleaner-to-carburetor boot poorly sealed. Look for cracks, holes or loose clamps, and replace or repair defective parts.

8   Float level too high or too low. Check float level and replace the float if necessary (Chapter 3).

9   Fuel tank air vent obstructed. Make sure the air vent passage in the filler cap is open.

10   Carburetor intake manifold loose. Check for cracks, breaks, tears or loose clamps or bolts. Repair or replace the rubber boots (Chapter 3).

11   Fuel tap clogged. Remove the tap and clean it (Chapter 1).

12   Fuel line clogged. Pull the fuel line loose and carefully blow through it.

16 Compression low

1   Spark plug loose. Remove the plug and inspect the threads. Reinstall and tighten to the specified torque (Chapter 1).

2   Cylinder head not sufficiently tightened down. If the cylinder head is suspected of being loose, then there's a chance that the gasket and head are damaged if the problem has persisted for any length of time. The head nuts and bolts should be tightened to the proper torque in the correct sequence (Chapter 2).

3   Improper valve clearance. This means that the valve is not closing completely and compression pressure is leaking past the valve. Check and adjust the valve clearances (Chapter 1).

4   Cylinder and/or piston worn. Excessive wear will cause compression pressure to leak past the rings. This is usually accompanied by worn rings as well. A top end overhaul is necessary (Chapter 2).

5   Piston rings worn, weak, broken, or sticking. Broken or sticking piston rings usually indicate a lubrication or carburetion problem that causes excess carbon deposits or seizures to form on the pistons and rings. Top end overhaul is necessary (Chapter 2).

6   Piston ring-to-groove clearance excessive. This is caused by excessive wear of the piston ring lands. Piston replacement is necessary (Chapter 2).

7   Cylinder head gasket damaged. If a head is allowed to become loose, or if excessive carbon build-up on the piston crown and combustion chamber causes extremely high compression, the head gasket may leak. Retorquing the head is not always sufficient to restore the seal, so gasket replacement is necessary (Chapter 2).

8   Cylinder head warped. This is caused by overheating or improperly tightened head nuts and bolts. Machine shop resurfacing or head replacement is necessary (Chapter 2).

9   Valve spring broken or weak. Caused by component failure or wear; the spring(s) must be replaced (Chapter 2).

10   Valve not seating properly. This is caused by a bent valve (from over-revving or improper valve adjustment), burned valve or seat (improper carburetion) or an accumulation of carbon deposits on the seat (from carburetion or lubrication problems). The valves must be cleaned and/or replaced and the seats serviced if possible (Chapter 2).

17 Knocking or pinging

1   Carbon build-up in combustion chamber. Use of a fuel additive that will dissolve the adhesive bonding the carbon particles to the crown and chamber is the easiest way to remove the build-up. Otherwise, the cylinder head will have to be removed and decarbonized (Chapter 2).

2   Incorrect or poor quality fuel. Old or improper grades of fuel can cause detonation. This causes the piston to rattle, thus the knocking or pinging sound. Drain old fuel and always use the recommended fuel grade.

3   Spark plug heat range incorrect. Uncontrolled detonation indicates the plug heat range is too hot. The plug in effect becomes a glow plug, raising cylinder temperatures. Install the proper heat range plug (Chapter 1).

4   Improper air/fuel mixture. This will cause the cylinder to run hot, which leads to detonation. Clogged jets or an air leak can cause this imbalance. See Chapter 3.

18 Miscellaneous causes

1   Throttle valve doesn't open fully. Adjust the cable slack (Chapter 1).

2   Clutch slipping. May be caused by improper adjustment or loose or worn clutch components. Refer to Chapter 1 for adjustment or Chapter 2 for cable replacement and clutch overhaul procedures.

3   Timing not advancing.

4   Engine oil viscosity too high. Using a heavier oil than the one recommended in Chapter 1 can damage the oil pump or lubrication system and cause drag on the engine.

5   Brakes dragging. Usually caused by debris which has entered the brake piston sealing boot, or from a warped disc or bent axle. Repair as necessary.

Overheating

19 Engine overheats

1   Engine oil level low. Check and add oil (Chapter 1).

2   Wrong type of oil. If you're not sure what type of oil is in the engine, drain it and fill with the correct type (Chapter 1).

3   Air leak at carburetor intake manifold. Check and tighten or replace as necessary (Chapter 3).

4   Fuel level low. Check and adjust if necessary (Chapter 3).

5   Worn oil pump or clogged oil passages. Replace pump or clean passages as necessary.

6   Clogged external oil line. Remove and check for foreign material (see Chapter 2).

7   Carbon build-up in combustion chambers. Use of a fuel additive that will dissolve the adhesive bonding the carbon particles to the piston crown and chambers is the easiest way to remove the build-up. Otherwise, the cylinder head will have to be removed and decarbonized (Chapter 2).

8   Operation in high ambient temperatures.

20 Firing incorrect

1   Spark plug fouled, defective or worn out. See Chapter 1 for spark plug maintenance.

2   Incorrect spark plug (see Chapter 1).

3   Faulty ignition coil (Chapter 4).

21 Fuel/air mixture incorrect

1   Pilot screw out of adjustment (Chapter 3).

2   Main jet clogged. Dirt, water and other contaminants can clog the main jets. Clean the fuel tap strainer, the float bowl area and the jets and carburetor orifices (Chapter 3).

3   Main jet wrong size. The standard jetting is for sea level atmospheric pressure and oxygen content. See Chapter 3 for high altitude settings.

4   Air cleaner poorly sealed or missing.

5   Air cleaner-to-carburetor boot poorly sealed. Look for cracks, holes or loose clamps and replace or repair.

6   Fuel level too low. Check float level and replace the float if necessary (Chapter 3).

7   Fuel tank air vent obstructed. Make sure that the air vent passage in the filler cap is open.

8   Carburetor intake manifold loose. Check for cracks or loose clamps or bolts. Inspect the gasket and O-ring (Chapter 3).

22   Compression too high

1   Carbon build-up in combustion chamber. Use of a fuel additive that will dissolve the adhesive bonding the carbon particles to the piston crown and chamber is the easiest way to remove the build-up. Otherwise, the cylinder head will have to be removed and decarbonized (Chapter 2).

2   Improperly machined head surface or installation of incorrect gasket during engine assembly.

23   Engine load excessive

1   Clutch slipping. Can be caused by damaged, loose or worn clutch components. Refer to Chapter 2 for overhaul procedures.

2   Engine oil level too high. The addition of too much oil will cause pressurization of the crankcase and inefficient engine operation. Check Specifications and drain to proper level (Chapter 1).

3   Engine oil viscosity too high. Using a heavier oil than the one recommended in Chapter 1 can damage the oil pump or lubrication system as well as cause drag on the engine.

4   Brakes dragging. Usually caused by a sticking caliper piston (disc brakes), brake cam (drum brakes), by a warped disc or drum or by a bent axle. Repair as necessary (Chapter 6).

24   Lubrication inadequate

1   Engine oil level too low. Friction caused by intermittent lack of lubrication or from oil that is overworked can cause overheating. The oil provides a definite cooling function in the engine. Check the oil level (Chapter 1).

2   Poor quality engine oil or incorrect viscosity or type. Oil is rated not only according to viscosity but also according to type. Some oils are not rated high enough for use in this engine. Check the Specifications section and change to the correct oil (Chapter 1).

3   Camshaft or journals worn. Excessive wear causing drop in oil pressure. Replace cam or cylinder head. Abnormal wear could be caused by oil starvation at high rpm from low oil level or improper viscosity or type of oil (Chapter 1).

4   Crankshaft and/or bearings worn. Same problems as paragraph 3. Check and replace crankshaft assembly if necessary (Chapter 2).

25   Miscellaneous causes

Modification to exhaust system. Most aftermarket exhaust systems cause the engine to run leaner, which makes it run hotter. When installing an aftermarket exhaust system, always rejet the carburetor.

Clutch problems

26   Clutch slipping

1   Friction plates worn or warped. Overhaul the clutch (Chapter 2).

2   Steel plates worn or warped (Chapter 2).

3   Clutch spring(s) broken or weak. Old or heat-damaged spring(s) (from slipping clutch) should be replaced with new ones (Chapter 2).

4   Clutch release mechanism defective. Replace any defective parts (Chapter 2).

5   Clutch center or housing unevenly worn. This causes improper engagement of the plates. Replace the damaged or worn parts (Chapter 2).

27   Clutch not disengaging completely

1   Clutch improperly adjusted (see Chapter 1).

2   Clutch plates warped or damaged. This will cause clutch drag, which in turn will cause the machine to creep. Overhaul the clutch assembly (Chapter 2).

3   Sagged or broken clutch spring(s). Check and replace the spring(s) (Chapter 2).

4   Engine oil deteriorated. Old, thin, worn out oil will not provide proper lubrication for the discs, causing the clutch to drag. Replace the oil and filter (Chapter 1).

5   Engine oil viscosity too high. Using a thicker oil than recommended in Chapter 1 can cause the clutch plates to stick together, putting a drag on the engine. Change to the correct viscosity oil (Chapter 1).

6   Clutch housing seized on shaft. Lack of lubrication, severe wear or damage can cause the housing to seize on the shaft. Overhaul of the clutch, and perhaps transmission, may be necessary to repair the damage (Chapter 2).

7   Clutch release mechanism defective. Worn or damaged release mechanism parts can stick and fail to apply force to the pressure plate. Overhaul the release mechanism (Chapter 2).

8   Loose clutch center snap-ring. Causes housing and center misalignment putting a drag on the engine. Engagement adjustment continually varies. Overhaul the clutch assembly (Chapter 2).

Gear shifting problems

28   Doesn't go into gear or lever doesn't return

1   Clutch not disengaging. See Section 27.

2   Shift fork(s) bent or seized. May be caused by lack of lubrication. Overhaul the transmission (Chapter 2).

3   Gear(s) stuck on shaft. Most often caused by a lack of lubrication or excessive wear in transmission bearings and bushings. Overhaul the transmission (Chapter 2).

4   Shift drum binding. Caused by lubrication failure or excessive wear. Replace the drum and bearing (Chapter 2).

5   Shift lever return spring weak or broken (Chapter 2).

6   Shift lever broken. Splines stripped out of lever or shaft, caused by allowing the lever to get loose. Replace necessary parts (Chapter 2).

7   Shift mechanism pawls broken or worn. Full engagement and rotary movement of shift drum results. Replace shaft assembly (Chapter 2).

8   Pawl spring broken. Allows pawl to float, causing sporadic shift operation. Replace spring (Chapter 2).

29   Jumps out of gear

1   Shift fork(s) worn. Overhaul the transmission (Chapter 2).

2   Gear groove(s) worn. Overhaul the transmission (Chapter 2).
3   Gear dogs or dog slots worn or damaged. The gears should be inspected and replaced. No attempt should be made to service the worn parts.

30   Overshifts

1   Pawl spring weak or broken (Chapter 2).
2   Shift drum stopper lever not functioning (Chapter 2).

Abnormal engine noise

31   Knocking or pinging

1   Carbon build-up in combustion chamber. Use of a fuel additive that will dissolve the adhesive bonding the carbon particles to the piston crown and chamber is the easiest way to remove the build-up. Otherwise, the cylinder head will have to be removed and decarbonized (Chapter 2).
2   Incorrect or poor quality fuel. Old or improper fuel can cause detonation. This causes the piston to rattle, thus the knocking or pinging sound. Drain the old fuel (Chapter 3) and always use the recommended grade fuel (Chapter 1).
3   Spark plug heat range incorrect. Uncontrolled detonation indicates that the plug heat range is too hot. The plug in effect becomes a glow plug, raising cylinder temperatures. Install the proper heat range plug (Chapter 1).
4   Improper air/fuel mixture. This will cause the cylinder to run hot and lead to detonation. Clogged jets or an air leak can cause this imbalance. See Chapter 3.

32   Piston slap or rattling

1   Cylinder-to-piston clearance excessive. Caused by improper assembly. Inspect and overhaul top end parts (Chapter 2).
2   Connecting rod bent. Caused by over-revving, trying to start a badly flooded engine or from ingesting a foreign object into the combustion chamber. Replace the damaged parts (Chapter 2).
3   Piston pin or piston pin bore worn or seized from wear or lack of lubrication. Replace damaged parts (Chapter 2).
4   Piston ring(s) worn, broken or sticking. Overhaul the top end (Chapter 2).
5   Piston seizure damage. Usually from lack of lubrication or overheating. Replace the pistons and bore the cylinder, as necessary (Chapter 2).
6   Connecting rod upper or lower end clearance excessive. Caused by excessive wear or lack of lubrication. Replace worn parts.

33   Valve noise

1   Incorrect valve clearances. Adjust the clearances by referring to Chapter 1.
2   Valve spring broken or weak. Check and replace weak valve springs (Chapter 2).
3   Camshaft or cylinder head worn or damaged. Lack of lubrication at high rpm is usually the cause of damage. Insufficient oil or failure to change the oil at the recommended intervals are the chief causes.

34   Other noise

1   Cylinder head gasket leaking.

2   Exhaust pipe leaking at cylinder head connection. Caused by improper fit of pipe, damaged gasket or loose exhaust flange. All exhaust fasteners should be tightened evenly and carefully. Failure to do this will lead to a leak.
3   Crankshaft runout excessive. Caused by a bent crankshaft (from over-revving) or damage from an upper cylinder component failure.
4   Engine mounting bolts or nuts loose. Tighten all engine mounting bolts and nuts to the specified torque (Chapter 2).
5   Crankshaft bearings worn (Chapter 2).
6   Camshaft chain tensioner defective. Replace according to the procedure in Chapter 2.
7   Camshaft chain, sprockets or guides worn (Chapter 2).

Abnormal driveline noise

35   Clutch noise

1   Clutch housing/friction plate clearance excessive (Chapter 2).
2   Loose or damaged pressure plate and/or bolts (Chapter 2).
3   Broken clutch springs (Chapter 2).

36   Transmission noise

1   Bearings worn. Also includes the possibility that the shafts are worn. Overhaul the transmission (Chapter 2).
2   Gears worn or chipped (Chapter 2).
3   Metal chips jammed in gear teeth. Probably pieces from a broken clutch, gear or shift mechanism that were picked up by the gears. This will cause early bearing failure (Chapter 2).
4   Engine oil level too low. Causes a howl from transmission. Also affects engine power and clutch operation (Chapter 1).

37   Final drive noise

1   Dry or dirty chain. Inspect, clean and lubricate (see Chapter 1).
2   Chain out of adjustment. Adjust chain slack (see Chapter 1).
3   Chain and sprockets damaged or worn. Inspect the chain and sprockets and replace them as necessary (see Chapter 4).
4   Sprockets loose (see Chapter 5).
5   On XR250L models, rubber dampers in the cush drive missing or deteriorated (see Chapter 5).

Abnormal chassis noise

38   Suspension noise

1   Spring weak or broken. Makes a clicking or scraping sound.
2   Steering head bearings worn or damaged. Clicks when braking. Check and replace as necessary (Chapter 5).
3   Front fork oil level incorrect. Check and correct oil level (see Chapter 5).
4   Front fork(s) assembled incorrectly. Disassemble the fork(s) and check for correct assembly (see Chapter 5).
5   Rear shock absorber fluid level incorrect. Indicates a leak caused by defective seal. Shock will be covered with oil. It may be possible to overhaul the shock and repair the damage; take the shock to a Honda dealer or motorcycle repair shop for inspection.
6   Defective shock absorber with internal damage. This is in the body of the shock. It may be possible to overhaul the shock and repair the damage; take the shock to a Honda dealer or motorcycle repair shop for inspection.
7   Bent or damaged shock body. Replace the shock with a new one (Chapter 5).

39 Brake noise

1   Squeal caused by pad shim not installed or positioned correctly (Chapter 7).
2   Squeal caused by dust on brake pads. Usually found in combination with glazed pads. Clean using brake cleaning solvent (see Chapter 6).
3   Contamination of brake pads. Oil, brake fluid or dirt causing pads to chatter or squeal. Clean or replace pads (see Chapter 6).
4   Pads glazed. Caused by excessive heat from prolonged use or from contamination. Do not use sandpaper, emery cloth or carborundum cloth or any other abrasives to roughen pad surface as abrasives will stay in the pad material and damage the disc. A very fine flat file can be used, but pad replacement is suggested as a cure (see Chapter 7).
5   Disc warped. Can cause a chattering, clicking or intermittent squeal. Usually accompanied by a pulsating lever and uneven braking. Replace the disc (see Chapter 6).
6   Drum brake linings worn or contaminated. Can cause scraping or squealing. Replace the shoes (Chapter 6).
7   Drum brake linings warped or worn unevenly. Can cause chattering. Replace the linings (Chapter 6).
8   Brake drum out of round. Can cause chattering. Replace brake drum (Chapter 6).
9   Loose or worn wheel bearings. Check and replace as needed (Chapter 6).

Excessive exhaust smoke

40 White smoke

1   Piston oil ring worn. The ring may be broken or damaged, causing oil from the crankcase to be pulled past the piston into the combustion chamber. Replace the rings with new ones (Chapter 2).
2   Cylinder worn, cracked, or scored. Caused by overheating or oil starvation. If worn or scored, the cylinder will have to be rebored and a new piston installed. If cracked, the cylinder block will have to be replaced (see Chapter 2).
3   Valve oil seal damaged or worn. Replace oil seals with new ones (Chapter 2).
4   Valve guide worn. Perform a complete valve job (Chapter 2).
5   Engine oil level too high, which causes the oil to be forced past the rings. Drain oil to the proper level (Chapter 1).
6   Head gasket broken between oil return and cylinder. Causes oil to be pulled into the combustion chamber. Replace the head gasket and check the head for warpage (Chapter 2).
7   Abnormal crankcase pressurization, which forces oil past the rings. Clogged breather or hoses usually the cause (Chapter 2).

41 Black smoke

1   Air cleaner clogged. Clean or replace the element (Chapter 1).
2   Main jet too large or loose. Compare the jet size to the Specifications (Chapter 3).
3   Choke stuck open (Chapter 3).
4   Fuel level too high. Check the float level and replace the float if necessary (Chapter 3).
5   Inlet needle held off needle seat. Clean the float chamber and fuel line and replace the needle and seat if necessary (Chapter 3).

42 Brown smoke

1   Main jet too small or clogged. Lean condition caused by wrong size main jet or by a restricted orifice. Clean float chamber and jets and compare jet size to Specifications (Chapter 3).
2   Fuel flow insufficient. Fuel inlet needle valve stuck closed due to chemical reaction with old fuel. Float level incorrect; check and replace float if necessary. Restricted fuel line. Clean line and float chamber.
3   Carburetor intake tube loose (Chapter 3).
4   Air cleaner poorly sealed or not installed (Chapter 1).

Poor handling or stability

43 Handlebar hard to turn

1   Steering stem adjusting nut too tight (Chapter 5).
2   Steering stem bearings damaged. Roughness can be felt as the bars are turned from side-to-side. Replace bearings and races (Chapter 5).
3   Races dented or worn. Denting results from wear in only one position (e.g. straight ahead), striking an immovable object or hole or from dropping the machine. Replace races and bearings (Chapter 5).
4   Steering stem bearing lubrication inadequate. Causes are grease getting hard from age or being washed out by high pressure car washes. Remove steering stem, clean and lubricate bearings (Chapter 5).
5   Steering stem bent. Caused by a collision, hitting a pothole or by dropping the machine. Replace damaged part. Don't try to straighten the steering stem (Chapter 5).
6   Front tire air pressure too low (Chapter 1).

44 Handlebar shakes or vibrates excessively

1   Tires worn or out of balance (Chapter 1 or 6).
2   Swingarm bearings worn. Replace worn bearings (Chapter 5).
3   Wheel rim(s) warped or damaged. Inspect wheels (Chapter 6).
4   Wheel bearings worn. Worn front or rear wheel bearings can cause poor tracking. Worn front bearings will cause wobble (Chapter 6).
5   Handlebar clamp bolts loose (Chapter 5).
6   Steering stem or triple clamps loose. Tighten them to the specified torque (Chapters 1 and 5).
7   Motor mount bolts loose. Will cause excessive vibration with increased engine rpm (Chapter 2).

45 Handlebar pulls to one side

1   Frame bent. Definitely suspect this if the machine has been dropped. May or may not be accompanied by cracking near the bend. Replace the frame (Chapter 5).
2   Front and rear wheels out of alignment. Caused by uneven adjustment of the drive chain adjusters (see Chapter 1). May also be caused by improper location of the axle spacers or from bent steering stem or frame (see Chapter 5).
3   Swingarm bent or twisted. Caused by age (metal fatigue) or impact damage. Replace the swingarm (Chapter 5).
4   Steering stem bent. Caused by impact damage or by dropping the motorcycle. Replace the steering stem (Chapter 5).

46 Poor shock absorbing qualities

1   Too hard:
a) Damping adjuster set too hard (cartridge forks) (see Chapter 5).
b) Fork oil level excessive (see Chapter 5).
c) Fork oil viscosity too high. Use a lighter oil (see the Specifications in Chapter 5).
d) Fork tube bent. Causes a harsh, sticking feeling (see Chapter 5).

e) *Fork internal damage (see Chapter 5).*
f) *Shock internal damage.*
g) *Tire pressures too high (Chapter 1).*
2   Too soft:
a) *Damping adjuster set too soft (cartridge forks) (see Chapter 5).*
b) *Fork or shock oil insufficient and/or leaking (Chapter 5).*
d) *Fork oil level too low (see Chapter 5).*
d) *Fork springs weak or broken (Chapter 5).*

Braking problems

47 Brakes are spongy or weak, don't hold

1   Air in brake line (disc brakes). Caused by inattention to master cylinder fluid level or by leakage. Locate problem and bleed brake (Chapter 6).
2   Pad or disc worn (Chapters 1 and 6).
3   Brake fluid leak. See paragraph 1.
4   Contaminated disc brake pads. Caused by contamination with oil, grease, brake fluid, etc. Clean or replace pads. Clean disc thoroughly with brake cleaner.
5   Brake fluid deteriorated (disc brakes). Fluid is old or contaminated. Drain system, replenish with new fluid and bleed the system (see Chapter 6).
6   Master cylinder internal parts worn or damaged, causing fluid to bypass (see Chapter 6).
7   Master cylinder bore scratched. From ingestion of foreign material or broken spring. Repair or replace master cylinder (see Chapter 6).
8   Disc warped. Replace disc (see Chapter 6).
9   Drum brake linings worn (Chapters 1 and 6).
10 Contaminated drum brake linings. Caused by contamination with oil, grease, etc. Clean or replace linings. Clean drum thoroughly with brake cleaner (Chapter 6).
11 Drum warped. Replace drum (Chapter 6).
12 Drum brake cable out of adjustment or stretched. Adjust or replace the cable (see Chapters 1 and 6).

48 Brake lever or pedal pulsates

1   Disc warped. Replace disc (see Chapter 6).
2   Axle bent. Replace axle (Chapter 5).
3   Brake caliper bolts loose (see Chapter 6).
4   Brake caliper shafts damaged or sticking, causing caliper to bind. Lube the shafts or replace them if they are corroded or bent (see Chapter 6).
5   Wheel warped or otherwise damaged (Chapter 6).
6   Wheel bearings damaged or worn (Chapter 6).
7   Brake drum out of round. Replace brake drum (Chapter 6).

49 Brakes drag

1   Master cylinder piston seized. Caused by wear or damage to piston or cylinder bore (see Chapter 6).
2   Lever or pedal balky or stuck. Check pivot and lubricate (see Chapter 7).
3   Brake caliper binds. Caused by inadequate lubrication or damage to caliper shafts (see Chapter 6).
4   Brake caliper piston seized in bore. Caused by wear or ingestion of dirt past deteriorated seal (see Chapter 6).
5   Brake pad or shoes damaged. Pad or lining material separated from backing plate or shoes. Usually caused by faulty manufacturing process or contact with chemicals. Replace pads (see Chapter 6).
6   Pads or shoes improperly installed (see Chapter 6).
7   Cable sticking. Lubricate or replace cable (see Chapters 1 and 6).
8   Shoes improperly installed (Chapter 6).
9   Brake pedal or lever freeplay insufficient (Chapter 1).
10 Drum brake springs weak. Replace brake springs (Chapter 6).

Electrical problems

50 Battery dead or weak (XR250L)

1   Battery faulty. Caused by sulfated plates which are shorted due to sedimentation or low electrolyte level. Also, broken battery terminal making only occasional contact (see Chapter 4).
2   Battery cables making poor contact (see Chapter 4).
3   Load excessive. Caused by addition of high wattage lights or other electrical accessories.
4   Ignition switch defective. Switch either grounds internally or fails to shut off system. Replace the switch (see Chapter 4).
5   Regulator/rectifier defective (see Chapter 4).
6   Stator coil open or shorted (see Chapter 4).
7   Wiring faulty. Wiring grounded or connections loose in ignition, charging or lighting circuits (see Chapter 4).

51 Battery overcharged (XR250L)

1   Regulator/rectifier defective. Overcharging is noticed when battery gets excessively warm or boils over (see Chapter 4).
2   Battery defective. Replace battery with a new one (see Chapter 4).
3   Battery amperage too low, wrong type or size. Install manufacturer's specified amp-hour battery to handle charging load (see Chapter 4).

Chapter 1
Tune-up and routine maintenance

Contents

Specifications

Engine

Spark plug type
XR250L
Standard .... NGK DPR8Z or ND X24GPR-U
Extended high speed riding .... NGK DPR9Z or ND X27GPR-U
Cold climates (below 5-degrees C/41-degrees F) .... NGK DPR7Z or ND X22GPR-U
1986 through 1995 XR250R
Standard .... NGK DPR9Z or ND X27GPR-U
Cold climates (below 5-degrees C/41-degrees F) .... NGK DPR8Z or ND X24GPR-U
1996 and later XR250R
Standard .... NGK CR9EH-9 or ND U27FER-9
Cold climates (below 5-degrees C/41-degrees F) .... NGK CR8EH-9 or ND U24FER-9
XR400R
Standard .... NGK DPR8Z or ND X24GPR-U
Extended high speed riding .... NGK DPR9Z or ND X27GPR-U
Spark plug gap
1996 and later XR250R .... 0.8 to 0.9 mm (0.031 to 0.035 inch)
All others .... 0.6 to 0.7 mm (0.02 to 0.03 inch)
Ignition timing full advance speed
All except XR400R .... 4300 rpm
XR400R .... Not specified

Engine (continued)

Engine idle speed	1300 +/- 100 rpm
Valve clearance (COLD engine)	
XR250L	
Intake	0.03 to 0.07 mm (0.001 to 0.003 inch)
Exhaust	0.06 to 0.10 mm (0.002 to 0.004 inch)
1986 through 1995 XR250R	
Intake	0.05 mm (0.002 inch)
Exhaust	0.08 mm (0.003 inch)
1996 and later XR250R, all XR400R	
Intake	0.10 mm +/- 0.02 mm (0.004 +/- 0.001 inch)
Exhaust	0.12 mm +/- 0.02 mm (0.005 +/- 0.001 inch)
Cylinder compression	
XR250L	11 to 13 kg/cm2 (156 to 185 psi)
1986 through 1995 XR250R	13 to 15 kg/cm2 (185 to 213 psi)
1996 and later XR250R	
Decompressor operating	6.5 to 7.5 kg/cm2 (92 to 107 psi)
Decompressor not operating, valve clearances at	
1.0 mm (0.04 inch)..	12 to 13 kg/cm2 (171 to 185 psi)
XR400R	7 to 10 kg/cm2 (100 to 142 psi)

Miscellaneous

Brake pad lining thickness limit...	See text
Rear brake shoe lining thickness (drum brakes)	
New	4 mm (0.16 inch)
Wear limit	2 mm (0.08 inch)
Front brake lever freeplay	
XR250L	Not specified
1986 through 1995 XR250R	
At lever tip	0.6 to 7.8 mm (1/16 to 5/8 inch)
At adjuster gap	1.4 mm (0.06 inch) minimum
1996 and later XR250R	10 to 20 mm (3/8 to 3/4 inch)
XR400R	20 mm (3/4 inch)
Rear brake pedal freeplay (drum brake models)	20 to 30 mm (3/4 to 1-1/4 inch)
Rear master cylinder bolt length (disc brake XR250R models)	
1986 through 1995	71 mm (2.8 inch)
1996 on	75 mm (2.95 inch)
Clutch lever freeplay..	10 to 20 mm (3/8 to 3/4 inch)
Throttle grip freeplay...	2 to 6 mm (1/8 to 1/4 inch)
Decompressor freeplay	
XR250L	1 to 2 mm (1/16 to 1/8 inch)
1986 through 1995 XR250R	
At engine lever	1 to 2 mm (1/16 to 1/8 inch)
At handlebar lever	5 to 8 mm (3/16 to 5/16 inch)
1996 and later XR250R, all XR400R	5 to 8 mm (3/16 to 5/16 inch)
Minimum tire tread depth	3 mm (1/8 inch)
Tire pressures (cold)	
XR250L	22 psi front and rear
XR250R, XR400R	15 psi front and rear
Tire sizes	
XL250R	
Early models	
Front	3.00-21-4PR
Rear	4.60-18-4PR
Later models	
Front	3.00-21-51P
Rear	4.60-18-63P
XR250R	
1986 through 1995	
Front	80/100-21 51 M
Rear	110/100-18 63 M
1996 on	
Front	80/100-21 51 M
Rear	100/100-18 59M
XR400R	
Front	80/100 21 51M
Rear	110/100 18 64M

Drive chain slack
    XR250L .... 20 to 30 mm (3/4 to 1-1/4 inch)
    XR250R
        1986 through 1995.. 35 to 45 mm (1-3/8 to 1-3/4 inch)
        1996 on .... 30 to 40 mm (1-1/4 to 1-5/8 inch)
    XR400R .... 35 to 45 mm (1-3/8 to 1-3/4 inch)

Recommended lubricants and fluids

Engine/transmission oil
    Type .... API grade SF or SG multigrade oil manufactured for use in motorcycles (without moly additives)
    Viscosity
        Standard 10W-40
        Optional
            10 to 90-degrees F 10W-30
            0-degrees F or above .... 20W-40 or 20W-50
    Capacity
        Oil change only
            XR250L, XR250R.. 1.3 liters (1.37 US qt)
            XR400R .... 1.7 liters (1.8 US qt)
        Oil and filter change
            XR250L, XR250R.. 1.4 liters (1.5 US qt)
            XR400R .... 1.8 liters (1.9 US qt)
        After engine overhaul
            XR250R, 1986 through 1995 XR250L .... 1.6 liters (1.7 US qt)
            1996 and later XR250R .... 1.7 liters (1.8 US qt)
            XR400R .... 2.2 liters (2.3 US qt)
Air cleaner filter oil .... Pro Honda Foam Filter Oil or equivalent
Brake fluid.. DOT 4
Drive chain lubricant .... Chain lube formulated for O-ring chains
Wheel bearings .... Medium weight, lithium-based multi-purpose grease (NLGI no. 3)
Swingarm pivot bushings .... Molybdenum disulfide paste grease containing 40 percent or more molybdenum disulfide
Cables and lever pivots .... Medium weight, lithium-based multi-purpose grease (NLGI no. 3)
Brake pedal/shift lever/throttle lever pivots...................................... Medium weight, lithium-based multi-purpose grease (NLGI no. 3)

Torque specifications

Oil drain plug in frame .... 39 Nm (29 ft-lbs)
Oil drain plug in crankcase .... 25 Nm (18 ft-lbs)
Oil filter cover bolts
    XR250L, 1986 through 1995 XR250R.. 10 Nm (86 inch-lbs)
    1996 and later XR250R, all XR400R.. 12 Nm (108 inch-lbs)
Oil strainer screen to frame .... 54 Nm (40 ft-lbs)
Hose fitting to oil strainer screen.. 37 Nm (27 ft-lbs)
Crankcase oil strainer screen bolt .... Not specified
Spark plug .... 17 Nm (144 inch-lbs)
Wheel spokes
    XR250L.. 4 Nm (35 inch-lbs)
    XR250R
        1986 through 1995.. 2.5 to 5.0 Nm (29 to 57 inch-lbs)
        1996 on .... 3.8 Nm (32 inch-lbs)
    XR400R .... 3.8 Nm (32 inch-lbs)
Rim lock locknut .... 15 Nm (132 in-lbs)
Steering stem adjusting nut
    Initial torque
        XR250L .... 25 Nm (18 ft-lbs)
        XR250R
            1986 through 1995 .... 20 to 30 Nm (14 to 22 ft-lbs)
            1996 on .... 5 Nm (43 inch-lbs)
        XR400R .... 29 Nm (22 ft-lbs)
    Final torque
        XR250L .... 5 Nm (43 inch-lbs)
        XR250R
            1986 through 1995 .... 1 to 2 Nm (8 to 16 inch-lbs)
            1996 on .... 5 Nm (43 inch-lbs)
        XR400R .... 4.5 Nm (40 inch-lbs)

1 Honda XR250/400 routine maintenance intervals

Note: *The pre-ride inspection outlined in the owner's manual covers checks and maintenance that should be carried out on a daily basis. It's condensed and included here to remind you of its importance. Always perform the pre-ride inspection at every maintenance interval (in addition to the procedures listed). The intervals listed below are the shortest intervals recommended by the manufacturer for each particular operation during the model years covered in this manual. Your owner's manual may have different intervals for your model.*

Daily or before riding

Check the engine oil level
Check the fuel level and inspect for leaks
Check the operation of both brakes - check the front brake lever and rear brake pedal for correct freeplay
Check the tires for damage, the presence of foreign objects and correct air pressure
Check the throttle for smooth operation and correct freeplay
Make sure the steering operates smoothly
Make sure the engine kill switch works properly
Check the air cleaner drain tube and clean it if necessary
Check all fasteners, including axle nuts, for tightness
Check for mud or debris that could start a fire or interfere with motorcycle operation

Every 300 miles

Lubricate and inspect the drive chain and sliders

Every 2,000 miles on XR250L models or every month (approximately 600 miles) on XR250R and XR400R models

Change the engine oil and filter

Every 4,000 miles on XR250L models or every month (approximately 600 miles) on XR250R and XR400R models

Perform all of the daily checks plus:
Inspect the brakes
Check the brake pads and shoes for wear
Check brake fluid level
Check and adjust the valve clearances
Check the decompressor system
Clean the air filter element (1)
Clean the air cleaner housing drain tube
Check the crankcase breather (XR250L)
Check/adjust the throttle lever freeplay
Check choke operation
Check/adjust the idle speed
Check the tightness of all fasteners
Inspect the suspension
Clean and gap the spark plug (2)
Check/adjust the clutch
Check the exhaust system for leaks and check fastener tightness; clean the spark arrester
Inspect the wheels and tires
Check the cleanliness of the fuel system and the condition of the fuel line
Clean the fuel tap strainer screen
Inspect the steering system and steering head bearings
Check the sidestand operation
Check the headlight aim

Every 12,000 miles

Check the evaporative emission control system (XR250L California models)

1. More often in dusty, sandy or wet conditions.
2. Replace the spark plugs every 8000 miles on XR250L models.

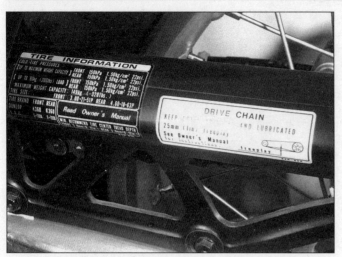

2.1a Decals on the motorcycle include maintenance information such as tire specifications and drive chain adjustment . . .

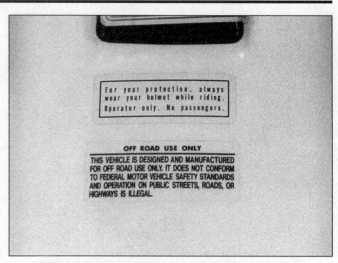

2.1b . . . as well as certification and safety information

2   Introduction to tune-up and routine maintenance

Refer to illustrations 2.1a and 2.1b

This Chapter covers in detail the checks and procedures necessary for the tune-up and routine maintenance of your motorcycle. Section 1 includes the routine maintenance schedule, which is designed to keep the machine in proper running condition and prevent possible problems. The remaining Sections contain detailed procedures for carrying out the items listed on the maintenance schedule, as well as additional maintenance information designed to increase reliability. Maintenance, certification and safety information is also printed on decals, which are mounted in various locations on the motorcycle **(see illustrations)**. Where information on the decals differs from that presented in this Chapter, use the decal information.

Since routine maintenance plays such an important role in the safe and efficient operation of your motorcycle, it is presented here as a comprehensive check list. For the rider who does all his own maintenance, these lists outline the procedures and checks that should be done on a routine basis.

Deciding where to start or plug into the routine maintenance schedule depends on several factors. If you have a motorcycle whose warranty has recently expired, and if it has been maintained according to the warranty standards, you may want to pick up routine maintenance as it coincides with the next mileage or calendar interval. If you have owned the machine for some time but have never performed any maintenance on it, then you may want to start at the nearest interval and include some additional procedures to ensure that nothing important is overlooked. If you have just had a major engine overhaul, then you may want to start the maintenance routine from the beginning. If you have a used machine and have no knowledge of its history or maintenance record, you may desire to combine all the checks into one large service initially and then settle into the maintenance schedule prescribed.

The Sections which actually outline the inspection and maintenance procedures are written as step-by-step comprehensive guides to the actual performance of the work. They explain in detail each of the routine inspections and maintenance procedures on the check list. References to additional information in applicable Chapters is also included and should not be overlooked.

Before beginning any actual maintenance or repair, the machine should be cleaned thoroughly, especially around the oil filter housing, spark plug, valve cover, side covers, carburetor, etc. Cleaning will help ensure that dirt does not contaminate the engine and will allow you to detect wear and damage that could otherwise easily go unnoticed.

3   Engine oil level - check

1   Start the engine and allow it to reach normal operating temperature. **Warning:** *Do not run the engine in an enclosed space such as a garage or shop.*

Wet sump models (XR250L and 1986 through 1995 XR250R)

2   Let the engine idle for a few minutes, then shut it off.
3   Stop the engine and allow the bike to sit undisturbed in a level position for about five minutes. Be sure it's upright, not on the side-stand.

Dry sump models (1996 and later XR250R, all XR400R)

4   Let the engine idle for five minutes, then shut it off. If you're working on an XR400R and the air temperature is below 50-degrees F or 10-degrees C, let it idle for 10 minutes; the external oil cooler and large oil capacity will cause the oil to warm more slowly. **Note:** *On dry sump models, check oil level immediately after shutting the engine off. Don't let the oil settle.*

All models

Refer to illustrations 3.5a and 3.5b
5   With the engine off, unscrew the dipstick **(see illustrations)**. It's

3.5a The dipstick on wet sump models is in the crankcase (right arrow); the oil filter housing is secured by three bolts (left arrows)

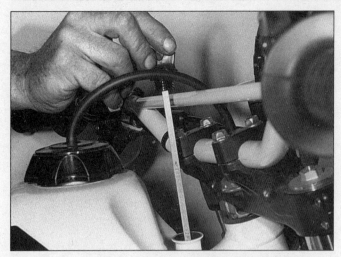

3.5b The dipstick on dry sump models is in the front part of the frame

4.4 The front and rear brake pads are equipped with wear grooves (arrow); replace both pads in the caliper if either of the pads is worn close to the groove

in the crankcase on wet sump models; on dry sump models, it's in the front center of the frame (the frame acts as an oil tank for the dry sump lubrication system). Pull it out, wipe it off with a clean rag, and reinsert it (let the dipstick rest on the threads; don't screw it back in).

6   Pull the dipstick out and check the oil level on the dipstick scale. The oil level should be between the Maximum and Minimum level marks on the scale.

7   If the level is below the Minimum mark, add oil through the dipstick hole. Add enough oil of the recommended grade and type to bring the level up to the Maximum mark. Do not overfill.

4   Brake system - general check

1   A routine general check of the brakes will ensure that any problems are discovered and remedied before the rider's safety is jeopardized.

2   Check the brake lever and pedal for loose connections, excessive play, bends, and other damage. Replace any damaged parts with new ones (see Chapter 6).

3   Make sure all brake fasteners are tight. Check the brakes for wear as described below.

Wear check

Disc brakes

Refer to illustration 4.4

4   There's a groove on the inside of each pad next to the metal backing **(see illustration)**. When the friction material is nearly worn down to the groove, it's time to replace the pads (even if only one pad is worn that far).

Rear drum brakes

Refer to illustration 4.6

5   Operate the brake pedal. If operation is rough or sticky, refer to Section 10 and lubricate the cable.

6   With the rear brake lever and pedal freeplay properly adjusted (see Section 5), check the wear indicator on the brake panel **(see illustration)**. If the pointer lines up with the indicator when the pedal is pressed, refer to Chapter 6 and replace the brake shoes.

Disc brake fluid

Front brake

Refer to illustrations 4.9, 4.10a and 4.10b

7   To ensure proper operation of the hydraulic disc brakes, the fluid

4.6 The wear indicator on rear drum brakes is at the rear of the panel (lower arrow); adjustments are made with the wingnut (upper arrow)

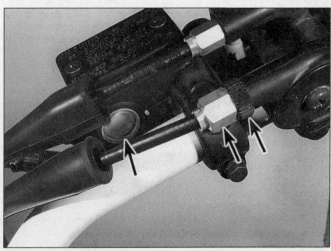

4.9 The front brake level should be at least up to the Lower mark next to the window (left arrow); the lockwheel and adjuster (right arrows) are used to set throttle cable freeplay

4.10a Remove the cover screws . . .

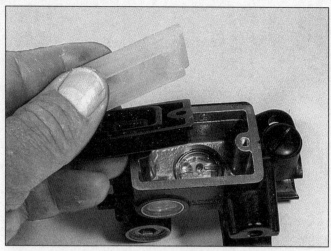

4.10b . . . and lift off the retainer and diaphragm to add brake fluid

level in the master cylinder reservoirs must be maintained within a safe range.

8   With the motorcycle supported in an upright position, turn the handlebars until the top of the front brake master cylinder is as level as possible.

9   The fluid level is visible in the window on the reservoir (see illustration). Make sure the fluid level is above the Lower mark cast on the master cylinder body next to the reservoir.

10   If the fluid level is low, clean the area around the reservoir cover. Remove the cover screws and take off the cover, diaphragm retainer and diaphragm (see illustrations). Add new clean brake fluid of the type listed in this Chapter's Specifications until the fluid level is even with the line cast inside the reservoir.

11   Install the diaphragm, retainer and cover, then tighten the cover screws securely.

Rear brake

Refer to illustration 4.12

12   The fluid level is visible through the master cylinder reservoir (see illustration). If it's below the Lower mark cast in the reservoir body, the fluid must be replenished.

13   Unscrew the reservoir cap and pour in fluid to bring the level up to the Upper mark cast in the reservoir. Install the cap and tighten it securely.

5   Brake lever and pedal - check and adjustment

Front brake lever

Refer to illustration 5.2

1   Squeeze the front brake lever and note how far the lever travels (measure at the tip of the lever). If it exceeds the limit listed in this Chapter's Specifications, adjust the front brake as described below.

2   Loosen the locknut and turn the adjusting screw (see illustration). Tighten the locknut after making the adjustment.

Rear brake pedal

Drum brake models

3   To adjust brake pedal height, loosen the locknut and turn the adjusting bolt (they're mounted in a boss on the right side of the frame behind the brake pedal). Honda doesn't specify pedal height.

4   Check the play of the brake pedal. If it exceeds the limit listed in this Chapter's Specifications, adjust it with the wingnut at the rear end of the brake rod (see illustration 4.6).

Disc brake models

Refer to illustrations 5.5 and 5.6

5   To adjust pedal height, loosen the locknut and turn the adjusting

4.12 The rear brake fluid level is visible through the reservoir; on some models the cap is held on by a retainer

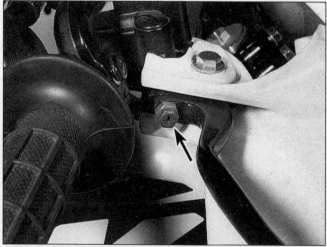

5.2 Front brake lever position on later models is adjusted by loosening the locknut and turning the screw (arrow)

5.5 Rear disc brake pedal height is adjusted by loosening the locknut (lower arrow) and turning the adjusting bolt (upper arrow); on XR250R models, pushrod length is measured from the center of the lower mounting bolt to the center of the clevis pin

5.6 On XR400R models, don't adjust the end of the pushrod (arrow) any closer than the specified distance to the clevis

bolt on the rear master cylinder **(see illustration)**. Although pedal height isn't specified, a dimension for the length of the clevis assembly for XR250R models is listed in this Chapter's Specifications.

6   If you're working on an XR400R, make sure the adjustment does not close the gap between the pushrod and clevis to less than 1 mm (0.04 inch) **(see illustration)**.

7   Pedal freeplay on disc brake models is automatic and no means of manual adjustment is provided.

Rear brake light switch

Refer to illustration 5.8

8   The rear brake light on XR250L models should illuminate just before the rear brake is activated. If the light comes on too soon or too late, turn the plastic nut that secures the switch to the bracket **(see illustration)**. Don't try to turn the switch itself.

6   Tires/wheels - general check

Refer to illustrations 6.4, 6.5 and 6.7

1   Routine tire and wheel checks should be made with the realization that your safety depends to a great extent on their condition.

2   Check the tires carefully for cuts, tears, embedded nails or other sharp objects and excessive wear. Operation of the motorcycle with excessively worn tires is extremely hazardous, as traction and handling are directly affected. Check the tread depth at the center of the tire and compare it to the value listed in this Chapter's Specifications. Honda doesn't specify a minimum tread depth for some models, but as a general rule, tires should be replaced with new ones when the tread knobs are worn to 3 mm (1/8-inch) or less.

3   Repair or replace punctured tires as soon as damage is noted. Do not try to patch a torn tire, as wheel balance and tire reliability may be impaired.

4   Check the tire pressures when the tires are cold and keep them properly inflated **(see illustration)**. Proper air pressure will increase tire life and provide maximum stability and ride comfort. Keep in mind that low tire pressures may cause the tire to slip on the rim or come off, while high tire pressures will cause abnormal tread wear and unsafe handling.

5   The wheels should be kept clean and checked periodically for cracks, bending, loose spokes and rust. Never attempt to repair damaged wheels; they must be replaced with new ones. Loose spokes can be tightened with a spoke wrench **(see illustration)**, but be careful not to overtighten and distort the wheel rim.

6   Check the valve stem locknuts to make sure they're tight. Also, make sure the valve stem cap is in place and tight. If it is missing,

5.8 Turn the plastic nut (arrow) to adjust the XR250L brake light switch

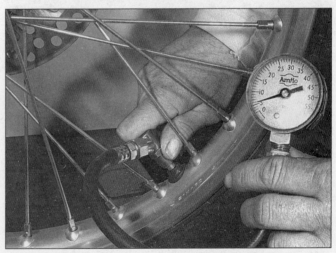

6.4 Check tire pressure with a gauge

6.5 Make sure the spokes are tight, but don't overtighten them

6.7 Tighten the locknut on the rim lock to the specified torque

install a new one made of metal or hard plastic.

7   Check the tightness of the locknut on the rim lock **(see illustration)**. Tighten it if necessary to the torque listed in this Chapter's Specifications.

7   Clutch - check and freeplay adjustment

Refer to illustrations 7.2, 7.4a and 7.4b

1   Operate the clutch lever and measure freeplay at the tip of the lever. If it's not within the range listed in this Chapter's Specifications, adjust it as follows.

2   Pull back the rubber cover from the adjuster at the handlebar **(see illustration)**. Loosen the lockwheel and turn the adjuster to change freeplay.

3   If freeplay can't be brought within specifications by using the handlebar adjuster, turn the handlebar adjuster in all the way, then back it out one turn.

4   Loosen the locknut on the lower cable adjuster and turn the adjuster to set freeplay **(see illustrations)**. Tighten the locknuts on the upper and lower adjusters.

5   If freeplay still can't be adjusted to within the specified range, the cable is probably stretched and should be replaced with a new one.

8   Throttle and choke operation/grip freeplay - check and adjustment

Throttle check

1   Make sure the throttle twistgrip moves easily from fully closed to fully open with the front wheel turned at various angles. The grip should return automatically from fully open to fully closed when released. If the throttle sticks, check the throttle cable for cracks or kinks in the housings. Also, make sure the inner cable is clean and well-lubricated.

2   Check for a small amount of freeplay at the twistgrip and compare the freeplay to the value listed in this Chapter's Specifications.

Throttle adjustment

Refer to illustration 8.5

3   Minor adjustments are made at the throttle lever end of the accelerator cable. Major adjustments are made at the carburetor end of the cable.

4   Pull back the rubber cover from the adjuster and loosen the lockwheel on the cable **(see illustration 4.9)**. Turn the adjuster until the desired freeplay is obtained, then retighten the lockwheel.

5   If the freeplay can't be adjusted at the grip end, loosen the lock-

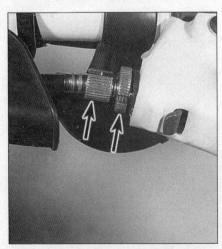

7.2 Loosen the lockwheel (right arrow) and turn the adjuster (left arrow) to make minor adjustments in clutch lever freeplay

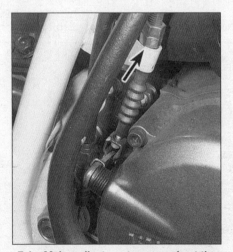

7.4a Major adjustments are made at the lower adjuster; it's behind the clutch cover on XR250L and XR250R models . . .

7.4b . . . and above it on XR400R models

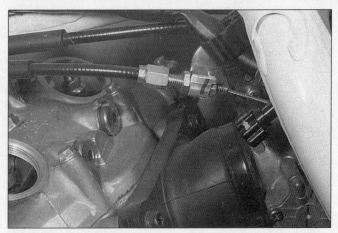

8.5 Major throttle cable adjustments are made at the adjuster near the carburetor

9.1 The XR250R choke knob is located near the left front fork

nuts at the carburetor end of the cable **(see illustration)**. Turn the adjuster to set freeplay, then tighten the locknuts securely.

9   Choke - operation check

XR250L

Refer to illustrations 9.1 and 9.2
1   Check that the choke knob moves smoothly **(see illustration)**. If not, refer to Section 10 and lubricate the cable.
2   Remove the seat and fuel tank (see Chapters 7 and 3). Locate the choke cable at its connection to the carburetor **(see illustration)**. Move the choke lever through its full stroke and make sure the choke valve operates. If it doesn't, refer to Chapter 3 and check the choke mechanism for worn or damaged parts.

XR250R and XR400R

3   Operate the choke lever on the carburetor while you feel for smooth operation.
4   If the lever doesn't move smoothly, refer to Chapter 3 and check the choke mechanism for worn or damaged parts.

10   Lubrication - general

Refer to illustrations 10.3, 10.5a and 10.5b
1   Since the controls, cables and various other components of a

motorcycle are exposed to the elements, they should be lubricated periodically to ensure safe and trouble-free operation.
2   The throttle twistgrip, brake lever, brake pedal, kickstarter pedal pivot and sidestand pivot should be lubricated frequently. In order for the lubricant to be applied where it will do the most good, the component should be disassembled. However, if chain and cable lubricant is being used, it can be applied to the pivot joint gaps and will usually work its way into the areas where friction occurs. If motor oil or light grease is being used, apply it sparingly as it may attract dirt (which could cause the controls to bind or wear at an accelerated rate). **Note:** *One of the best lubricants for the control lever pivots is a dry-film lubricant (available from many sources by different names).*
3   The throttle and clutch cables (and the brake and choke cables, if equipped) should be removed and treated with a commercially available cable lubricant which is specially formulated for use on motorcycle control cables. Small adapters for pressure lubricating the cables with spray can lubricants are available and ensure that the cable is lubricated along its entire length **(see illustration)**. When attaching the cable to the lever, be sure to lubricate the barrel-shaped fitting at the end with multi-purpose grease.
4   To lubricate the cables, disconnect them at the upper end, then lubricate the cable with a pressure lube adapter **(see illustration 10.3)**. See Chapter 2 (decompressor cable) and Chapter 3 (throttle and choke cables).
5   The swingarm and rear suspension linkage pivots can be lubricated with a grease gun through the grease fittings **(see illustrations)**.
6   Refer to Chapter 5 for the following lubrication procedures:

  a) *Swingarm bearings and dust seals*
  b) *Steering head bearings*

9.2 The choke cable is attached to this bracket on the carburetor

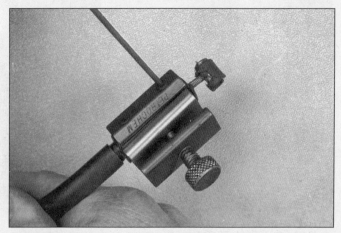

10.3 Lubricating a cable with a pressure lube adapter (make sure the tool seats around the inner cable)

10.5a There's a grease fitting on the swingarm (left arrow) and on the shock arm pivot (right arrow)

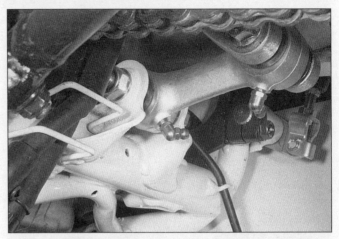

10.5b Lubricate the suspension linkage relay arm through the two grease fittings

7　Refer to Chapter 6 for the following lubrication procedures:

a) *Front and rear wheel bearings*
b) *Brake pedal pivot*

11 Engine oil change and filter screen cleaning

Refer to illustrations 11.5a, 11.5b, 11.6a, 11.6b and 11.6c

1　Consistent routine oil changes and filter screen cleaning are the single most important maintenance procedure you can perform on these models. The oil not only lubricates the internal parts of the engine, transmission and clutch, but it also acts as a coolant, a cleaner, a sealant, and a protectant. Because of these demands, the oil takes a terrific amount of abuse and should be replaced often with new oil of the recommended grade and type. Saving a little money on the difference in cost between a good oil and a cheap oil won't pay off if the engine is damaged. Honda recommends against using the following:

a) *Oils with graphite or molybdenum additives*
b) *Non-detergent oils*
c) *Castor or vegetable based oils*
d) *Oil additives*

2　Before changing the oil and cleaning the filter screens, warm up the engine so the oil will drain easily. Be careful when draining the oil, as the exhaust pipe, the engine and the oil itself can cause severe burns.

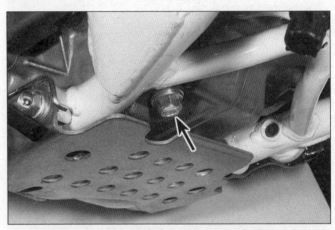

11.5a The crankcase drain plug on XR250L and XR250R models is on the bottom of the engine . . .

3　Park the motorcycle over a clean drain pan.
4　Remove the dipstick/oil filler cap to vent the crankcase and act as a reminder that there is no oil in the engine.
5　Next, remove the drain plugs from the frame and crankcase **(see illustrations)** and allow the oil to drain into the pan. Do not lose the sealing washers on the drain plugs.
6　Remove the filter cover and O-ring from the right side of the

11.5b . . . on XR400R models, it's on the left side

11.6a Remove the Allen bolts (some models use only two), then pull off the oil filter cover and O-ring . . .

11.6b . . . pull out the filter; the OUT SIDE mark must face outward on installation to prevent engine damage . . .

11.6c . . . and the spring - it fits like this when installed

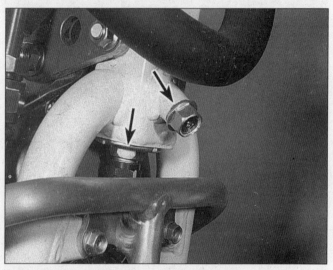

11.7a The oil tank drain plug on dry sump models is located in the bottom of the front frame member (right arrow); the oil hose strainer screen is behind it (left arrow)

crankcase, then pull out the filter and spring **(see illustration 3.5a and the accompanying illustrations).**

Dry sump models (1996 and later XR250R, all XR400R)

Refer to illustrations 11.7a and 11.7b

7   As the oil is draining, unscrew the hose fitting from the frame oil screen, then unscrew the strainer screen from the bottom of the frame oil tank **(see illustrations)**. If additional maintenance is planned for this time period, check or service another component while the oil is allowed to drain completely.

All models

Refer to illustrations 11.8a, 11.8b and 11.8c

8   Remove the right engine cover (see Chapter 2). Remove the retainer or mounting bolt (if equipped) and pull the filter screen out of its slot in the crankcase **(see illustrations)**.

9   Clean the strainer screen(s) thoroughly with a high flash point solvent, then dry them completely (blow dry with compressed air, if available).

10   Check the condition of the drain plug threads. Replace the plug if the threads are damaged.

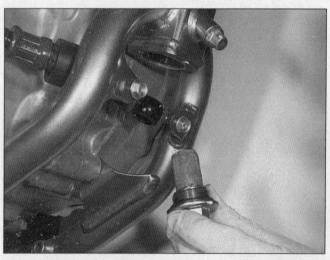

11.7b With the hose detached, unscrew the strainer screen from the frame

11.8a The right engine cover must be removed for access to the crankcase strainer screen; on some models it's secured directly by a bolt (arrow) . . .

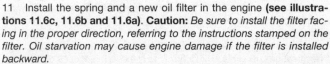

11.8b . . . while on others, it's held in by a retainer

11.8c The screen slides out of the crankcase

11   Install the spring and a new oil filter in the engine **(see illustrations 11.6c, 11.6b and 11.6a)**. **Caution:** *Be sure to install the filter facing in the proper direction, referring to the instructions stamped on the filter. Oil starvation may cause engine damage if the filter is installed backward.*

12   Install the crankcase filter screen in its slot. Install the retainer or mounting bolt (if equipped), then refer to Chapter 2 and install the right engine cover.

13   If you're working on a dry sump model, place a new O-ring on the frame strainer screen. Install the strainer screen in the frame and tighten it to the torque listed in this Chapter's Specifications. Install new sealing washers on the hose fitting, connect the hose to the strainer screen and tighten the hose fitting to the torque listed in this Chapter's Specifications.

14   Slip a new sealing washer over the drain plug(s), then install and tighten the plugs to the torque listed in this Chapter's Specifications. Avoid overtightening, as damage to the threads or engine case will result.

15   Before refilling the engine, check the old oil carefully. If the oil was drained into a clean pan, small pieces of metal or other material can be easily detected. If the oil is very metallic colored, then the engine is experiencing wear from break-in (new engine) or from insufficient lubrication. If there are flakes or chips of metal in the oil, then something is drastically wrong internally and the engine will have to be disassembled for inspection and repair.

16   If there are pieces of fiber-like material in the oil, the clutch is experiencing excessive wear and should be checked.

17   If the inspection of the oil turns up nothing unusual, refill the engine as described below.

Wet sump models

18   Fill the crankcase to the proper level with the recommended oil and install the dipstick/filler cap. Start the engine and let it run.

19   Shut the engine off, wait a few minutes, then check the oil level with the bike upright. Add more oil if necessary to bring the level up to the upper level mark on the dipstick.

Dry sump models

20   Dry sump models will accept only part of the recommended amount of oil at this stage. Refer to this Chapter's Specifications and add the specified initial amount to the frame oil tank.

21   Support the bike upright (not on the sidestand). Start the engine and let it idle for a few minutes. Don't rev the engine during this time or the level reading won't be accurate.

22   Shut the engine off. Holding the bike upright, add the remainder of the total amount of oil listed in this Chapter's Specifications.

23   Refer to Section 3 and recheck the oil level. The level check procedure must be followed exactly for accurate readings.

All models

24   Check around the drain plugs and filter cover for leaks.

25   The old oil drained from the engine cannot be reused in its present state and should be disposed of. Check with your local refuse disposal company, disposal facility or environmental agency to see if they will accept the oil for recycling. Don't pour used oil into drains or onto the ground. After the oil has cooled, it can be drained into a suitable container (capped plastic jugs, topped bottles, milk cartons, etc.) for transport to one of these disposal sites.

12 Air cleaner - filter element and drain tube cleaning

Element cleaning

Refer to illustrations 12.1, 12.2, 12.3a, 12.3b and 12.3c

1   If you're working on an XR250L or a 1986 through 1995 XR250R, remove the left side cover (see Chapter 7). If the air cleaner has an inlet dust cap, you'll need to remove the seat as well to remove the dust cap. On 1990 and later models, take the cover off the housing **(see illustration)**.

2   If you're working on a 1996 or later XR250R or an XR400R, undo the quick-release cover fasteners and open the cover (it's hinged at the

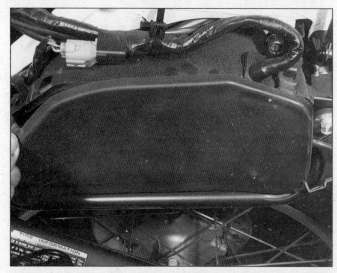

12.1 Lift off the air filter cover on XR250L and 1990 through 1995 XR250R models

12.2   On later XR250R and XR400R models, undo the fasteners and lower the cover

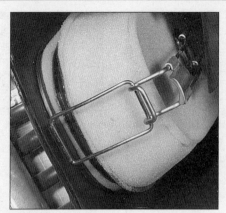

12.3a   On XR250L and early XR250R models, unclip the filter retaining band and pull the filter out of the case . . .

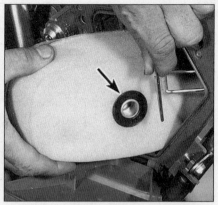

12.3b   . . . on later XR250R and XR400R models, unclip the retainer from the case - align the filter hole (arrow) with the protrusion on the band when you install the filter

bottom) **(see illustration).**

3   Unclip the retaining band that secures the filter, pull the filter out and separate the foam element from the metal core **(see illustrations).**

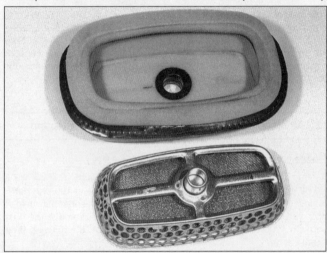

12.3c   Separate the foam element from the core for cleaning and re-oiling

4   Clean the element and holder or core in a high flash point solvent, squeeze the solvent out of the foam and let the core and element dry completely.

5   Soak the foam element in the type of oil listed in this Chapter's Specifications, then squeeze it firmly to remove the excess oil.

6   Place the element on the holder or core.

7   The remainder of installation is the reverse of the removal steps.

Drain tube cleaning

Refer to illustrations 12.8a and 12.8b

8   Squeeze the drain tube to let accumulated water and oil run out **(see illustrations).** If the tube is clogged, squeeze its clamp, remove it from the air cleaner housing and clean it out. Install the drain tube on the housing and secure it with the clamp.

---

13   Fuel system - check and filter cleaning

Refer to illustrations 13.1a and 13.1b

Warning: *Gasoline is extremely flammable, so take extra precautions when you work on any part of the fuel system. Don't smoke or allow open flames or bare light bulbs near the work area, and don't work in a garage where a natural gas-type appliance (such as a water heater or clothes dryer) is present. Since gasoline is carcinogenic, wear latex gloves when there's a possibility of being exposed to fuel, and if you*

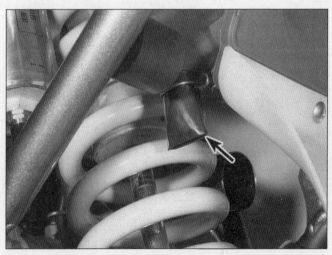

12.8a   Open the drain tube (arrow) to release accumulated oil and water; if it's clogged, remove it for cleaning . . .

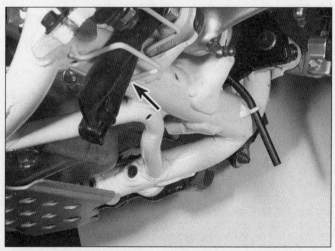

12.8b   . . . the longer drain tubes on some models fit through retainers on the frame

13.1a The fuel tap on XR250R and XR400R models is bolted to the tank

13.1b There's a drain hose connected to the bottom of the float chamber and a vent hose connected to the top

spill any fuel on your skin, rinse it off immediately with soap and water. Mop up any fuel spills immediately and do not store fuel-soaked rags where they could ignite. When you perform any kind of work on the fuel system, wear safety glasses and have a Class B type fire extinguisher (flammable liquids) on hand.

1   Check the carburetor, fuel tank, the fuel tap and line and the carburetor hoses for leaks and evidence of damage (see illustrations).

2   If carburetor gaskets are leaking, the carburetor should be disassembled and rebuilt (refer to Chapter 3).

3   If the fuel tap is leaking at the gasket, tightening the screws may help. If leakage persists, the tap should be removed and a new gasket installed. The tap can't be disassembled, so if it's leaking around the handle, it should be replaced with a new one.

4   If the fuel line or drain hose is cracked or otherwise deteriorated, replace it with a new one.

5   Place the fuel tap lever in the Off position.

XL250R

Refer to illustrations 13.6a and 13.6b

6   Place a wrench on the hex at the bottom of the fuel tap and remove the cup, strainer and O-ring (see illustrations).

7   Clean the strainer. If it's heavily clogged, remove the fuel tank (see Chapter 3). Unscrew the fuel valve nut (see illustration 13.6a), then remove the fuel tank and clean the in-tank strainer.

XR250R and XR400R

8   Drain the fuel from the fuel tank. This can be done by removing

the tank and pouring the fuel into an approved fuel container, or by turning the fuel tap lever to the Off position, detaching the fuel line from the tap and attaching a hose to the tap, then directing the hose into an approved fuel container and turning the fuel tap On.

9   Disconnect and plug the fuel line, remove the bolts and take the tap out of the fuel tank (see illustration 13.1a).

10   Clean the strainer. If it's too heavily clogged to clean, replace the fuel tap.

All models

11   Installation is the reverse of the removal steps. Tighten the fuel tap or tap screws securely, but don't overtighten them and strip out the threads.

12   After installation, run the engine and check for fuel leaks.

13   If the motorcycle will be stored for a month or more, remove and drain the fuel tank. Also loosen the float chamber drain screw and drain the fuel from the carburetor (see Chapter 3).

14   Exhaust system - inspection and spark arrester cleaning

Refer to illustrations 14.4a, 14.4b, 14.5a and 14.5b

Warning: Make sure the exhaust system is cool before doing this procedure.

1   Periodically check the exhaust system for leaks and loose fasteners (see Chapter 3). If tightening the holder nuts at the cylinder head

13.6a On XR250L models, turn the hex (lower arrow) counterclockwise to unscrew the cup from the fuel tap; drain the fuel tank and remove the fuel tap nut (upper arrow) if it's necessary to remove the in-tank strainer

13.6b Pull the O-ring and plastic strainer from the fuel tap; on installation, line up the match mark on the strainer with the mark on the fuel tap

14.4a Unbolt the plate . . .

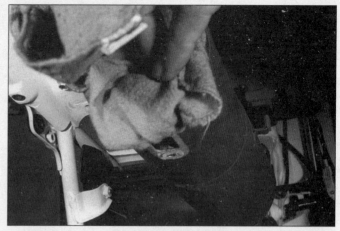

14.4b . . . then hold a rag against the muffler opening and rev the engine a few times to blow carbon out of the spark arrester

fails to stop any leaks, replace the gaskets with new ones (a procedure which requires removal of the system).

2   The exhaust pipe flange nuts at the cylinder head are especially prone to loosening, which could cause damage to the head. Check them frequently and keep them tight.

3   At the specified interval, clean the spark arrester as described below.

4   If there's a plate on the underside of the muffler, remove it **(see illustration)**. Hold a rag firmly over the normal exhaust outlet at the rear end of the muffler **(see illustration)**. Have an assistant start the engine and rev it a few times to blow carbon out of the plate hole, then shut the engine off. After the exhaust system has cooled, install the plate and gasket. Tighten the bolts securely.

5   If there are bolts in the rear end of the muffler and no plate on the underside, remove the bolts **(see illustration)**. Pull out the spark arrester and clean it with a wire brush **(see illustration)**. Install a new gasket and the spark arrester, then tighten the bolts securely.

15   Spark plug - replacement

Refer to illustrations 15.1, 15.6a and 15.6b

1   Twist the spark plug cap to break it free from the plug, then pull it off **(see illustration)**.

2   If available, use compressed air to blow any accumulated debris from around the spark plug. Remove the plug. **Note:** *The plug is difficult to reach on XR400R models. The plug socket in the bike's tool kit is designed to work in the space available.*

3   Inspect the electrodes for wear. Both the center and side electrodes should have square edges and the side electrode should be of uniform thickness. Look for excessive deposits and evidence of a cracked or chipped insulator around the center electrode. Compare your spark plug to the color spark plug chart on the inside of the back cover. Check the threads, the washer and the ceramic insulator body for cracks and other damage.

4   If the electrodes are not excessively worn, and if the deposits can be easily removed with a wire brush, the plug can be regapped and reused (if no cracks or chips are visible in the insulator). If in doubt concerning the condition of the plug, replace it with a new one, as the expense is minimal.

5   Cleaning the spark plug by sandblasting is permitted, provided you clean the plug with a high flash-point solvent afterwards.

6   Before installing a new plug, make sure it is the correct type and heat range. Check the gap between the electrodes, as it is not preset. For best results, use a wire-type gauge rather than a flat gauge to check the gap **(see illustration)**. If the gap must be adjusted, bend the side electrode only and be very careful not to chip or crack the insulator nose **(see illustration)**. Make sure the washer is in place before installing the plug.

7   Since the cylinder head is made of aluminum, which is soft and easily damaged, thread the plug into the head by hand. Slip a short length of hose over the end of the plug to use as a tool to thread it into place. The hose will grip the plug well enough to turn it, but will start to slip if the plug begins to cross-thread in the hole - this will prevent damaged threads and the accompanying repair costs.

8   Once the plug is finger tight, the job can be finished with a socket.

14.5a Remove the Allen bolts at the end of the muffler . . .

14.5b . . . and pull the spark arrester out; use a new gasket on installation

15.1 Twist the spark plug cap back and forth to free it, then pull it off the plug

15.6a Spark plug manufacturers recommend using a wire type gauge when checking the gap - if the wire doesn't slide between the electrodes with a slight drag, adjustment is required

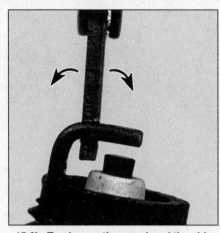

15.6b To change the gap, bend the side electrode only, as indicated by the arrows, and be very careful not to crack or chip the ceramic insulator surrounding the center electrode

16.5 A compression gauge with a threaded fitting for the spark plug hole is preferred over the type that requires hand pressure to maintain the seal

Tighten the spark plug to the torque listed in this Chapter's Specifications.

9   Reconnect the spark plug cap.

16   Cylinder compression - check

Refer to illustration 16.5

1   Among other things, poor engine performance may be caused by leaking valves, incorrect valve clearances, a leaking head gasket, or worn piston, rings and/or cylinder wall. A cylinder compression check will help pinpoint these conditions and can also indicate the presence of excessive carbon deposits in the cylinder head.

2   The only tools required are a compression gauge and a spark plug wrench. Depending on the outcome of the initial test, a squirt-type oil can may also be needed.

3   Start the engine and allow it to reach normal operating temperature, then remove the spark plug (see Section 15, if necessary). Work carefully - don't strip the spark plug hole threads and don't burn your hands.

4   Disable the ignition by disconnecting the primary (low tension) wires from the coil (see Chapter 4). Be sure to mark the locations of the wires before detaching them.

5   Install the compression gauge in the spark plug hole **(see illustration)**. Hold or block the throttle wide open.

6   Kick the engine over a minimum of four or five revolutions (or until the gauge reading stops increasing) and observe the initial movement of the compression gauge needle as well as the final total gauge reading. Compare the results to the value listed in this Chapter's Specifications.

7   If the compression built up quickly and evenly to the specified amount, you can assume the engine upper end is in reasonably good mechanical condition. Worn or sticking piston rings and worn cylinders will produce very little initial movement of the gauge needle, but compression will tend to build up gradually as the engine spins over. Valve and valve seat leakage, or head gasket leakage, is indicated by low initial compression which does not tend to build up.

8   To further confirm your findings, add a small amount of engine oil to the cylinder by inserting the nozzle of a squirt-type oil can through the spark plug hole. The oil will tend to seal the piston rings if they are leaking.

9   If the compression increases significantly after the addition of the oil, the piston rings and/or cylinder are definitely worn. If the compression does not increase, the pressure is leaking past the valves or the head gasket. Leakage past the valves may be due to insufficient valve

clearances, burned, warped or cracked valves or valve seats or valves that are hanging up in the guides.

10   If compression readings are considerably higher than specified, the combustion chamber is probably coated with excessive carbon deposits. It is possible (but not very likely) for carbon deposits to raise the compression enough to compensate for the effects of leakage past rings or valves. Refer to Chapter 2, remove the cylinder head and carefully decarbonize the combustion chamber.

17   Valve clearances - check and adjustment

Refer to illustrations 17.3, 17.4, 17.5a and 17.5b

1   The engine must be completely cool for this maintenance procedure (below 35-degrees C/95-degrees F), so if possible let the machine sit overnight before beginning. Also, make sure there's at least some clearance in the decompressor lever (see Section 18). Adjust the decompressor cable if necessary.

2   Refer to Section 15 and remove the spark plug. This will make it easier to turn the engine.

3   Remove the valve adjusting hole plugs from the cylinder head cover **(see illustration)**.

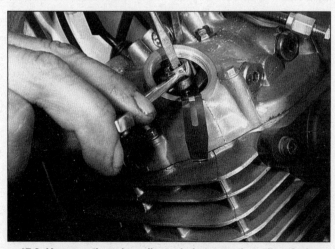

17.3 Unscrew the valve adjuster hole cover, then slip a feeler gauge between the rocker arm and valve stem to measure the clearance; to change it, loosen the locknut and turn the adjuster with a screwdriver

17.4 Unscrew the timing hole cover to look at the timing marks (don't forget to inspect its O-ring); the center cover (arrow) provides access to the alternator rotor bolt, which you can use to turn the engine

17.5a The line next to the T on the alternator rotor should be aligned with the timing hole notch for valve adjustment

17.5b The line next to the T indicates top dead center; the line next to the F is the ignition timing mark at idle speed; the two parallel lines form the advance timing mark (left engine cover removed for clarity)

4   Remove the timing hole plug and center access plug from the left engine cover **(see illustration)**.
5   Position the piston at Top Dead Center (TDC) on the compression stroke. Do this by turning the crankshaft until the T mark on the rotor is aligned with the timing pointer on the crankcase **(see illustrations)**. **Note:** *Turn the crankshaft counterclockwise only; turning it clockwise will operate the decompressor and give an inaccurate reading on one of the exhaust valves.* Reach through the access holes and try to wiggle the rocker arms. They should have some play. If they don't, the piston is on the exhaust stroke; rotate the crankshaft one full turn to bring the marks into alignment again and recheck to make sure there's now some play in the rocker arms. **Caution:** *Be sure the engine is on the compression stroke, not the exhaust stroke; engine damage may occur if the valves are adjusted with the piston on the exhaust stroke. If you're still in doubt, place a thumb over the spark plug hole while you turn the engine. As the piston rises on its compression stroke, you'll feel the compression build up.*
6   With the engine in this position, all four of the valves can be checked.
7   To check, insert a feeler gauge of the thickness listed in this Chapter's Specifications between the valve stem and rocker arm **(see illustration 17.3)**. Pull the feeler gauge out slowly - you should feel a slight drag. If there's no drag, the clearance is too loose. If there's a heavy drag, the clearance is too tight.
8   If the clearance is incorrect, loosen the adjuster locknut with a box wrench (ring spanner). Turn the adjusting screw until the correct clearance is achieved, then tighten the locknut. The adjusting screws have square heads. They can be turned with a special tool (Honda part no. 07708-0030100 or equivalent), or with an open-end wrench if you don't have the special tool.
9   After adjusting, recheck the clearance with the feeler gauge to make sure it wasn't changed when the locknut was tightened.
10   Now measure the other valves, following the same procedure you used for the first valve. Make sure to use a feeler gauge of the specified thickness.
11   With all of the clearances within the Specifications, install the adjusting hole plugs, center access cover and the timing hole plug.
12   Always check the adjustment of the decompressor after adjusting the valve clearances.

18 Decompressor freeplay - check and adjustment

1   Refer to Section 17 and make sure the engine is at top dead center on its compression stroke. Make the adjustments in the following order.

XR250L, 1986 through 1995 XR250R

Refer to illustrations 18.2 and 18.3
2   Measure play at the end of the kickstarter decompressor cable **(see illustration)**. If it's not within the range listed in this Chapter's Specifications, loosen the locknut, turn the adjusting nut to obtain the correct freeplay and tighten the locknut.
3   If you're working on a 1986 through 1995 XR250R, operate the decompressor lever on the left handlebar and note the amount of freeplay at the outer end of the lever (how far the lever travels before it starts to pull the decompressor) **(see illustration)**. If it's not within the range listed in this Chapter's Specifications, loosen the locknut(s) at the engine. Turn the adjuster to obtain correct freeplay then tighten the locknut(s).

1996 and later XR250R, all XR400R

Refer to illustration 18.4
4   Operate the decompressor lever on the left handlebar and note the amount of freeplay at the outer end of the lever (how far the lever travels before it starts to pull the decompressor). If it's not within the range listed in this Chapter's Specifications, loosen the locknut at the engine **(see illustration)**. Turn the adjuster to obtain correct freeplay and tighten the locknut.

18.2 XR250L decompressor freeplay is measured at the lever

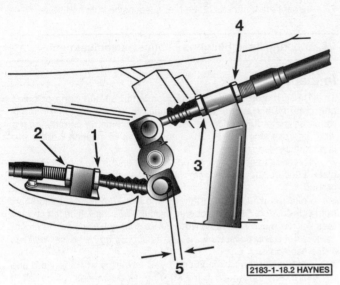

2183-1-18.2 HAYNES

**18.3 Kickstarter decompressor details
(1986 through 1995 XR250R)**

1 Locknut (kickstarter decompressor)
2 Adjusting nut (kickstarter decompressor)
3 Locknut (manual decompressor)
4 Adjusting nut (manual decompressor)
5 Freeplay (kickstarter decompressor)

19 Ignition timing

1   Ignition timing is fixed and can't be adjusted.
2   Connect a timing light and tune-up tachometer to the engine, following manufacturer's instructions.
3   Remove the timing hole plug from the left engine cover **(see illustration 17.4)**.
4   Start the engine. Let it idle and compare idle speed with this Chapter's Specifications. If necessary, adjust idle speed (see Section 20).
5   At idle, the timing light should flash when the F mark on the alternator rotor is aligned with the timing pointer on the crankcase **(see illustration 17.5b)**.
6   Operate the throttle to slowly increase engine speed to the full advance speed listed in this Chapter's Specifications. At that point, the timing light should flash when the timing pointer on the crankcase is between the full advance marks (parallel lines) on the alternator rotor **(see illustration 17.5b)**.
7   If the light doesn't flash at the proper time, there's a problem in the electronic ignition system (possibly a defective CDI unit). Have the system tested by a Honda dealer or motorcycle repair shop.

20 Idle speed - check and adjustment

Refer to illustration 20.3
1   Before adjusting the idle speed, make sure the valve clearances and spark plug gap are correct. Also, turn the handlebars back-and-forth and see if the idle speed changes as this is done. If it does, the throttle cable may not be adjusted correctly, or it may be worn out. Be sure to correct this problem before proceeding.
2   The engine should be at normal operating temperature, which is usually reached after 10 to 15 minutes of stop and go riding. Make sure the transmission is in Neutral.
3   Turn the throttle stop screw **(see illustration)** until the idle speed listed in this Chapter's Specifications is obtained.
4   Snap the throttle open and shut a few times, then recheck the idle speed. If necessary, repeat the adjustment procedure.

18.4 On 1996 and later XR250R and all XR400R models, loosen the locknut (left arrow) and turn the adjusting nut (right arrow) to set decompressor lever freeplay

20.3 Turn the throttle stop screw to set idle speed

5   If a smooth, steady idle can't be achieved, the fuel/air mixture may be incorrect. Refer to Chapter 3 for additional carburetor information.

21 Fasteners - check

1   Since vibration of the machine tends to loosen fasteners, all nuts, bolts, screws, etc. should be periodically checked for proper tightness. Also make sure all cotter pins or other safety fasteners are correctly installed.
2   Pay particular attention to the following:

Spark plug
Engine oil drain plugs
Gearshift pedal
Brake lever and pedal
Kickstarter pedal
Footpegs
Engine mounting bolts
Steering stem locknut
Front axle nut
Rear axle nut
Skid bar or skid plate bolts

3   If a torque wrench is available, use it along with the torque specifications at the beginning of this or other Chapters.

22.4 Remove the air valve cap to check fork air pressure

22 Suspension - check

Refer to illustration 22.4

1   The suspension components must be maintained in top operating condition to ensure rider safety. Loose, worn or damaged suspension parts decrease the motorcycle's stability and control.

2   Lock the front brake and push on the handlebars to compress the front forks several times. See if they move up-and-down smoothly without binding. If binding is felt, the forks should be disassembled and inspected as described in Chapter 6.

3   Check the tightness of all front suspension nuts and bolts to be sure none have worked loose.

4   If you're working on an XR250L or a 1986 through 1995 XR250R, with the front forks cold and fully extended, remove the air valve caps from the forks and check air pressure with a pressure gauge **(see illustration)**. Compare with the reading listed in this Chapter's Specifications.

5   Inspect the rear shock absorber for fluid leakage and tightness of the mounting nuts and bolts. If leakage is found, the shock should be replaced.

6   Support the motorcycle securely upright with its rear wheel off the ground. Grab the swingarm on each side, just ahead of the axle. Rock the swingarm from side to side - there should be no discernible movement at the rear. If there's a little movement or a slight clicking can be heard, make sure the swingarm pivot shaft is tight. If the pivot shaft is tight but movement is still noticeable, the swingarm will have to be removed and the bearings replaced as described in Chapter 5.

7   Inspect the tightness of the rear suspension nuts and bolts.

23 Steering head bearings - check and adjustment

Inspection

1   These motorcycles are equipped with ball-and-cone or roller-and-cone type steering head bearings, which can become dented, rough or loose during normal use of the machine. In extreme cases, worn or loose steering head bearings can cause steering wobble that is potentially dangerous.

2   To check the bearings, lift up the front end of the motorcycle and place a secure support beneath the engine so the front wheel is off the ground.

3   Point the wheel straight ahead and slowly move the handlebars from side-to-side. Dents or roughness in the bearing will be felt and the bars will not move smoothly. **Note:** *Make sure any hesitation in movement is not being caused by the cables and wiring harnesses that run to the handlebars.*

4   Next, grasp the fork legs and try to move the wheel forward and backward. Any looseness in the steering head bearings will be felt. If play is felt in the bearings, adjust the steering head as follows.

Adjustment

Refer to illustrations 23.6 and 23.9

5   Remove the handlebars and upper triple clamp (see Chapter 5).

6   Loosen the bearing adjusting nut, then tighten it to the torque listed in this Chapter's Specifications **(see illustration)**.

7   Turn the lower triple clamp from lock-to-lock (all the way to the left and all the way back to the right) four or five times to seat the bearings.

8   Loosen the adjusting nut all the way, then tighten it to the final torque listed in this Chapter's Specifications.

9   An adjustable spanner wrench can be used to adjust the bearings if you don't have the special socket **(see illustration)**. Since this tool can't be used with a torque wrench, it will be necessary to estimate the tightness of the nut. Be sure the final result is that the steering stem turns from side-to-side freely, but there is no side-to-side or vertical play of the steering stem in the bearings.

10.   Install the upper triple clamp and handlebars (see Chapter 5).

24 Drive chain and sprockets - check, adjustment and lubrication

Refer to illustrations 24.3 and 24.6

1   A neglected drive chain won't last long and can quickly damage

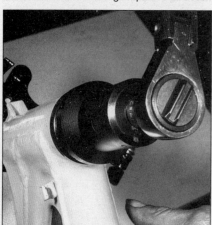

23.6 The best way to adjust the steering stem bearings is with a torque wrench and a special socket . . .

23.9 . . . but an adjustable spanner can also be used; be very sure there's no binding or looseness in the bearings

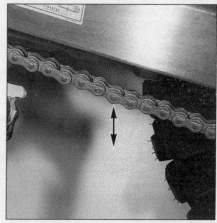

24.3 Check drive chain freeplay midway along the lower chain run

24.6 Inspect the slider at the front of the swingarm and replace it if it's worn; also inspect the sliders on the top and bottom of the swingarm

the sprockets. Routine chain adjustment isn't difficult and will ensure maximum chain and sprocket life.

2   To check the chain, support the bike securely with the rear wheel off the ground. Place the transmission in neutral.

3   Push up on the bottom run of the chain and measure the slack midway between the two sprockets **(see illustration)**, then compare the measurements to the value listed in this Chapter's Specifications. As wear occurs, the chain will actually stretch, which means adjustment by removing some slack from the chain. In some cases where lubrication has been neglected, corrosion and galling may cause the links to bind and kink, which effectively shortens the chain's length. If the chain is tight between the sprockets, rusty or kinked, it's time to replace it with a new one. **Note:** *Repeat the chain slack measurement along the length of the chain - ideally, every inch or so. If you find a tight area, mark it with a felt pen or paint and repeat the measurement after the bike has been ridden. If the chain's still tight in the same areas, it may be damaged or worn. Because a tight or kinked chain can damage the transmission countershaft bearing, it's a good idea to replace it.*

4   Check the entire length of the chain for damaged rollers, loose links and loose pins.

5   Look through the slots in the engine sprocket cover and inspect the engine sprocket. Check the teeth on the engine sprocket and the rear sprocket for wear (see Chapter 5). Refer to Chapter 5 for the sprocket replacement procedure if the sprockets appear to be worn excessively.

6   Check the chain slider on the swingarm near the front **(see illustration)**. Also check the slider on top of the swingarm. If it's worn, measure its thickness. If it's less than the value listed in the Chapter 5 Specifications, replace it (see Chapter 5). Look through the small hole in the chain guide bolted to the underside of the swingarm. If you can see the chain through the hole, the slider is worn. Replace it.

Adjustment

Refer to illustration 24.8

7   Rotate the rear wheel until the chain is positioned with the least amount of slack present.

8   Loosen the rear axle nut (see *Wheels - inspection, removal and installation* in Chapter 6). Turn the snail adjuster on each side of the swingarm evenly until the proper chain tension is obtained (get the adjuster on the chain side close, then set the adjuster on the opposite side) **(see illustration)**. Be sure to turn the adjusters evenly to keep the wheel in alignment. If the adjusters reach the end of their travel, the chain is excessively worn and should be replaced with a new one (see Chapter 5).

9   When the chain has the correct amount of slack, make sure the marks on the adjusters correspond to the same relative marks on each side of the swingarm **(see illustration 24.8)**. Tighten the axle nut to the torque listed in the Chapter 6 Specifications.

Lubrication

Note: *If the chain is dirty, it should be removed and cleaned before it's lubricated* (see Chapter 5).

10   Use a good quality chain lubricant of the type listed in this Chapter's Specifications. Be sure the lubricant is intended for use with O-ring chains - if the lubricant causes the O-rings to deteriorate, the chain will lose its internal lubricant and dirt will find its way into the rollers. Apply the lubricant along the top of the lower chain run, so that when the bike is ridden centrifugal force will move the lubricant into the chain, rather than throwing it off.

11   After applying the lubricant, let it soak in a few minutes before wiping off any excess.

25   Crankcase breather system - check

Refer to illustrations 25.1 and 25.2

1   Check the breather hoses for damage, deterioration and loose connections **(see illustration)**.

2   At the bottom end of the drain hose, either remove the plug or squeeze the fitting to open it so any breather deposits can drain out **(see illustration)**. If the hose is clogged, remove it and clean out the deposits.

24.8 Turn the chain adjuster to tighten or loosen the chain

25.1 Inspect the breather hoses

25.2 Squeeze the fitting at the bottom end of the breather drain hose (arrow) to let out accumulated oil and water

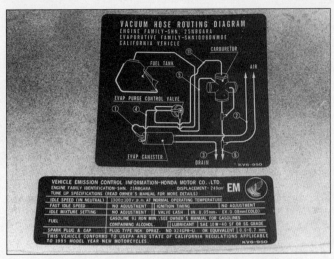

26.2 Evaporative emission control system sticker (California XR250L models)

27.6 Some models have a fork oil drain bolt (arrow)

26 Evaporative emission control system - check

Refer to illustration 26.2

1   This system is used on XR250L models first sold in California. It stores gasoline vapor from the fuel system in a canister filled with activated charcoal. The stored vapor is pulled into the engine for combustion when the engine is run.

2   To inspect the system, check the hoses for misconnection, cracks and general deterioration and connect or replace them as necessary. There's a hose diagram on the inside of the side cover **(see illustration)**.

3   Remove the canister from the hoses and turn it upside down. If liquid gasoline runs out, the canister should be replaced.

27 Front fork oil change

Refer to illustration 27.6

1   Although fork oil changes are not a regularly scheduled maintenance procedure, the oil should be changed if it becomes contaminated. The following steps apply to models equipped with fork drain screws. If you're working on a bike that doesn't have a drain screw, you'll need to disassemble the forks part-way to drain the oil (see Chapter 5).

2   Support the motorcycle securely upright.

3   Remove the handlebars (see Chapter 5).

4   Remove the fork cap bolts.

5   Wrap a rag around the top of the fork to catch dripping oil, then lift out the fork spring from each fork.

6   Place a pan under the fork drain bolt and remove the drain bolt and gasket **(see illustration)**. **Warning:** *Do not allow the fork oil to drip onto the tire or brake disc. If it does, wash it off with soap and water*

before riding the motorcycle.

7   After most of the oil has drained, slowly compress and release the forks to pump out the rest of the oil. An assistant may be needed to do this.

8   Check the drain bolt gasket for damage and replace it if necessary. Clean the threads of the drain bolt with solvent and let it dry, then reinstall the bolt and gasket, tightening it securely.

9   Pour the type and amount of fork oil listed in the Chapter 5 Specifications into the fork tube through the opening at the top. Slowly pump the forks a few times to purge air from the upper and lower chambers.

10   Fully compress the front forks (you may need an assistant to do this). Insert a stiff tape measure into the fork tube and measure the distance from the oil to the top of the fork tube (see Chapter 5). Compare your measurement to the value listed in the Chapter 5 Specifications, Drain or add oil as necessary until the level is correct.

11   Check the O-ring on the fork cap bolt and replace it with a new one if it's deteriorated, broken or otherwise damaged. Install the fork spring. Install the cap bolt and tighten it to the Chapter 5 Specifications.

12   Repeat the procedure for the other fork. It is essential that the oil quantity and level are identical in each fork.

13   Install the handlebar, being sure to locate it correctly in the brackets, and tighten the handlebar bracket bolts to the torque listed in the Chapter 5 Specifications.

28 Sidestand - check

The sidestand should be checked to make sure it stays down when extended and up when retracted. Refer to Chapter 8 and check tightness of the sidestand mounting bolts. Check the spring for cracks or rust and replace it if any problems are found.

Chapter 2
Engine, clutch and transmission

Contents

Specifications

XR250L

Main rocker arms

Rocker arm inside diameter
  Standard... 11.500 to 11.518 mm (0.4528 to 0.4535 inch)
  Limit... 11.53 mm (0.454 inch)
Rocker shaft outside diameter
  Standard... 11.466 to 11.484 mm (0.4514 to 0.4521 inch)
  Limit... 11.41 mm (0.449 inch)
Shaft-to-arm clearance
  Standard... 0.016 to 0.052 mm (0.0006 to 0.0020 inch)
  Limit... 0.10 mm (0.004 inch)

Sub-rocker arms

Rocker arm inside diameter (intake and exhaust)
  Standard... 7.000 to 7.015 mm (0.2756 to 0.2762 inch)
  Limit... 7.05 mm (0.278 inch)
Rocker shaft outside diameter (intake and exhaust)
  Standard... 6.972 to 6.987 mm (0.2745 to 0.2762 inch)
  Limit... 6.92 mm (0.272 inch)
Shaft-to-arm clearance
  Standard... 0.013 to 0.043 mm (0.0005 to 0.0017 inch)
  Limit... 0.10 mm (0.004 inch)

XR250L (continued)

Camshaft

Lobe height
   Intake
      Standard .... 29.377 to 29.537 mm (1.1566 to 1.1629 inch)
      Limit .... 29.27 mm (1.152 inch)
   Exhaust
      Standard .... 29.178 to 29.338 mm (1.1487 to 1.1550 inch)
      Limit .... 29.07 mm (1.144 inch)
Journal diameter .... Not specified
Bearing journal inside diameter .... Not specified
Journal oil clearance .... Not specified
Camshaft runout limit .... 0.04 mm (0.002 inch)
Camshaft side clearance .... Not specified

Cylinder head, valves and valve springs

Cylinder head warpage limit .... 0.10 mm (0.004 inch)
Valve stem runout .... Not specified
Valve stem diameter
   Intake
      Standard .... 5.475 to 5.490 mm (0.2156 to 0.2161 inch)
      Limit .... 5.46 mm (0.2149 inch)
   Exhaust
      Standard .... 5.467 to 5.477 mm (0.2152 to 0.2156 inch)
      Limit .... 5.45 mm (0.2145 inch)
Valve guide inside diameter (intake and exhaust)
   Standard .... 5.500 to 5.512 mm (0.2165 to 0.2170 inch)
   Limit .... 5.53 mm (0.218 inch)
Stem-to-guide clearance
   Intake
      Standard .... 0.010 to 0.037 mm (0.0004 to 0.0015 inch)
      Limit .... 0.07 mm (0.003 inch)
   Exhaust
      Standard .... 0.023 to 0.045 mm (0.0009 to 0.0018 inch)
      Limit .... 0.08 mm (0.003 inch)
Valve seat width (intake and exhaust)
   Standard .... 1.2 to 1.4 mm (0.05 to 0.06 inch)
   Limit .... 2.0 mm (0.08 inch)
Valve spring free length
   Inner spring
      Standard .... 38.83 mm (1.529 inches)
      Limit .... 37.9 mm (1.49 inches)
   Outer spring
      Standard .... 38.30 mm (1.508 inches)
      Limit .... 37.1 mm (1.46 inches)
Valve face width .... Not specified

Cylinder

Bore
   Standard .... 73.000 to 73.010 mm (2.8740 to 2.8744 inches)
   Limit .... 73.11 mm (28.78 inches)
Taper and out-of-round limits .... 0.05 mm (0.002 inch)
Surface warpage limit .... 0.10 mm (0.004 inch)

Piston

Piston diameter
   Standard .... 72.960 to 72.985 mm (2.8724 to 2.8734 inches)
   Limit .... 72.88 mm (2.869 inches)
Piston diameter measuring point (above bottom of piston) .... 10 mm (0.40 inch)
Piston-to-cylinder clearance
   Standard .... 0.015 to 0.050 mm (0.0006 to 0.0020 inch)
   Limit .... 0.10 mm (0.004 inch)
Piston pin bore in piston
   Standard .... 17.002 to 17.008 mm (0.6694 to 0.6696 inch)
   Limit .... 17.07 mm (0.672 inch)
Piston pin bore in connecting rod
   Standard .... 17.016 to 17.034 mm (0.6699 to 0.6706 inch)
   Limit .... 17.06 mm (0.672 inch)

Piston pin outer diameter
    Standard.. 17.000 to 17.006 mm (0.6693 to 0.6695 inch)
    Limit... 16.97 mm (0.668 inch)
Piston pin-to-piston clearance
    Standard.. 0.002 to 0.004 mm (0.0001 to 0.0002 inch)
    Limit... 0.07 mm (0.003 inch)
Piston pin-to-connecting rod clearance
    Standard.. 0.016 to 0.040 mm (0.0006 to 0.0016 inch)
    Limit... 0.09 mm (0.004 inch)
Top and second ring side clearance
    Standard.. 0.015 to 0.045 mm (0.0006 to 0.0018 inch)
    Limit... 0.12 mm (0.006 inch)
Oil ring side clearance .... Not specified
Ring end gap
    Top and second
        Standard .... 0.25 to 0.45 mm (0.010 to 0.018 inch)
        Limit .... 0.56 mm (0.022 inch)
    Oil ring side rails
        Standard .... 0.20 to 0.70 mm (0.008 to 0.038 inch)
        Limit .... 0.86 mm (0.034 inch)

Clutch

Spring free length
    Standard.. 33.7 mm (1.33 inches)
    Limit... 32.2 mm (1.27 inches)
Friction plate thickness
    Standard.. 2.92 to 3.08 mm (0.115 to 0.121 inch)
    Limit... 2.69 mm (0.106 inch)
Friction and metal plate warpage limit .... 0.30 mm (0.012 inch)
Clutch housing bushing inside diameter
    Standard.. 20.010 to 20.035 mm (0.7878 to 0.7888 inch)
    Limit... 20.05 mm (0.789 inch)
Clutch housing bushing outside diameter
    Standard.. 24.959 to 24.980 mm (0.9826 to 0.9835 inch)
    Limit... 24.17 mm (0.952 inch)
Clutch housing bushing clearance to mainshaft .... Not specified
Clutch housing inside diameter
    Standard.. 25.00 to 25.021 mm (0.9843 to 0.9851 inch)
    Limit... 25.04 mm (0.986 inch)

Oil pump

Outer rotor-to-body clearance
    Standard.. 0.10 to 0.21 mm (0.004 to 0.008 inch)
    Limit... 0.25 mm (0.010 inch)
Inner-to-outer rotor clearance
    Standard.. 0.15 mm (0.006 inch) or less
    Limit... 0.20 mm (0.008 inch)
Side clearance (rotors-to-straightedge)
    Standard.. 0.02 to 0.09 mm (0.001 to 0.004 inch)
    Limit... 0.12 mm (0.005 inch)

Kickstarter

Spindle outside diameter
    Standard.. 21.959 to 21.980 mm (0.8645 to 0.8654 inch)
    Limit... 22.91 mm (0.863 inch)
Pinion gear inside diameter
    Standard.. 22.020 to 22.041 mm (0.8669 to 0.8678 inch)
    Limit... 22.12 mm (0.871 inch)
Idler gear bushing inside diameter
    Standard.. 15.000 to 15.018 mm (0.5906 to 0.5913 inch)
    Limit... 14.97 mm (0.589 inch)
Idler gear bushing outside diameter
    Standard.. 18.959 to 18.980 mm (0.7464 to 0.7472 inch)
    Limit... 18.92 mm (0.745 inch)
Idler gear inside diameter
    Standard.. 19.010 to 19.034 mm (0.7484 to 0.7494 inch)
    Limit... 19.13 mm (0.753 inch)
Countershaft diameter at idler gear bushing surface
    Standard.. 14.966 to 14.984 mm (0.5892 to 0.5899 mm)

XR250L (continued)

Shift drum and forks

Fork inside diameter
  Standard.. 13.000 to 13.021 mm (0.5118 to 0.5126 inch)
  Limit.. 13.05 mm (0.514 inch)
Fork shaft outside diameter
  Standard.. 12.966 to 12.983 mm (0.5105 to 0.5111 inch)
  Limit.. 12.90 mm (0.508 inch)
Fork ear thickness
  Standard.. 4.930 to 5.000 mm (0.1941 to 0.1969 inch)
  Limit.. 4.50 mm (0.18 inch)
Shift drum groove width limit... Not specified

Transmission

Gear inside diameters
  Mainshaft fifth
    Standard .... 20.020 to 20.041 mm (0.7882 to 0.7890 inch)
    Limit .... 20.08 mm (0.791 inch)
  Mainshaft sixth
    Standard .... 23.020 to 23.041 mm (0.9063 to 0.9071 inch)
    Limit .... 23.09 mm (0.909 inch)
  Countershaft first
    Standard .... 23.000 to 23.021 mm (0.9055 to 0.9063 inch)
    Limit .... 23.07 mm (0.908 inch)
  Countershaft second
    Standard .... 25.020 to 25.041 mm (0.9850 to 0.9859 inch)
    Limit .... 25.09 mm (0.988 inch)
  Countershaft third
    Standard .... 22.020 to 22.041 mm (0.8669 to 0.8678 inch)
    Limit .... 22.08 mm (0.869 inch)
  Countershaft fourth
    Standard .... 22.014 to 22.020 mm (0.8667 to 0.8669 inch)
    Limit .... 22.08 mm (0.869 inch)
Bushing inside diameters
  Countershaft first
    Standard .... 18.000 to 18.018 mm (0.7087 to 0.7094 inch)
    Limit .... 18.08 mm (0.712 inch)
  Countershaft second
    Standard .... 22.020 to 22.041 mm (0.8669 to 0.8678 inch)
    Limit .... 22.12 mm (0.871 inch)
Bushing outside diameters
  Mainshaft sixth
    Standard .... 22.959 to 22.980 mm (0.9039 to 0.9047 inch)
    Limit .... 22.92 mm (0.902 inch)
  Countershaft first
    Standard .... 22.951 to 22.980 mm (0.9036 to 0.9047 inch)
    Limit .... 22.90 mm (0.902 inch)
  Countershaft second
    Standard .... 24.972 to 24.993 mm (0.9831 to 0.9840 inch)
    Limit .... 24.90 mm (0.980 inch)
Gear-to-bushing clearances
  Mainshaft sixth
    Standard .... 0.040 to 0.082 mm (0.0016 to 0.0032 inch)
    Limit .... 0.10 mm (0.004 inch)
  Countershaft first
    Standard .... 0.020 to 0.070 mm (0.0008 to 0.0028 inch)
    Limit .... 0.10 mm (0.004 inch)
  Countershaft second
    Standard .... 0.027 to 0.067 mm (0.0011 to 0.0027 inch)
    Limit .... 0.10 mm (0.040 inch)
Mainshaft diameter (at fifth gear and clutch outer guide)
  Standard.. 19.959 to 19.980 mm (0.7858 to 0.7866 inch)
  Limit.. 19.91 mm (0.784 inch)
Countershaft diameter (at second and fourth gears)
  Standard.. 21.959 to 21.980 mm (0.8645 to 0.8654 inch)
  Limit.. 21.91 mm (0.863 inch)
Shaft-to-gear clearance (mainshaft fifth, countershaft fourth)
  Standard.. 0.040 to 0.082 mm (0.0016 to 0.0032 inch)
  Limit.. 0.15 mm (0.006 inch)

Shaft-to-bushing clearance (countershaft second)
    Standard.. 0.040 to 0.080 mm (0.0016 to 0.0031 inch)
    Limit.. 0.15 mm (0.006 inch)

Crankshaft and balancer

Connecting rod side clearance
    Standard.. 0.050 to 0.650 mm (0.0020 to 0.0256 inch)
    Limit.. 0.80 mm (0.031 inch)
Connecting rod big end radial clearance
    Standard.. 0.006 to 0.018 mm (0.0002 to 0.0007 inch)
    Limit.. 0.05 mm (0.002 inch)
Runout measuring points
    At alternator end.. 6 mm (0.24 inch) in from end
    At clutch end.. 8 mm (0.31 inch) in from end
Runout limit.. 0.1 mm (0.004 inch)
Balancer shaft diameter... Not specified

Torque specifications

Engine mounting bolts
    Top hanger plate nuts and bolts
        To frame.. 27 Nm (20 ft-lbs)
        To engine... 65 Nm (47 ft-lbs)
    Front hanger plate
        To frame.. 27 Nm (20 ft-lbs)
        To engine... 65 Nm (47 ft-lbs)
    Lower front and rear through-bolts.................................... 65 Nm (47 ft-lbs)
    Upper rear hanger plate
        Small bolts.. 27 Nm (20 ft-lbs)
        Nut and through-bolt.. 65 Nm (47 ft-lbs)
External oil pipe union bolts .... 10 Nm (86 inch-lbs)
Cylinder head cover bolts
    6 mm bolts .... 12 Nm (108 inch-lbs)
    8 mm bolt .... 23 Nm (17 ft-lbs)
Cam sprocket bolts .... 20 Nm (14 ft-lbs)
Main rocker shafts .... 28 Nm (20 ft-lbs) (1)
Sub-rocker shafts
    Intake .... 28 Nm (20 ft-lbs)
    Exhaust .... 23 Nm (17 ft-lbs)
Cylinder head 10 mm bolts .... 40 Nm (29 ft-lbs) (2)
Cylinder head 6 mm bolts .... 12 Nm (108 inch-lbs)
Cam chain tensioner bolt... Not specified
Cylinder main bolts... 40 Nm (29 ft-lbs) (2)
Cylinder small bolts .... 10 Nm (86 inch-lbs)
Right and left engine cover bolts and nuts................................ 12 Nm (108 inch-lbs)
Clutch spring bolts .... 10 Nm (86 inch-lbs)
Primary drive gear locknut... 60 Nm (43 ft-lbs)
Clutch locknut.. 60 Nm (43 ft-lbs) (3)
Shift cam plate to shift drum bolt .... Not specified (4)
Shift drum stopper arm bolt .... 12 Nm (108 inch-lbs)
Shift pedal pinch bolt.. 12 Nm (108 inch-lbs)
Crankcase bolts... 12 Nm (108 inch-lbs)

1. *Apply non-hardening sealant to the threads.*
2. *Apply oil to the threads.*
3. *Stake after tightening.*
4. *Apply non-permanent thread locking agent to the threads.*

XR250R

Main rocker arms

Rocker arm inside diameter
    Standard.. 11.500 to 11.518 mm (0.4528 to 0.4535 inch)
    Limit.. 11.53 mm (0.454 inch)
Rocker shaft outside diameter
    Standard.. 11.466 to 11.484 mm (0.4514 to 0.4521 inch)
    Limit.. 11.41 mm (0.449 inch)
Shaft-to-arm clearance
    Standard.. 0.016 to 0.052 mm (0.0006 to 0.0020 inch)
    Limit.. 0.10 mm (0.004 inch)

XR250R (continued)

Sub-rocker arms

Rocker arm inside diameter (intake and exhaust)
    Standard.. 7.000 to 7.015 mm (0.2756 to 0.2762 inch)
    Limit.. 7.05 mm (0.278 inch)
Rocker shaft outside diameter (intake and exhaust)
    Standard.. 6.972 to 6.987 mm (0.2745 to 0.2751 inch)
    Limit.. 6.92 mm (0.272 inch)
Shaft-to-arm clearance
    Standard.. 0.013 to 0.043 mm (0.0005 to 0.0017 inch)
    Limit.. 0.10 mm (0.004 inch)

Camshaft

Lobe height
    1986 through 1995
        Intake
            Standard.. 29.529 mm (1.1626 inches)
            Limit.. 29.34 mm (1.155 inches)
        Exhaust
            Standard.. 29.330 mm (1.1547 inches)
            Limit.. 29.14 mm (1.147 inches)
    1996 on
        Intake
            Standard.. 30.772 mm (1.2115 inches)
            Limit.. 30.583 mm (1.2041 inches)
        Exhaust
            Standard.. 30.819 mm (1.2133 inches)
            Limit.. 30.269 mm (1.2059 inches)
Journal diameter... Not specified
Bearing journal inside diameter... Not specified
Journal oil clearance.. Not specified
Camshaft runout limit
    1986 through 1995... 0.04 mm (0.002 inch)
    1996 on.. 0.03 mm (0.001 inch)
Camshaft side clearance.. Not specified

Cylinder head, valves and valve springs

Cylinder head warpage limit... 0.10 mm 0.004 inch)
Valve stem runout... Not specified
Valve stem diameter
    1986 through 1995
        Intake
            Standard .... 5.475 to 5.490 mm (0.2156 to 0.2161 inch)
            Limit.. 5.46 mm (0.2149 inch)
        Exhaust
            Standard.. 5.467 to 5.477 mm (0.2152 to 0.2156 inch)
            Limit.. 5.45 mm (0.2145 inch)
    1996 on
        Intake
            Standard.. 4.975 to 4.990 mm (0.1959 to 0.1965 inch)
            Limit.. 4.96 mm (0.195 inch)
        Exhaust
            Standard.. 4.955 to 4.970 mm (0.1951 to 0.1957 inch)
            Limit.. 4.94 mm (0.194 inch)
Valve guide inside diameter (intake and exhaust)
    1986 through 1995
        Standard.. 5.500 to 5.512 mm (0.2165 to 0.2170 inch)
        Limit.. 5.53 mm (0.218 inch)
    1996 on
        Standard.. 5.000 to 5.012 mm (0.1969 to 0.1973 inch)
        Limit.. 5.03 mm (0.198 inch)
Stem-to-guide clearance
    1986 through 1995
        Intake
            Standard.. 0.010 to 0.037 mm (0.0004 to 0.0015 inch)
            Limit.. 0.07 mm (0.003 inch)
        Exhaust
            Standard.. 0.023 to 0.045 mm (0.0009 to 0.0018 inch)
            Limit.. 0.08 mm (0.003 inch)

Stem-to-guide clearance
    1996 on
        Intake
            Standard .... 0.010 to 0.037 mm (0.0004 to 0.0015 inch)
            Limit .... 0.07 mm (0.003 inch)
        Exhaust
            Standard .... 0.030 to 0.057 mm (0.0012 to 0.0022 inch)
            Limit .... 0.09 mm (0.004 inch)
Valve seat width (intake and exhaust)
    1986 through 1995
        Standard .... 1.2 to 1.4 mm (0.05 to 0.06 inch)
        Limit .... 2.0 mm (0.08 inch)
    1996 on
        Standard .... 1.1 to 1.2 mm (0.04 to 0.05 inch)
        Limit .... 2.0 mm (0.08 inch)
Valve spring free length
    1986 through 1995
        Inner spring
            Standard .... 38.83 mm (1.529 inches)
            Limit .... 37.9 mm (1.49 inches)
        Outer spring
            Standard .... 38.30 mm (1.508 inches)
            Limit .... 37.1 mm (1.46 inches)
    1996 on
        Inner spring
            Standard .... 43.44 mm (1.710 inches)
            Limit .... 42.51 mm (1.673 inches)
        Outer spring
            Standard .... 44.03 mm (1.733 inches)
            Limit .... 42.83 mm (1.686 inches)
Valve face width
    1986 through 1995
        Standard .... 1.2 to 1.4 mm (0.05 to 0.06 inch)
        Limit .... 2.0 mm (0.08 inch)
    1996 on
        Standard .... Not specified
        Limit .... 2.0 mm (0.08 inch)

Cylinder

Bore
    Standard.. 73.000 to 73.010 mm (2.8740 to 2.8744 inches)
    Limit... 73.11 mm (2.878 inches)
Taper and out-of-round limits .... 0.05 mm (0.002 inch)
Surface warpage limit.. 0.10 mm (0.004 inch)

Piston

Piston diameter
    1986 through 1995
        Standard .... 72.960 to 72.985 mm (2.8724 to 2.8734 inches)
        Limit .... 72.88 mm (2.869 inches)
    1996 on
        Standard .... 72.965 to 72.985 mm (2.8726 to 2.8734 inches)
        Limit .... 72.88 mm (2.869 inches)
Piston diameter measuring point (above bottom of piston)
    1986 through 1995 .... 10 mm (0.40 inch)
    1996 on .... 19 mm (0.70 inch)
Piston-to-cylinder clearance
    1986 through 1995
        Standard .... 0.015 to 0.050 mm (0.0006 to 0.0020 inch)
        Limit .... 0.10 mm (0.004 inch)
    1996 on
        Standard .... 0.015 to 0.045 mm (0.0006 to 0.0018 inch)
        Limit .... 0.10 mm (0.004 inch)
Piston pin bore in piston
    Standard.. 17.002 to 17.008 mm (0.6694 to 0.6696 inch)
    Limit... 17.07 mm (0.672 inch)
Piston pin bore in connecting rod
    Standard.. 17.016 to 17.034 mm (0.6699 to 0.6706 inch)
    Limit... 17.06 mm (0.672 inch)

XR250R (continued)

Piston pin outer diameter
    1986 through 1995
        Standard .... 17.000 to 17.006 mm (0.6693 to 0.6695 inch)
        Limit .... 16.97 mm (0.668 inch)
    1996 on
        Standard .... 16.994 to 17.000 mm (0.6691 to 0.6693 inch)
        Limit .... 16.97 mm (0.668 inch)
Piston pin-to-piston clearance
    1986 through 1995
        Standard .... 0.002 to 0.004 mm (0.0001 to 0.0002 inch)
        Limit .... 0.07 mm (0.003 inch)
    1996 on
        Standard .... 0.002 to 0.014 mm (0.0001 to 0.0006 inch)
        Limit .... 0.07 mm (0.003 inch)
Piston pin-to-connecting rod clearance
    1986 through 1995 .... Not specified
    1996 on
        Standard .... 0.016 to 0.040 mm (0.0006 to 0.0016 inch)
        Limit .... 0.09 mm (0.004 inch)
Top and second ring side clearance
    1986 through 1995
        Standard .... 0.015 to 0.045 mm (0.0006 to 0.0018 inch)
        Limit .... 0.12 mm (0.005 inch)
    1996 on
        Standard .... 0.015 to 0.050 mm (0.0006 to 0.0020 inch)
        Limit .... 0.12 mm (0.005 inch)
Oil ring side clearance .... Not specified
Ring end gap
    1986 through 1995
        Top and second
            Standard .... 0.25 to 0.45 mm (0.010 to 0.018 inch)
            Limit .... 0.56 mm (0.022 inch)
        Oil ring side rails
            Standard .... 0.20 to 0.70 mm (0.008 to 0.028 inch)
            Limit .... 0.86 mm (0.034 inch)
    1996 on
        Top
            Standard .... 0.15 to 0.30 mm (0.006 to 0.012 inch)
            Limit .... 0.40 mm (0.016 inch)
        Second
            Standard .... 0.30 to 0.45 mm (0.012 to 0.018 inch)
            Limit .... 0.55 mm (0.022 inch)
        Oil ring side rails
            Standard .... 0.20 to 0.70 mm (0.008 to 0.028 inch)
            Limit .... 0.86 mm (0.034 inch)

Clutch

Spring free length
    1986 through 1995
        Standard .... 33.7 mm (1.33 inches)
        Limit .... 32.2 mm (1.27 inches)
    1996 on
        Standard .... 37.2 mm (1.46 inches)
        Limit .... 33.5 mm (1.32 inches)
Friction plate thickness
    Standard .... 2.92 to 3.08 mm (0.115 to 0.121 inch)
    Limit .... 2.69 mm (0.106 inch)
Friction and metal plate warpage limit .... 0.30 mm (0.012 inch)
Clutch housing bushing inside diameter
    1986 through 1995
        Standard .... 20.010 to 20.035 mm (0.7878 to 0.7888 inch)
        Limit .... 20.05 mm (0.789 inch)
    1996 on
        Standard .... 19.990 to 20.010 mm (0.7870 to 0.7878 inch)
        Limit .... 20.03 mm (0.788 inch)
Clutch housing bushing outside diameter
    Standard .... 24.959 to 24.980 mm (0.9826 to 0.9835 inch)
    Limit .... 24.17 mm (0.952 inch)

Clutch housing bushing clearance to mainshaft .... Not specified
Clutch housing inside diameter
    Standard... 25.00 to 25.021 mm (0.9843 to 0.9851 inch)
    Limit... 25.04 mm (0.986 inch)

Oil pump

Outer rotor-to-body clearance
    1986 through 1995
        Standard .... 0.10 to 0.21 mm (0.004 to 0.008 inch)
        Limit... 0.25 mm (0.010 inch)
    1996 on
        Standard .... 0.15 to 0.22 mm (0.006 to 0.009 inch)
        Limit... 0.25 mm (0.010 inch)
Inner to outer rotor clearance
    Standard... 0.15 mm (0.006 inch) or less
    Limit... 0.20 mm (0.008 inch)
Side clearance (rotors to straightedge)
    Standard... 0.02 to 0.09 mm (0.001 to 0.004 inch)
    Limit... 0.12 mm (0.005 inch)

Kickstarter

Spindle outside diameter
    Standard... 21.959 to 21.980 mm (0.8645 to 0.8654 inch)
    Limit .... 21.91 mm (0.863 inch)
Pinion gear inside diameter
    1986 through 1995
        Standard .... 22.020 to 22.041 mm (0.8669 to 0.8678 inch)
        Limit... 22.12 mm (0.871 inch)
    1996 on
        Standard .... 22.000 to 22.021 mm (0.8661 to 0.8670 inch)
        Limit... 22.10 mm (0.870 inch)
Idler gear bushing inside diameter
    Standard... 15.000 to 15.018 mm (0.5906 to 0.5913 inch)
    Limit
        1986 through 1995.. 14.97 mm (0.589 inch)
        1995 on .... 15.04 mm (0.592 inch)
Idler gear bushing outside diameter
    Standard... 18.959 to 18.980 mm (0.7464 to 0.7472 inch)
    Limit .... 18.92 mm (0.745 inch)
Idler gear inside diameter
    Standard... 19.010 to 19.034 mm (0.7484 to 0.7494 inch)
    Limit .... 19.13 mm (0.753 inch)

Shift drum and forks

Fork inside diameter
    Standard... 13.000 to 13.021 mm (0.5118 to 0.5126 inch)
    Limit .... 13.05 mm (0.514 inch)
Fork shaft outside diameter
    Standard... 12.966 to 12.983 mm (0.5105 to 0.5111 inch)
    Limit .... 12.90 mm (0.508 inch)
Fork ear thickness
    1986 through 1995
        Standard .... 4.930 to 5.000 mm (0.1941 to 0.1969 inch)
        Limit... 4.50 mm (0.18 inch)
    1996 on (right and left forks)
        Standard .... 4.930 to 5.000 mm (0.1941 to 0.1969 inch)
        Limit... 4.50 mm (0.18 inch)
    1996 on (center fork)
        Standard .... 4.90 to 5.000 mm (0.193 to 0.1969 inch)
        Limit... 4.50 mm (0.18 inch)
Shift drum groove width limit... Not specified

Transmission (1986 through 1995)

Gear inside diameters
    Mainshaft fifth
        Standard .... 20.020 to 20.041 mm (0.7882 to 0.7890 inch)
        Limit .... 20.08 mm (0.791 inch)
    Mainshaft sixth
        Standard .... 23.020 to 23.041 mm (0.9063 to 0.9071 inch)
        Limit .... 23.09 mm (0.909 inch)

XR250R (continued)

Transmission (1986 through 1995) (continued)

Countershaft first
  Standard .... 23.000 to 23.021 mm (0.9055 to 0.9063 inch)
  Limit .... 23.07 mm (0.908 inch)
Countershaft second
  Standard .... 25.020 to 25.041 mm (0.9850 to 0.9859 inch)
  Limit .... 25.09 mm (0.988 inch)
Countershaft third
  Standard .... 22.020 to 22.041 mm (0.8669 to 0.8678 inch)
  Limit .... 22.08 mm (0.869 inch)
Countershaft fourth
  Standard .... 22.014 to 22.020 mm (0.8667 to 0.8669 inch)
  Limit .... 22.08 mm (0.869 inch)
Bushing inside diameters
  Countershaft first
    Standard .... 18.000 to 18.018 mm (0.7087 to 0.7094 inch)
    Limit .... 18.08 mm (0.712 inch)
  Countershaft second
    Standard .... 22.020 to 22.041 mm (0.8669 to 0.8678 inch)
    Limit .... 22.12 mm (0.871 inch)
Bushing outside diameters
  Mainshaft sixth
    Standard .... 22.959 to 22.980 mm (0.9039 to 0.9047 inch)
    Limit .... 22.92 mm (0.902 inch)
  Countershaft first
    Standard .... 22.951 to 22.980 mm (0.9036 to 0.9047 inch)
    Limit .... 22.90 mm (0.902 inch)
  Countershaft second
    Standard .... 24.972 to 24.993 mm (0.9831 to 0.9840 inch)
    Limit .... 24.90 mm (0.980 inch)
Gear-to-bushing clearances
  Mainshaft sixth
    Standard .... 0.040 to 0.082 mm (0.0016 to 0.0032 inch)
    Limit .... 0.10 mm (0.004 inch)
  Countershaft first
    Standard .... 0.020 to 0.070 mm (0.0008 to 0.0028 inch)
    Limit .... 0.10 mm (0.004 inch)
  Countershaft second
    Standard .... 0.027 to 0.069 mm (0.0011 to 0.0027 inch)
    Limit .... 0.10 mm (0.004 inch)
Mainshaft diameter (at fifth gear and clutch housing bushing)
  Standard... 19.959 to 19.980 mm (0.7858 to 0.7866 inch)
  Limit... 19.91 mm (0.784 inch)
Countershaft diameter (at second and fourth gears)
  Standard... 21.959 to 21.980 mm (0.8645 to 0.8654 inch)
  Limit... 21.91 mm (0.863 inch)
Shaft-to-gear clearance (mainshaft fifth, countershaft fourth)
  Standard... 0.040 to 0.082 mm (0.0016 to 0.0032 inch)
  Limit... 0.15 mm (0.006 inch)
Shaft-to-bushing clearance (countershaft second)
  Standard... 0.040 to 0.080 mm (0.0016 to 0.0031 inch)
  Limit... 0.15 mm (0.006 inch)

Transmission (1996 on)

Gear inside diameters
  Mainshaft fifth
    Standard .... 20.000 to 20.021 mm (0.7874 to 0.7882 inch)
    Limit .... 20.08 mm (0.791 inch)
  Mainshaft sixth
    Standard .... 23.000 to 23.021 mm (0.9055 to 0.9063 inch)
    Limit .... 23.07 mm (0.908 inch)
  Countershaft first
    Standard .... 23.000 to 23.021 mm (0.9055 to 0.9063 inch)
    Limit .... 23.07 mm (0.908 inch)
  Countershaft second
    Standard .... 25.020 to 25.041 mm (0.9850 to 0.9859 inch)
    Limit .... 25.09 mm (0.988 inch)

Countershaft third
    Standard .... 25.000 to 25.021 mm (0.9843 to 0.9851 inch)
    Limit .... 25.07 mm (0.987 inch)
Countershaft fourth
    Standard .... 22.000 to 22.021 mm (0.8661 to 0.8670 inch)
    Limit .... 22.07 mm (0.869 inch)
Bushing inside diameters
  Countershaft first
    Standard .... 18.000 to 18.018 mm (0.7087 to 0.7094 inch)
    Limit .... 18.08 mm (0.712 inch)
  Countershaft second
    Standard .... 22.000 to 22.021 mm (0.8661 to 0.8670 inch)
    Limit .... 22.10 mm (0.870 inch)
Bushing outside diameters
  Mainshaft sixth
    Standard .... 22.959 to 22.980 mm (0.9039 to 0.9047 inch)
    Limit .... 22.92 mm (0.902 inch)
  Countershaft first
    Standard .... 22.959 to 22.980 mm (0.9039 to 0.9047 inch)
    Limit .... 22.90 mm (0.902 inch)
  Countershaft second
    Standard .... 24.979 to 25.000 mm (0.9834 to 0.9843 inch)
    Limit .... 24.90 mm (0.980 inch)
Gear-to-bushing clearances
    Standard .... 0.020 to 0.062 mm (0.0008 to 0.0022 inch)
    Limit .... 0.10 mm (0.004 inch)
Mainshaft diameter (at fifth gear and clutch housing bushing)
    Standard .... 19.959 to 19.980 mm (0.7858 to 0.7866 inch)
    Limit .... 19.91 mm (0.784 inch)
Countershaft diameter (at second and fourth gears)
    Standard .... 21.959 to 21.980 mm (0.8645 to 0.8654 inch)
    Limit .... 21.91 mm (0.863 inch)
Countershaft diameter (at first gear)
    Standard .... 17.966 to 17.984 mm (0.7073 to 0.7080 inch)
    Limit .... 17.91 mm (0.705 inch)
Countershaft diameter (at kickstarter idler gear)
    Standard .... 14.966 to 14.984 mm (0.5892 to 0.5899 inch)
    Limit .... 14.91 mm (0.587 inch)
Shaft-to-gear clearance (mainshaft fifth, countershaft fourth)
    Standard .... 0.020 to 0.062 mm (0.0008 to 0.0022 inch)
    Limit .... 0.15 mm (0.006 inch)
Shaft-to-bushing clearance (countershaft second)
    Standard .... 0.020 to 0.062 mm (0.0008 to 0.0022 inch)
    Limit .... 0.15 mm (0.006 inch)
Shaft-to-bushing clearance (countershaft first)
    Standard .... 0.016 to 0.052 mm (0.0006 to 0.0020 inch)
    Limit .... 0.10 mm (0.004 inch)

Crankshaft and balancer

Connecting rod side clearance
    Standard .... 0.050 to 0.500 mm (0.0020 to 0.0197 inch)
    Limit .... 0.80 mm (0.031 inch)
Connecting rod big end radial clearance
    Standard .... 0.006 to 0.018 mm (0.0002 to 0.0007 inch)
    Limit .... 0.05 mm (0.002 inch)
Runout limit .... 0.05 mm (0.002 inch)
Balancer shaft diameter .... Not specified

Torque specifications

Engine mounting bolts
  Top hanger plate
    To frame .... 27 Nm (20 ft-lbs)
    To engine
      1986 through 1989 .... 40 Nm (29 ft-lbs)
      1990 on.. 65 Nm (47 ft-lbs)
  Front hanger plate
    To frame .... 27 Nm (20 ft-lbs)
    To engine
      1986 through 1989
      1990 on.. 65 Nm (47 ft-lbs)

XR250R (continued)

Torque specifications (continued)

Lower front and rear through-bolts	
1986 through 1989	40 Nm (29 ft-lbs)
1990 on	65 Nm (47 ft-lbs)
Upper rear hanger plate	
Small bolts	27 Nm (20 ft-lbs)
Nut and through-bolts	65 Nm (47 ft-lbs)
Oil cooler union bolts (1986 through 1995 models)	
1986 through 1989	18 Nm (156 inch-lbs)
1990 through 1995	32 to 40 Nm (23 to 29 ft-lbs)
External oil hose bolts (1996 on)	
End fitting bolts at engine	Not specified
Upper ends to frame	Not specified
Lower end to frame oil tank (below strainer)	37 Nm (27 ft-lbs)
Cylinder head cover bolts	
1986 through 1995	
6 mm bolts	8 to 12 Nm (72 to 108 inch-lbs)
8 mm bolt	26 to 30 Nm (19 to 22 ft-lbs)
1996 on	
6 mm bolts	12 Nm (108 inch-lbs)
8 mm bolt	23 Nm (17 ft-lbs)
Cam sprocket bolts	20 Nm (14 ft-lbs) (1)
Main rocker shafts	28 Nm (20 ft-lbs) (1)
Sub-rocker shafts	
1986 through 1995	
Intake	28 Nm (20 ft-lbs) (1)
Exhaust	23 Nm (17 ft-lbs) (1)
1996 on	23 Nm (17 ft-lbs) (1)
Cylinder head 10 mm bolts	40 Nm (29 ft-lbs) (2)
Cylinder head 6 mm bolts	
1986 through 1995	12 Nm (108 inch-lbs)
1996 on	10 Nm (86 inch-lbs)
Cam chain tensioner	
Top bolts	
1986 through 1995	10 to 14 Nm (86 to 120 inch-lbs)
1996 on	10 Nm (86 inch-lbs)
Bottom bolt	Not specified
Cylinder main bolts	40 Nm (29 ft-lbs)
Cylinder small bolts	10 Nm (86 inch-lbs)
Right and left engine cover bolts and nuts	12 Nm (108 inch-lbs)
Clutch spring bolts	Not specified
Primary drive gear locknut	
1986 through 1995	60 Nm (43 ft-lbs)
1996 on	88 Nm (65 ft-lbs)
Clutch locknut	
1986 through 1995	60 Nm (43 ft-lbs) (3)
1996 on	108 Nm (80 ft-lbs) (3)
Shift cam plate to shift drum bolt	
1986 through 1995	10 to 14 Nm (86 to 120 inch-lbs) (1)
1996 on	24 Nm (17 ft-lbs)
Shift drum stopper arm bolt	
1986 through 1995	22 to 26 Nm (16 to 19 ft-lbs)
1996 on	12 Nm (108 inch-lbs)
Shift pedal pinch bolt	
1986 through 1995	14 to 18 Nm (120 to 156 inch-lbs)
1996 on	27 Nm (20 ft-lbs)
Kickstarter pinch bolt	27 Nm (20 ft-lbs)
Crankcase bolts	12 Nm (108 inch-lbs)

1. *Apply non-permanent thread locking agent to the threads.*
2. *Apply engine oil to the threads.*
3. *Stake after tightening.*

XR400R

Main rocker arms
Rocker arm inside diameter
  Standard .... 11.500 to 11.518 mm (0.4528 to 0.4535 inch)
  Limit .... 11.53 mm (0.454 inch)
Rocker shaft outside diameter
  Standard .... 11.466 to 11.484 mm (0.4514 to 0.4521 inch)
  Limit .... 11.41 mm (0.449 inch)
Shaft-to-arm clearance
  Standard .... 0.016 to 0.052 mm (0.0006 to 0.0020 inch)
  Limit .... 0.10 mm (0.004 inch)

Sub-rocker arms
Rocker arm inside diameter (intake and exhaust)
  Standard .... 7.000 to 7.015 mm (0.2756 to 0.2762 inch)
  Limit .... 7.05 mm (0.278 inch)
Rocker shaft outside diameter (intake and exhaust)
  Standard .... 6.972 to 6.987 mm (0.2745 to 0.2751 inch)
  Limit .... 6.92 mm (0.272 inch)
Shaft-to-arm clearance
  Standard .... 0.013 to 0.043 mm (0.0005 to 0.0017 inch)
  Limit .... Not specified

Camshaft
Lobe height
  Intake
    Standard .... 30.295 to 31.025 mm (1.2175 to 1.2215 inches)
    Limit .... 30.82 mm (1.213 inches)
  Exhaust
    Standard .... 30.827 to 30.927 mm (1.2137 to 1.2176 inches)
    Limit .... 30.72 mm (1.209 inches)
Journal diameter .... Not specified
Bearing journal inside diameter .... Not specified
Journal oil clearance .... Not specified
Camshaft runout limit .... 0.03 mm (0.001 inch)
Camshaft side clearance .... Not specified

Cylinder head, valves and valve springs
Cylinder head warpage limit .... 0.10 mm 0.004 inch)
Valve stem runout .... Not specified
Valve stem diameter
  Intake
    Standard .... 5.475 to 5.490 mm (0.2156 to 0.2161 inch)
    Limit .... 5.46 mm (0.2149 inch)
  Exhaust
    Standard .... 5.455 to 5.470 mm (0.2148 to 0.2154 inch)
    Limit .... 5.44 mm (0.214 inch)
Valve guide inside diameter (intake and exhaust)
  Standard .... 5.500 to 5.512 mm (0.2165 to 0.2170 inch)
  Limit .... 5.52 mm (0.217 inch)
Stem to guide clearance
  Intake
    Standard .... 0.010 to 0.037 mm (0.0004 to 0.0015 inch)
    Limit .... 0.12 mm (0.005 inch)
  Exhaust
    Standard .... 0.030 to 0.057 mm (0.0012 to 0.0022 inch)
    Limit .... 0.14 mm (0.006 inch)
Valve seat width (intake and exhaust)
  Standard .... 1.0 to 1.1 mm (0.039 to 0.043 inch)
  Limit .... 2.0 mm (0.078 inch)
Valve spring free length
  Inner spring
    Standard .... 37.19 mm (1.464 inches)
    Limit .... 36.3 mm (1.43 inches)
  Outer spring
    Standard .... 44.20 mm (1.740 inches)
    Limit .... 43.1 mm (1.70 inches)
Valve face width
  Standard .... 1.0 to 1.1 mm (0.039 to 0.43 inch)
  Limit .... 2.0 mm (0.078 inch)

XR400R (continued)

Cylinder

Bore
  Standard.. 85.000 to 85.010 mm (3.3465 to 3.3468 inches)
  Limit... 85.10 mm (3.350 inches)
Taper and out-of-round limits.. 0.05 mm (0.002 inch)
Surface warpage limit.. 0.10 mm (0.004 inch)

Piston

Piston diameter
  Standard.. 84.960 to 84.985 mm (3.3449 to 3.3459 inches)
  Limit... 84.88 mm (3.3417 inches)
Piston diameter measuring point (above bottom of piston) .... 15 mm (0.6 inch)
Piston-to-cylinder clearance
  Standard.. 0.015 to 0.050 mm (0.0006 to 0.0020 inch)
  Limit... 0.10 mm (0.004 inch)
Piston pin bore in piston
  Standard.. 20.002 to 20.008 mm (0.7875 to 0.7877 inch)
  Limit... 20.060 mm (0.7898 inch)
Piston pin bore in connecting rod
  Standard.. 20.020 to 20.041 mm (0.7882 to 0.7890 inch)
  Limit... 20.067 mm (0.790 inch)
Piston pin outer diameter
  Standard.. 19.994 to 20.000 mm (0.7872 to 0.7874 inch)
  Limit... 19.964 mm (0.786 inch)
Piston pin-to-piston clearance
  Standard.. 0.002 to 0.014 mm (0.0001 to 0.0006 inch)
  Limit... 0.096 mm (0.0038 inch)
Piston pin-to-connecting rod clearance
  Standard.. 0.020 to 0.047 mm (0.0008 to 0.0019 inch)
  Limit... 0.103 mm (0.0041 inch)
Top ring side clearance
  Standard.. 0.030 to 0.065 mm (0.0012 to 0.0026 inch)
  Limit... 0.14 mm (0.006 inch)
Second ring side clearance
  Standard.. 0.015 to 0.050 mm (0.0006 to 0.0020 inch)
  Limit... 0.12 mm (0.005 inch)
Oil ring side clearance .... Not specified
Ring end gap
  Top
    Standard .... 0.20 to 0.35 mm (0.008 to 0.014 inch)
    Limit .... 0.50 mm (0.020 inch)
  Second
    Standard .... 0.35 to 0.50 mm (0.014 to 0.020 inch)
    Limit .... 0.65 mm (0.026 inch)
  Oil ring side rails
    Standard .... 0.20 to 0.70 mm (0.008 to 0.028 inch)
    Limit .... 0.9 mm (0.04 inch)

Clutch

Spring free length
  1996
    Standard .... 45.5 mm (1.79 inches)
    Limit .... 44.5 mm (1.64 inches)
  1997 and later
    Standard .... 43.2 mm (1.70 inches)
    Limit .... 41.6 mm (1.64 inches)
Friction plate thickness
  Standard.. 2.92 to 3.08 mm (0.115 to 0.121 inch)
  Limit... 2.69 mm (0.106 inch)
Friction and metal plate warpage limit .... 0.30 mm (0.012 inch)
Clutch housing bushing inside diameter
  Standard.. 22.010 to 22.035 mm (0.8665 to 0.8675 inch)
  Limit... 22.05 mm (0.868 inch)
Clutch housing bushing outside diameter
  Standard.. 27.959 to 27.980 mm (1.1007 to 1.1016 inches)
  Limit... 27.90 mm (1.098 inches)
Clutch housing bushing clearance to mainshaft .... Not specified

Clutch housing inside diameter
  Standard... 28.00 to 28.021 mm (1.1024 to 1.1032 inches)
  Limit... 28.04 mm (1.104 inches)

Oil pump

Outer rotor-to-body clearance
  Standard... 0.15 to 0.22 mm (0.006 to 0.009 inch)
  Limit... 0.25 mm (0.010 inch)
Inner-to-outer rotor clearance
  Standard... 0.15 mm (0.006 inch) or less
  Limit... 0.20 mm (0.008 inch)
Side clearance (rotors-to-straightedge)
  Standard... 0.02 to 0.09 mm (0.001 to 0.004 inch)
  Limit... 0.12 mm (0.005 inch)

Kickstarter

Spindle outside diameter
  Standard... 21.959 to 21.980 mm (0.8645 to 0.8654 inch)
  Limit... 21.91 mm (0.863 inch)
Pinion gear inside diameter
  Standard... 22.020 to 22.041 mm (0.8669 to 0.8678 inch)
  Limit... 22.12 mm (0.871 inch)
Idler gear bushing inside diameter
  Standard... 14.000 to 14.018 mm (0.5512 to 0.5519 inch)
  Limit... 14.05 mm (0.553 inch)
Idler gear bushing outside diameter
  Standard... 18.959 to 18.980 mm (0.7464 to 0.7472 inch)
  Limit... 18.92 mm (0.745 inch)
Idler gear inside diameter
  Standard... 19.010 to 19.034 mm (0.7484 to 0.7494 inch)
  Limit... 19.13 mm (0.753 inch)

Shift drum and forks

Fork inside diameter
  Standard... 13.000 to 13.021 mm (0.5118 to 0.5126 inch)
  Limit... 13.05 mm (0.514 inch)
Fork shaft outside diameter
  Standard... 12.966 to 12.984 mm (0.5105 to 0.5112 inch)
  Limit... 12.90 mm (0.508 inch)
Fork ear thickness
  Standard... 5.930 to 6.000 mm (0.233 to 0.236 inch)
  Limit... 5.50 mm (0.22 inch)
Shift drum groove width limit.. Not specified

Transmission (1986 through 1995)

Gear inside diameters
  Mainshaft fourth
    Standard .... 25.020 to 25.041 mm (0.9850 to 0.9859 inch)
    Limit .... 25.08 mm (0.987 inch)
  Mainshaft fifth
    Standard .... 25.000 to 25.021 mm (0.9843 to 0.9851 inch)
    Limit .... 25.06 mm (0.98 inch)
  Countershaft first
    Standard .... 23.000 to 23.021 mm (0.9055 to 0.9063 inch)
    Limit .... 23.07 mm (0.908 inch)
  Countershaft second and third
    Standard .... 28.020 to 28.041 mm (1.1031 to 1.1040 inches)
    Limit .... 28.08 mm (1.106 inches)
Bushing inside diameters
  Mainshaft fourth
    Standard .... 22.000 to 22.021 mm (0.8661 to 0.8670 inch)
    Limit .... 22.10 mm (0.870 inch)
  Countershaft first
    Standard .... 22.020 to 22.041 mm (0.7882 to 0.7890 inch)
    Limit .... 20.08 mm (0.791 inch)
  Countershaft second and third
    Standard .... 25.000 to 25.021 mm (0.9843 to 0.9851 inch)
    Limit .... 25.06 mm (0.987 inch)

XR400R (continued)

Bushing outside diameters
   Mainshaft fourth
      Standard .... 24.979 to 25.000 mm (0.9834 to 0.9843 inch)
      Limit .... 24.90 mm (0.980 inch)
   Mainshaft fifth
      Standard .... 24.959 to 24.980 mm (0.9826 to 0.9835 inch)
      Limit .... 24.90 mm (0.980 inch)
   Countershaft first
      Standard .... 22.959 to 22.980 mm (0.9039 to 0.9047 inch)
      Limit .... 22.90 mm (0.902 inch)
   Countershaft second and third
      Standard .... 27.979 to 28.000 mm (1.1015 to 1.1024 inches)
      Limit .... 27.94 mm (1.100 inches)
Gear-to-bushing clearance
   Standard .... 0.020 to 0.062 mm (0.0008 to 0.0062 inch)
   Limit... 0.10 mm (0.004 inch)
Bushing-to-shaft clearance
   Standard .... 0.020 to 0.062 mm (0.0008 to 0.0062 inch)
   Limit... 0.10 mm (0.004 inch)
Mainshaft diameter (at fourth gear)
   Standard... 21.959 to 21.980 mm (0.8645 to 0.8654 inch)
   Limit   .... 21.92 mm (0.863 inch)
Countershaft diameter (at first gear)
   Standard... 19.979 to 20.000 mm (0.7866 to 0.7874 inch)
   Limit... 19.94 mm (0.785 inch)
Countershaft diameter (at second and gears)
   Standard... 24.959 to 24.980 mm (0.9826 to 0.9835 inch)
   Limit... 24.92 mm (0.981 inch)

Crankshaft and balancer

Connecting rod side clearance
   Standard... 0.05 to 0.45 mm (0.0020 to 0.018 inch)
   Limit... 0.60 mm (0.02 inch)
Connecting rod big end radial clearance
   Standard... 0.006 to 0.018 mm (0.0002 to 0.0007 inch)
   Limit... 0.05 mm (0.002 inch)
Runout limit... 0.05 mm (0.002 inch)
Balancer shaft diameter... Not specified

Torque specifications

Engine mounting bolts
   Top and front hanger plates
      To frame.. 27 Nm (20 ft-lbs)
      To engine .... 54 Nm (40 ft-lbs)
   Lower front through-bolt .... 54 Nm (40 ft-lbs)
External oil hose bolts
   End fitting bolts at engine .... Not specified
   Lower end to frame oil tank (below strainer)............... 37 Nm (27 ft-lbs)
   Oil cooler flare nuts .... 20 Nm (14 ft-lbs)
Oil pump assembly bolts... 13 Nm (108 inch-lbs)
Cylinder head cover bolts
   6 mm bolts .... Not specified
   8 mm bolt .... 27 Nm (20 ft-lbs)
Cam sprocket bolts.. 27 Nm (20 ft-lbs) (1)
Cylinder head nuts.. 44 Nm (33 ft-lbs) (2)
Cam chain tensioner
   Plug .... 4 Nm (35 inch-lbs)
   Mounting bolts .... Not specified
   Bottom bolt .... Not specified
Cylinder bolts... 44 Nm (29 ft-lbs)
Right and left engine cover bolts and nuts..................... Not specified
Clutch spring bolts .... Not specified
Primary drive gear locknut.. 88 Nm (65 ft-lbs) (3)
Clutch locknut.. 108 Nm (80 ft-lbs) (4)
Shift cam plate to shift drum bolt .... Not specified (1)
Shift drum stopper arm bolt .... 12 Nm (108 inch-lbs)
Shift pedal pinch bolt... Not specified
Kickstarter pinch bolt .... 27 Nm (20 ft-lbs)

Crankcase bolts	12 Nm (108 inch-lbs)
Transmission bearing retainer (inside crankcase)	12 Nm (108 inch-lbs)
Return spring pin	24 Nm (18 ft-lbs)

1. Apply non-permanent thread locking agent to the threads.
2. Apply engine oil to the threads.
3. Apply engine oil to the threads and locknut face.
4. Stake after tightening.

1   General information

The engine/transmission unit is of the air-cooled, single-cylinder four-stroke design. The four valves are operated by an overhead camshaft which is chain driven off the crankshaft. The valves are arranged in a circle, rather than in the parallel pairs more commonly used in four-valves-per-cylinder engines. To accommodate this arrangement, the camshaft operates four main rocker arms, each of which in turn operates its valve through a sub-rocker arm rather than directly. Honda refers to this design as Radial Four Valve Combustion (RFVC).

The engine/transmission assembly is constructed from aluminum alloy. The crankcase is divided vertically.

The lubrication system incorporates a wet sump (XR250L and 1986 through 1995 XR250R) or dry sump (1996 and later XR250R and all XR400R models). Oil is pressure-fed by a gear-driven rotor-type oil pump, through an oil filter and separate strainer screen (or more than one screen, depending on model). On wet sump models, oil not circulating through the engine is stored in the crankcase. On dry sump models, oil not circulating through the engine is stored inside the upper and front frame member, which acts as an oil tank. The oil pump has two sets of rotors, one to circulate oil under pressure to the engine and the other to scavenge oil from the engine.

Power from the crankshaft is routed to the transmission via a wet, multi-plate type clutch. The transmission has six forward gears on 250 models and five forward gears on 400 models.

A decompressor reduces the effort required to kick start the engine.

2   Operations possible with the engine in the frame

The components and assemblies listed below can be removed without having to remove the engine from the frame. If, however, a number of areas require attention at the same time, removal of the engine is recommended.

Camshaft, rocker arms and cylinder head
Cam chain tensioner
Cylinder and piston
External shift mechanism
Clutch
External oil hoses
Oil pump and pipe
Kickstarter

3   Operations requiring engine removal

It is necessary to remove the engine/transmission assembly from the frame and separate the crankcase halves to gain access to the following components:

Crankshaft, balancer and connecting rod
Transmission shafts
Internal shift mechanism (shift shaft, shift drum and forks)
Crankcase bearings

4   Major engine repair - general note

1   It is not always easy to determine when or if an engine should be completely overhauled, as a number of factors must be considered.
2   High mileage is not necessarily an indication that an overhaul is needed, while low mileage, on the other hand, does not preclude the need for an overhaul. Frequency of servicing is probably the single most important consideration. An engine that has regular and frequent oil and filter changes, as well as other required maintenance, will most likely give many miles of reliable service. Conversely, a neglected engine, or one which has not been broken in properly, may require an overhaul very early in its life.
3   Exhaust smoke and excessive oil consumption are both indications that piston rings and/or valve guides are in need of attention. Make sure oil leaks are not responsible before deciding that the rings and guides are bad. Refer to Chapter 1 and perform a cylinder compression check to determine for certain the nature and extent of the work required.
4   If the engine is making obvious knocking or rumbling noises, the connecting rod and/or main bearings are probably at fault.
5   Loss of power, rough running, excessive valve train noise and high fuel consumption rates may also point to the need for an overhaul, especially if they are all present at the same time. If a complete tune-up does not remedy the situation, major mechanical work is the only solution.
6   An engine overhaul generally involves restoring the internal parts to the specifications of a new engine. During an overhaul the piston rings are replaced and the cylinder walls are bored and/or honed. If a rebore is done, then a new piston is also required. The crankshaft and connecting rod are permanently assembled, so if one of these components needs to be replaced, both must be. Generally the valves are serviced as well, since they are usually in less than perfect condition at this point. While the engine is being overhauled, other components such as the carburetor can be rebuilt also. The end result should be a like-new engine that will give as many trouble-free miles as the original.
7   Before beginning the engine overhaul, read through all of the related procedures to familiarize yourself with the scope and requirements of the job. Overhauling an engine is not all that difficult, but it is time consuming. Plan on the motorcycle being tied up for a minimum of two weeks. Check on the availability of parts and make sure that any necessary special tools, equipment and supplies are obtained in advance.
8   Most work can be done with typical shop hand tools, although a number of precision measuring tools are required for inspecting parts to determine if they must be replaced. Often a dealer service department or repair shop will handle the inspection of parts and offer advice concerning reconditioning and replacement. As a general rule, time is the primary cost of an overhaul so it doesn't pay to install worn or sub-standard parts.
9   As a final note, to ensure maximum life and minimum trouble from a rebuilt engine, everything must be assembled with care in a spotlessly clean environment.

5   Engine - removal and installation

Note: Engine removal and installation should be done with the aid of an

5.11 The oil overflow hose on dry sump models runs between the frame oil tank and the cylinder head cover (arrows)

5.14a On XR250L and early XR250R models, pull the rubber cover off the top mount; note the directions of the nuts and bolts, then unscrew them . . .

assistant to avoid damage or injury that could occur if the engine is dropped. A hydraulic floor jack should be used to support and lower the engine if possible (they can be rented at low cost).

Removal

Refer to illustrations 5.11, 5.14a through 5.14e, 5.15a, 5.15b, 5.15c and 5.16

1   Drain the engine oil (see Chapter 1).
2   Remove the seat, both side covers, the skid plate or bars and the right footpeg (see Chapter 7).
3   Remove the fuel tank, exhaust system and carburetor (see Chapter 3).
4   Disconnect the spark plug wire (see Chapter 1).
5   Label and disconnect the alternator and pulse generator wires (refer to Chapter 4 for component location if necessary). Detach the wires from their retainers. If you're working on an XR400R, remove the ignition control module and the AC regulator.
6   Remove the drive chain and sprocket (see Chapter 5).
7   Remove the brake pedal (see Chapter 6). If you're working on an XR400R, unbolt the rear brake fluid reservoir and tie it out of the way. Make sure the reservoir stays level so brake fluid doesn't leak.
8   Disconnect the clutch cable (see Section 16).
9   Remove the kickstarter pedal (see Section 21). If you're working on an XR400R, remove the gearshift pedal (see Section 19).

10   Disconnect the decompressor cable(s) from the engine (see Section 20).
11   Disconnect the crankcase breather hose from engine (see Chapter 1). If you're working on a dry sump model, disconnect the oil overflow hose from the top of the engine **(see illustration)**. Refer to Section 22 and disconnect the external oil hoses and pipes from the engine.
12   If you're working on a 1986 through 1995 XR250R, detach the rear shock absorber reservoir from the frame and tie it out of the way (see Chapter 5).
13   Support the bike securely upright so it can't fall over during the remainder of this procedure. Support the engine with a jack, using a block of wood between the jack and the engine to protect the crankcase.

XR250L and 1986 through 1995 XR250R

Refer to illustrations 5.14a through 5.14e

14   Remove the engine mounting bolts, nuts and brackets at the top, upper front, upper rear, lower front and lower rear **(see illustrations)**. **Note:** *Raise and lower the jack as needed to relieve strain on the mounting bolts.*

1996 and later XR250R, all XR400R

Refer to illustrations 5.15a, 5.15b and 5.15c

15   Remove the engine mounting bolts, nuts and brackets at the top,

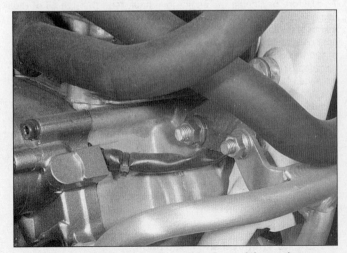

5.14b . . . remove the bracket at the front of the engine . . .

5.14c . . . unbolt the bracket from the upper rear on the right side of the bike . . .

5.14d ... and remove the through-bolt that passes from the left side of the bike through the bracket ...

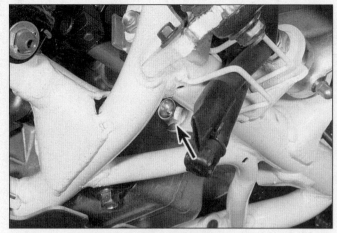

5.14e ... then remove the through-bolt from the lower rear of the engine

upper front and lower front (see illustrations). You'll also need to remove the swingarm pivot bolt; it passes through the rear of the crankcase to act as an engine support (see Chapter 5).

All models

Refer to illustration 5.16

16   Have an assistant help you lift the engine out of the right side of the frame (see illustration).

17   Slowly lower the engine to a suitable work surface.

Installation

18   Have an assistant help lift the engine into the frame so it rests on the jack and block of wood. Use the jack to align the mounting bolt holes, then install the brackets, bolts and nuts. Tighten them to the torques listed in this Chapter's Specifications. If you're working on a 1996 or later XR250R or an XR400R, refer to the Chapter 5 Specifications for the swingarm pivot bolt torque.

19   The remainder of installation is the reverse of the removal steps, with the following additions:

a) *The two plates that form the upper mount are labeled L for left side and R for right side.*

b) *Use new gaskets at all exhaust pipe connections.*

c) *Adjust the throttle cable, decompression cable(s) and clutch cable following the procedures in Chapter 1.*

d) *Fill the engine with oil, also following the procedures in Chapter 1.*

d) *Run the engine and check for oil or exhaust leaks.*

5.15a On later XR250R and all XR400R models, pull off the rubber cover and remove the bolts from the top mount ...

6   Engine disassembly and reassembly - general information

Refer to illustrations 6.2 and 6.3

1   Before disassembling the engine, clean the exterior with a degreaser and rinse it with water. A clean engine will make the job eas-

5.15b ... unbolt the brackets on each side of the frame at the upper front ...

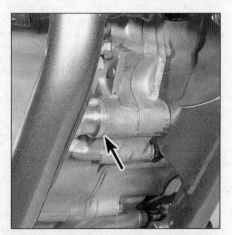

5.15c ... and remove the through-bolt from the lower front; note the location of the spacer (arrow)

5.16 Have an assistant help you lift the engine out of the frame

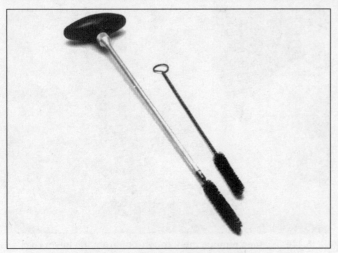

6.2 A selection of brushes is required for cleaning holes and passages in the engine components

6.3 An engine stand can be made from short lengths of lumber and lag bolts or nails

ier and prevent the possibility of getting dirt into the internal areas of the engine.

2   In addition to the precision measuring tools mentioned earlier, you will need a torque wrench, a valve spring compressor, oil gallery brushes **(see illustration)**, a piston ring removal and installation tool and a piston ring compressor. Some new, clean engine oil of the correct grade and type, some engine assembly lube (or moly-based grease) and a tube of RTV (silicone) sealant will also be required.

3   An engine support stand made from short lengths of 2 x 4's bolted together will facilitate the disassembly and reassembly procedures **(see illustration)**. If you have an automotive-type engine stand, an adapter plate can be made from a piece of plate, some angle iron and some nuts and bolts.

4   When disassembling the engine, keep "mated" parts together (including gears, rocker arms and shafts, etc.) that have been in contact with each other during engine operation. These "mated" parts must be reused or replaced as an assembly.

5   Engine/transmission disassembly should be done in the following general order with reference to the appropriate Sections.

Remove the cylinder head cover and rocker assembly
Remove the cam sprocket and camshaft
Remove the cylinder head and cam chain tensioner
Remove the cylinder
Remove the piston
Remove the clutch
Remove the primary drive gear
Remove the kickstarter
Remove the oil pump
Remove the external shift mechanism
Remove the alternator rotor
Separate the crankcase halves
Remove the internal shift mechanism
Remove the transmission shafts/gears
Remove the crankshaft, connecting rod and balancer

6   Reassembly is accomplished by reversing the general disassembly sequence.

---

7   Cylinder head cover and rocker arms - removal, inspection and installation

---

Removal

Refer to illustration 7.6

1   Refer to the valve adjustment procedure in Chapter 1 and place the engine at top dead center on its compression stroke.

2   Remove the seat and fuel tank (see Chapters 7 and 3).

7.6 Loosen the cover bolts evenly in two or three stages

3   If you're working on a later XR250R or an XR400R, disconnect the oil overflow hose from the cover **(see illustration 5.11)**.

4   Disconnect the decompressor cable from the cover (see Section 20).

5   If you're working on an XR400R, remove the AC regulator (see Chapter 4).

6   Loosen the cover bolts in a criss-cross pattern, in two or three stages **(see illustration)**. Some of the bolts secure cable and hose retainers; note which ones these are. It's a good idea to punch holes in a piece of cardboard in the shape of the cover and place the bolts in the same positions they're in when installed.

7   Lift the cover off the engine. If it's stuck, don't attempt to pry it off - tap around its sides with a plastic hammer to dislodge it.

8   Remove the gasket from the cylinder head cover. Use a new gasket whenever the cover is removed.

Inspection

Refer to illustrations 7.9, 7.10 and 7.11

9   Refer to Section 9 and check the cam bearing surfaces in the cylinder head and its cover for wear or damage. Check the rocker arms for wear at the cam contact surfaces and at the tips of the valve adjusting screws **(see illustration)**. Also check the decompression shaft for wear at the point where it contacts the exhaust rocker arm. Try to twist the rocker arms from side-to-side on the shafts. If they're loose on the shafts or if there's visible wear, remove them as described below.

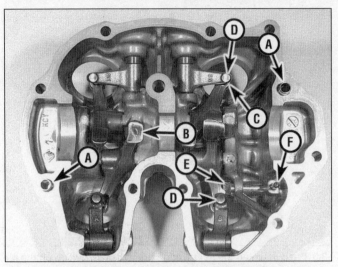

7.9 Lift off the cover, remove the gasket and note the locations of the dowels; they may come off with the cover or stay in the head (XR400R shown)

- A Dowels
- B Main rocker arm camshaft contact surfaces
- C Main rocker arm to sub-rocker arm contact surfaces
- D Sub-rocker arm valve stem contact surfaces
- E Decompressor lever contact surface
- F Decompressor shaft retaining pin

10 Pull out the decompression shaft retaining pin **(see illustration 7.9)**. Unbolt the cable bracket/spring retainer and pull the decompression shaft out of the cover **(see illustration)**.

11 Unscrew the rocker shafts and sub-rocker shafts and pull them out of the cover **(see illustration**. Remove the sealing washers, wave washers (sub-rocker arms only) and the rocker arms. **Note:** *Some of the rocker arms (all of the rocker arms on some models) have identification marks so they can be returned to their original positions. Look for the marks, and make your own if they aren't clearly visible. It's a good idea to label all of the rocker arms and sub-rocker arms so they can be reinstalled in their original locations. In addition to developing wear patterns with their shafts, some of the rocker arms are shaped differently from the others and won't work in the wrong location.*

12 Check the decompression lever and its shaft for wear, damage or a broken spring. If any problems are found, replace the shaft or spring. Pry the shaft oil seal out of its bore.

13 Measure the outer diameter of each rocker shaft and the inner

7.11 Remove the rocker shafts

7.10 Note how the cable bracket secures the spring, then remove the bracket bolt (arrow)

diameter of the rocker arms with a micrometer and compare the measurements to the values listed in this Chapter's Specifications. If rocker arm-to-shaft clearance is excessive, replace the rocker arm or shaft, whichever is worn.

Installation

Refer to illustrations 7.17a and 7.17b

14 Press a new decompression shaft oil seal into the bore with a seal driver or a socket the same diameter as the seal. Install the shaft, securing its spring with the cable bracket **(see illustration 7.10)**. Install the retaining pin.

15 Coat the main rocker shafts and rocker arm bores with moly-based grease containing 40-percent or more molybdenum disulfide. Apply non-hardening gasket sealant to the threads of the main rocker shafts. Install the rocker shafts and rocker arms in the cylinder head cover, using new copper sealing washers on the shafts. Depending on model, the main rocker arms will be marked as follows:
- a) *No marks*
- b) *A and B*
- c) *A, B, C and D*

16 If the rocker arms are unmarked, you'll need to refer to the labels made on disassembly. Note that the exhaust rocker arm with the lug for the decompressor goes next to the decompressor shaft bore.

17 If the rocker arms have factory markings, install them in the specified locations **(see illustrations)**.

7.17a Intake sub-rocker shaft wave washer locations; both intake sub-rocker arms are labeled IN

7.17b Exhaust sub-rocker shaft wave washer locations; the exhaust sub-rocker arms are labeled A and B

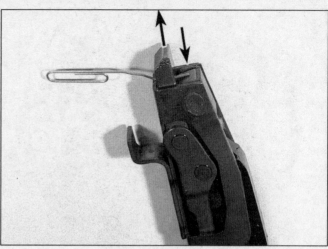

8.3 Push down on the near wedge (right arrow), pull up on the far wedge (left arrow) and insert a paper clip

18   Coat new sub-rocker shaft sealing rings with clean engine oil and install them on the shafts. Coat the shaft threads with non-hardening gasket sealant. Install the sub-rocker arms and their wave washers in the correct locations in the cylinder head cover, then install the shafts and sealing washers.

19   Install the decompressor shaft in the cylinder head cover. Align the groove in the shaft with the retaining pin, then install the retaining pin through the groove.

20   Clean the mating surfaces of the cylinder head and cover with lacquer thinner, acetone or brake system cleaner. Install a new gasket, taking care not to damage its silicone coating.

21   Make sure the piston is still at top dead center on its compression stroke (both cam lobes pointing downward). Fill the oil pockets in the top of the cylinder head with clean engine oil so the oil covers the cam lobes.

22   Loosen the valve adjusting screws all the way, then install the cover on the cylinder head. Install the bolts and tighten them evenly in two or three stages to the torques listed in this Chapter's Specifications. Note that there are different types of bolts with different torque settings.

23   Adjust the valve clearances (see Chapter 1).

24   Refer to Section 20 and reconnect the decompressor cable.

25   The remainder of installation is the reverse of the removal steps.

26   Refer to Chapter 1 and adjust the decompressor cable.

8   Cam chain tensioner - removal, inspection and installation

XR250L, XR250R

Removal

Refer to illustrations 8.3 and 8.6

1   Refer to Section 7 and remove the cylinder head cover.

2   Unbolt the tensioner retaining plate from the top of the cylinder head.

3   Push down on the tensioner wedge closest to the camshaft **(see illustration)**. At the same time, pull up on the farther wedge with pliers and insert a paper clip through the hole. This releases tension on the cam chain.

4   Refer to Section 9 and remove the cam sprocket.

5   Remove the right engine cover and the clutch (see Section 16).

6   Remove the shouldered tensioner bolt and lift the tensioner out of the engine. Don't lose the bearing retainer that's held in place by the tensioner bolt **(see illustration)**.

Inspection

Refer to illustration 8.7

7   Check for wear along the tensioner friction surface **(see illustra-**

8.6 Remove the shouldered bolt; be sure the bearing retainer (arrow) is in place on installation

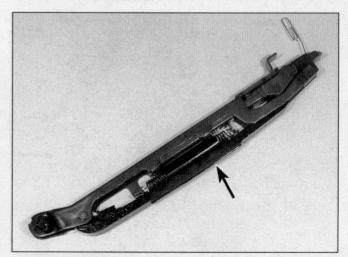

8.7 Check the guide surface (arrow) for wear and make sure the spring is in good condition

8.9 Loosen the cover screw (arrow) while the tensioner is
on the engine

8.10 Pull the tensioner out of the engine and remove the gasket

tion). Make sure the spring is in place and is not broken. If any problems are found, replace the tensioner.

Installation

8   Installation is the reverse of the removal steps. Be sure the bearing retainer is install under the tensioner. Tighten the tensioner bolt
securely, but don't overtighten it and strip the threads.

XR400R

Removal
Refer to illustrations 8.9 and 8.10

9   You'll need to remove the tensioner cover screw to reset the tensioner for installation, so loosen the screw while the tensioner is still on
the engine **(see illustration)**.
10   Remove two bolts and take the tensioner and its gasket off the
cylinder **(see illustration)**. Clean all traces of old gasket from the tensioner and engine.

Inspection
Refer to illustration 8.11

11   Check the tensioner for visible wear and damage and replace it if
any problems are found. Replace the sealing washers and O-ring
whenever the tensioner is removed **(see illustration)**.

Installation

12   Place a new gasket on the tensioner. Insert a small screwdriver
into the tensioner and turn it clockwise to retract the tensioner piston.
Caution: *If you try to tighten the tensioner bolts without retracting the
piston, the tensioner body or cam chain will be damaged.*
13   Hold the tensioner piston in the retracted position and install the
tensioner on the engine. Install the bolts, using new sealing washers.
Tighten the bolts securely, but don't overtighten them and strip the
threads. Release the screwdriver.
14   Install the tensioner cover screw, using a new O-ring. Tighten it to
the torque listed in this Chapter's Specifications.

---

9   Camshaft, guides and chain - removal and installation

Removal
Refer to illustrations 9.3, 9.4 and 9.5

1   Remove the cylinder head cover. If you're working on an XR400R,
remove the cam chain tensioner (see Sections 7 and 8).
2   Stuff rags into the cam chain opening so the camshaft bolts won't
fall into the crankcase.
3   Position the engine at TDC on the compression stroke **(see illustration)**. Now rotate the crankshaft one revolution (clockwise) and

8.11 Use a new O-ring and sealing washers on installation

9.3 Rotate the camshaft sprocket so the Top Dead Center mark
is straight up and the timing marks are aligned with the cylinder
head surface, then rotate the crankshaft one turn and remove the
exposed bolt (on early 250 models, the bolts are on the other side
of the camshaft) . . .

A   Top Dead Center mark (punch mark on early 250 models)
B   Timing marks (align with cylinder head surface)

9.4 ... rotate the sprocket, remove the other bolt and disengage the sprocket from the chain (its OUT mark (arrow) faces outward on installation); then turn the camshaft back to its original position

9.5 On XR250R and XR400R models with a one-way decompressor on the camshaft, pull the decompressor pin and spring out of the cylinder head

9.6 Check the cam bearing surfaces (arrows) for scoring or wear

remove the exposed cam sprocket bolt. Turn the crankshaft one more revolution (to TDC compression) so the other bolt is accessible, then unscrew the bolt.

4   Disengage the sprocket from the cam chain **(see illustration)**. Support the cam chain so it won't drop into the engine and remove the sprocket.

5   Lift the camshaft out of the cylinder head, then remove the decompressor pin and spring **(see illustration)**.

Inspection

Refer to illustrations 9.6, 9.7a, 9.7b, 9.8a, 9.8b, 9.8c and 9.11

Note: *Before replacing camshaft or the cylinder head cover and cylinder head because of damage, check with local machine shops specializing in motorcycle engine work. In the case of the camshaft, it may be possible for cam lobes to be welded, reground and hardened, at a cost far lower than that of a new camshaft. If the bearing surfaces in the center of the cylinder head or cover are damaged, it may be possible for them to be bored out to accept bearing inserts. Due to the cost of a new cylinder head it is recommended that all options be explored before condemning it as trash!*

6   Inspect the cam bearing surfaces of the cylinder head and cover **(see illustration 7.9 and the accompanying illustration)**. Look for score marks, deep scratches and evidence of spalling (a pitted appearance). The bearing surfaces that support the ends of the camshaft contain ball bearings, so the surfaces shouldn't be scored or worn. If they are, the bearings may have spun in their bores due to seizure or a loose cylinder head cover.

7   Check the camshaft lobes for heat discoloration (blue appearance), score marks, chipped areas, flat spots and spalling **(see illustration)**. Measure the height of each lobe with a micrometer **(see illustration)** and compare the results to the minimum lobe height listed in this Chapter's Specifications. If damage is noted or wear is excessive, the camshaft must be replaced. Also, be sure to check the condition of the rocker arms, as described in Section 7.

8   Check the chain guides for wear or damage. If they are worn or damaged, replace them. To remove the exhaust side (front) chain guide, you'll need to remove the cylinder head (see Section 10), then lift the guide out of its notches **(see illustration)**. The intake side guide on XR250L and XR250R models is part of the cam chain tensioner (see Section 8). To remove the intake side guide on XR400R models, you'll need to remove the right engine cover and clutch (see Section 16), then unscrew the bolt and take off the chain guide, collar and washer **(see illustrations)**.

9.7a Check the cam lobes for wear - here's a good example of lobe damage which will require replacement (or repair) of the camshaft

9.7b Measure the height of the cam lobes with a micrometer

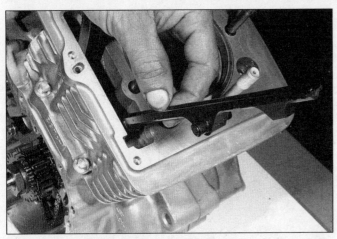

9.8a The front chain guide fits in notches in the cylinder head

9.8b The rear chain guide on XR400R models is secured by a bolt and pivot collar; there's a washer between the chain guide and crankcase

9   Except in cases of oil starvation, the camshaft chain wears very little. If the chain has stretched excessively, which makes it difficult to maintain proper tension, replace it with a new one. To remove the chain from the crankshaft sprocket, it's necessary to remove the chain guides as described above, as well as the oil pump (see Section 17). Once this is done, the chain can be lowered away from the sprocket.

10   Check the sprocket for wear, cracks and other damage, replacing it if necessary. If the sprocket is worn, the chain is also worn, and possibly the sprocket on the crankshaft. If wear this severe is apparent, the entire engine should be disassembled for inspection.

11   Slip the ball bearings off the ends of the camshaft **(see illustration)**. Hold the center race of each bearing with fingers and turn the outer race. The bearing should spin freely without roughness, looseness or noise. If it has obvious problems, or if you aren't sure it's in good condition, replace the bearing. If you're working on a 1996 or later XR250R or an XR400R, spin the outer race of the decompressor one-way clutch and make sure it turns in only one direction. If not, have it pressed off and a new one pressed on by a Honda dealer or motorcycle repair shop.

Installation

Refer to illustrations 9.14a and 9.14b

12   Install the cam chain guides, cylinder head, oil pump, clutch and right engine cover if they were removed.

13   Make sure the bearing surfaces in the cylinder head and cylinder head cover are clean. Install the ball bearings on the ends of the camshaft **(see illustration 9.11)**. If there's only one sealed bearing,

9.8c The finger on the front chain guide fits in a pocket in the crankcase (arrow)

install it on the sprocket end of the camshaft with its sealed side facing away from the center of the engine. If both bearings are sealed, install both with their sealed sides facing away from the center of the engine.

14   Lubricate the cam bearing journals with molybdenum disulfide grease. Lay the camshaft in the cylinder head with the lobes downward

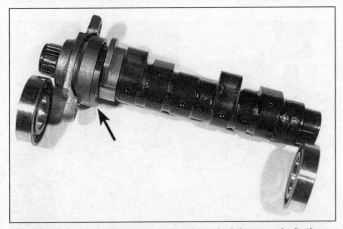

9.11 There's a ball bearing on each end of the camshaft; the sealed side of the bearing at the sprocket end faces away from the camshaft - later XR250R and all XR400R models have a one-way decompressor clutch (arrow)

9.14a Coat the cam lobes with moly-based grease

9.14b Position the bearing in its saddle and make sure the dowel is in position, then do the same at the other end of the camshaft

10.3a The cylinder head is secured by four bolts on 250 models or four nuts on 400 models (arrows); 250 models also have four small bolts - on 1986 through 1995 XR250R models, the two large bolts at the front and right are colored white and the two large bolts at the left and rear are colored black

(see illustration). Install the bearing retaining dowels in the cylinder head at each end of the camshaft **(see illustration)**.

15 Engage the sprocket with the chain so its timing mark will be straight up and its OUT mark faces away from the center of the engine **(see illustration 9.4)**. Place the sprocket on the camshaft so its bolt holes align with the camshaft bolt holes. Rotate the sprocket as needed for access, install the bolts and tighten them to the torque listed in this Chapter's Specifications.

16 Turn the sprocket so its timing mark is straight up and the marks are aligned with the cylinder head gasket surface **(see illustration 9.3)**.

17 Recheck the crankshaft timing mark on the alternator rotor to make sure it's still at the TDC position (see *Valve clearance - check and adjustment* in Chapter 1). If it's out of position and the camshaft sprocket is aligned as described in Step 3, you'll need to remove the chain from the sprocket and reposition it. Don't run the engine with the marks out of alignment or severe engine damage could occur.

18 Remove the holder from the cam chain tensioner.

19 Adjust the valve clearances (see Chapter 1).

20 The remainder of installation is the reverse of removal.

10 Cylinder head - removal and installation

Caution: *The engine must be completely cool before beginning this procedure, or the cylinder head may become warped.*

10.3b On XR400R models, the washer near the spark plug hole is thicker than the others

Removal

Refer to illustrations 10.3a, 10.3b and 10.5

1 Remove the cylinder head cover, cam chain tensioner and camshaft (Sections 7, 8 and 9).

2 On XR250L and XR250R models, there four small head bolts (6 mm shaft diameter) on the camshaft sprocket side of the head. Two of these bolts secure the cam chain tensioner retainer, so they're removed when the tensioner is removed. Unscrew the two remaining small bolts.

3 Loosen the main cylinder head bolts (XR250L and XR250R) or nuts (XR400R) in two or three stages, in a criss-cross pattern **(see illustration)**. Remove the bolts or nuts and their washers. On XR400R models, the washer nearest the spark plug hole is thicker than the others **(see illustration)**.

4 Lift the cylinder head off the cylinder. If the head is stuck, use wooden dowels inserted into the intake or exhaust ports to lever the head off. Don't attempt to pry the head off by inserting a screwdriver between the head and the cylinder - you'll damage the sealing surfaces. Don't hammer against the side of the head or the cooling fins may be broken.

5 Support the cam chain so it won't drop into the cam chain tunnel, and stuff a clean rag into the tunnel to prevent the entry of debris.

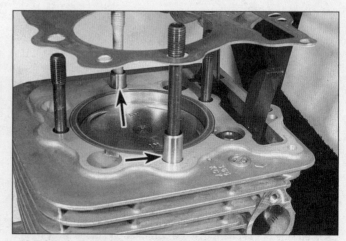

10.5 Lift the head off, remove the gasket and locate the dowels (arrows); they may come off with the head or stay in the cylinder

Once this is done, remove the gasket and two dowel pins from the cylinder **(see illustration)**.

6   If the front (exhaust) side chain guide is worn, lift it out of its notches **(see illustration 9.8a)**.

7   Check the cylinder head gasket and the mating surfaces on the cylinder head and cylinder for leakage, which could indicate warpage. Refer to Section 11 and check the flatness of the cylinder head.

8   Clean all traces of old gasket material from the cylinder head and cylinder. Be careful not to let any of the gasket material fall into the crankcase, the cylinder bore or the bolt holes.

Installation

9   Install the two dowel pins, then lay the new gasket in place on the cylinder **(see illustration 10.5)**. Never reuse the old gasket and don't use any type of gasket sealant.

10   Make sure the cam chain front guide fits in its notches **(see illustration 9.8a)**.

11   Carefully lower the cylinder head over the dowels. It's helpful to have an assistant support the camshaft chain with a piece of wire so it doesn't fall and become kinked or detached from the crankshaft. When the head is resting on the cylinder, wire the cam chain to another component to keep tension on it.

12   If you're working on an XR250L or XR250R, install the head bolts and their washers in the proper holes (they're different lengths). Tighten the bolts in two or three stages, in a criss-cross pattern, to the torque listed in this Chapter's Specifications.

13   Install the cylinder head nuts and tighten them securely, but don't overtighten them and strip the threads.

14   The remainder of installation is the reverse of the removal steps.

15   Change the engine oil (see Chapter 1).

11 Valves/valve seats/valve guides - servicing

1   Because of the complex nature of this job and the special tools and equipment required, servicing of the valves, the valve seats and the valve guides (commonly known as a valve job) is best left to a professional.

2   The home mechanic can, however, remove and disassemble the head, do the initial cleaning and inspection, then reassemble and deliver the head to a dealer service department or properly equipped motorcycle repair shop for the actual valve servicing. Refer to Section 12 for those procedures.

3   The service department will remove the valves and springs, recondition or replace the valves and valve seats, replace the valve guides, check and replace the valve springs, spring retainers and keepers (as necessary), replace the valve seals with new ones and reassemble the valve components.

4   After the valve job has been performed, the head will be in like-new condition. When the head is returned, be sure to clean it again very thoroughly before installation on the engine to remove any metal particles or abrasive grit that may still be present from the valve service operations. Use compressed air, if available, to blow out all the holes and passages.

12 Cylinder head and valves - disassembly, inspection and reassembly

1   As mentioned in the previous Section, valve servicing and valve guide replacement should be left to a dealer service department or motorcycle repair shop. However, disassembly, cleaning and inspection of the valves and related components can be done (if the necessary special tools are available) by the home mechanic. This way no expense is incurred if the inspection reveals that service work is not required at this time.

2   To properly disassemble the valve components without the risk of damaging them, a valve spring compressor is absolutely necessary. If the special tool is not available, have a dealer service department or motorcycle repair shop handle the entire process of disassembly, inspection, service or repair (if required) and reassembly of the valves.

Disassembly

Refer to illustrations 12.7a, 12.7b and 12.7c

3   Remove the intake manifold from the cylinder head (see Chapter 3).

4   Before the valves are removed, scrape away any traces of gasket material from the head gasket sealing surface. Work slowly and do not nick or gouge the soft aluminum of the head. Gasket removing solvents, which work very well, are available at most motorcycle shops and auto parts stores.

5   Carefully scrape all carbon deposits out of the combustion chamber area. A hand-held wire brush or a piece of fine emery cloth can be used once most of the deposits have been scraped away. Do not use a wire brush mounted in a drill motor, or one with extremely stiff bristles, as the head material is soft and may be eroded away or scratched by the wire brush.

6   Before proceeding, arrange to label and store the valves along with their related components so they can be kept separate and reinstalled in the same valve guides they are removed from (plastic bags work well for this).

7   Compress the valve spring(s) on the first valve with a spring compressor, then remove the keepers and the retainer from the valve assembly **(see illustrations)**. Do not compress the spring(s) any more

12.7a Install a valve spring compressor and compress the valve springs, then remove the keepers, the valve spring retainer, springs, spring seat and valve

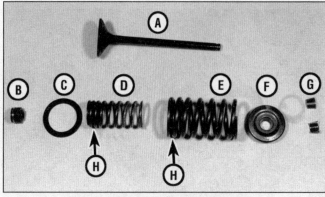

12.7b Valve and related components

A Valve stem	E Outer valve spring
B Oil seal	F Valve spring retainer
C Spring seat	G Keepers
D Inner valve spring	H Tightly wound coils

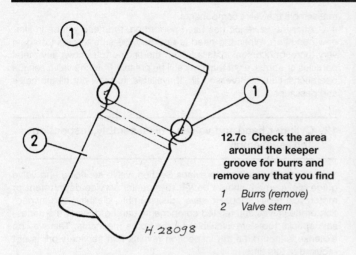

12.7c Check the area around the keeper groove for burrs and remove any that you find

1 *Burrs (remove)*
2 *Valve stem*

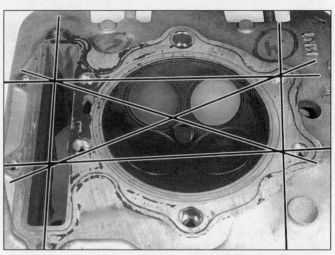

12.14 Check the gasket surface for flatness with a straightedge and feeler gauge in the directions shown

than is absolutely necessary. Carefully release the valve spring compressor and remove the spring(s), spring seat and valve from the head. If the valve binds in the guide (won't pull through), push it back into the head and deburr the area around the keeper groove with a very fine file or whetstone **(see illustration)**.

8   Repeat the procedure for the remaining valves. Remember to keep the parts for each valve together so they can be reinstalled in the same location.

9   Once the valves have been removed and labeled, pull off the valve stem seals with pliers and discard them (the old seals should never be reused).

10   Next, clean the cylinder head with solvent and dry it thoroughly. Compressed air will speed the drying process and ensure that all holes and recessed areas are clean.

11   Clean all of the valve springs, keepers, retainers and spring seats with solvent and dry them thoroughly. Do the parts from one valve at a time so that no mixing of parts between valves occurs.

12   Scrape off any deposits that may have formed on the valve, then use a motorized wire brush to remove deposits from the valve heads and stems. Again, make sure the valves do not get mixed up.

Inspection

Refer to illustrations 12.14, 12.15, 12.16, 12.17, 12.18a, 12.18b, 12.19a and 12.19b

13   Inspect the head very carefully for cracks and other damage. If cracks are found, a new head will be required. Check the cam bearing surfaces for wear and evidence of seizure. Check the camshaft for

wear as well (see Section 9).

14   Using a precision straightedge and a feeler gauge, check the head gasket mating surface for warpage. Lay the straightedge lengthwise, across the head and diagonally (corner-to-corner), intersecting the head bolt holes, and try to slip a feeler gauge under it, on either side of the combustion chamber **(see illustration)**. The feeler gauge thickness should be the same as the cylinder head warpage limit listed in this Chapter's Specifications. If the feeler gauge can be inserted between the head and the straightedge, the head is warped and must either be machined or, if warpage is excessive, replaced with a new one.

15   Examine the valve seats in each of the combustion chambers. If they are pitted, cracked or burned, the head will require valve service that is beyond the scope of the home mechanic. Measure the valve seat width **(see illustration)** and compare it to this Chapter's Specifications. If it is not within the specified range, or if it varies around its circumference, valve service work is required.

16   Clean the valve guides to remove any carbon buildup, then measure the inside diameters of the guides (at both ends and the center of the guide) with a small hole gauge and a micrometer **(see illustration)**. Record the measurements for future reference. The guides are measured at the ends and at the center to determine if they are worn in a bell-mouth pattern (more wear at the ends). If they are, guide replacement is an absolute must.

17   Carefully inspect each valve face for cracks, pits and burned

12.15 Measuring valve seat width

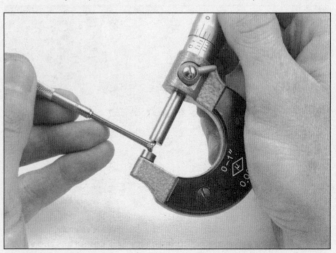

12.16 Measure the valve guide inside diameter with a hole gauge, then measure the gauge with a micrometer

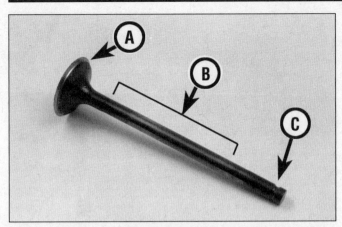

12.17 Check the valve face (A), stem (B) and keeper groove (C) for wear and damage

12.18a Measuring valve stem diameter

spots. Check the valve stem and the keeper groove area for cracks **(see illustration)**. Rotate the valve and check for any obvious indication that it is bent. Check the end of the stem for pitting and excessive wear. The presence of any of the above conditions indicates the need for valve servicing.

18   Measure the valve stem diameter **(see illustration)**. If the diameter is less than listed in this Chapter's Specifications, the valves will have to be replaced with new ones. Also check the valve stem for bending. Set the valve in a V-block with a dial indicator touching the middle of the stem **(see illustration)**. Rotate the valve and look for a reading on the gauge (which indicates a bent stem). If the stem is bent, replace the valve.

19   Check the end of each valve spring for wear and pitting. Measure the free length **(see illustration)** and compare it to this Chapter's Specifications. Any springs that are shorter than specified have sagged and should not be reused. Stand the spring on a flat surface and check it for squareness **(see illustration)**.

20   Check the spring retainers and keepers for obvious wear and cracks. Any questionable parts should not be reused, as extensive damage will occur in the event of failure during engine operation.

21   If the inspection indicates that no service work is required, the valve components can be reinstalled in the head.

Reassembly

Refer to illustrations 12.23, 12.24a, 12.24b, 12.26 and 12.27

22   If the valve seats have been ground, the valves and seats should be lapped before installing the valves in the head to ensure a positive seal between the valves and seats. This procedure requires coarse and

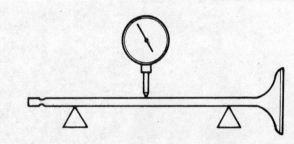

12.18b Check the valve stem for bends with a V-block (or V-blocks, as shown here) and a dial indicator

fine valve lapping compound (available at auto parts stores) and a valve lapping tool. If a lapping tool is not available, a piece of rubber or plastic hose can be slipped over the valve stem (after the valve has been installed in the guide) and used to turn the valve.

23   Apply a small amount of coarse lapping compound to the valve face **(see illustration)**, then slip the valve into the guide. **Note:** *Make sure the valve is installed in the correct guide and be careful not to get any lapping compound on the valve stem.*

24   Attach the lapping tool (or hose) to the valve and rotate the tool between the palms of your hands. Use a back-and-forth motion rather than a circular motion. Lift the valve off the seat and turn it at regular intervals to distribute the lapping compound properly. Continue the lapping procedure until the valve face and seat contact area is of uni-

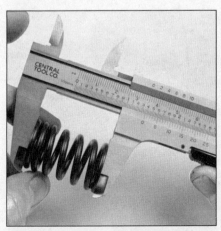

12.19a Measuring the free length of the valve springs

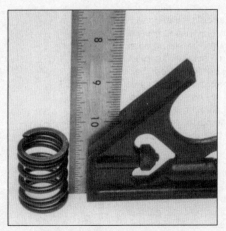

12.19b Checking the valve springs for squareness

12.23 Apply the lapping compound very sparingly, in small dabs, to the valve face only

12.24a After lapping, the valve face should exhibit a uniform, unbroken contact pattern (arrow) . . .

12.24b . . . and the seat (arrow) should be the specified width with a smooth, unbroken appearance

12.26 Push the oil seal onto the valve guide (arrow)

12.27 A small dab of grease will help hold the keepers in place on the valve while the spring compressor is released

form width and unbroken around the entire circumference of the valve face and seat **(see illustrations)**. Once this is accomplished, lap the valves again with fine lapping compound.

25   Carefully remove the valve from the guide and wipe off all traces of lapping compound. Use solvent to clean the valve and wipe the seat area thoroughly with a solvent soaked cloth. Repeat the procedure for the remaining valves.

26   Lay the spring seat in place in the cylinder head, then install a new valve stem seal on the guide **(see illustration)**. Use an appropriate size deep socket to push the seals into place until they are properly seated. Don't twist or cock them, or they will not seal properly against the valve stems. Also, don't remove them again or they will be damaged.

27   Coat the valve stems with assembly lube or moly-based grease, then install one of them into its guide. Next, install the spring seat, springs and retainers, compress the springs and install the keepers. **Note:** *Install the springs with the tightly wound coils at the bottom (next to the spring seat).* When compressing the springs with the valve spring compressor, depress them only as far as is absolutely necessary to slip the keepers into place. Apply a small amount of grease to the keepers **(see illustration)** to help hold them in place as the pressure is released from the springs. Make certain that the keepers are securely locked in their retaining grooves.

28   Support the cylinder head on blocks so the valves can't contact the workbench top, then very gently tap each of the valve stems with a soft-faced hammer. This will help seat the keepers in their grooves.

29   Once all of the valves have been installed in the head, check for proper valve sealing by pouring a small amount of solvent into each of the valve ports. If the solvent leaks past the valve(s) into the combustion chamber area, disassemble the valve(s) and repeat the lapping procedure, then reinstall the valve(s) and repeat the check. Repeat the procedure until a satisfactory seal is obtained.

13   Cylinder - removal, inspection and installation

Removal

Refer to illustrations 13.2, 13.3, 13.4 and 13.5

1   Remove the cylinder head cover, camshaft and cylinder head (see Sections 7, 9 and 10). Make sure the crankshaft is positioned at Top Dead Center (TDC).

2   Remove two small bolts securing the cylinder to the crankcase **(see illustration)**.

13.2 Remove the two small bolts that secure the cylinder to the crankcase . . .

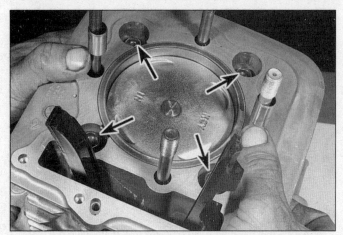

13.3 ... then lift off the dowels if they're still in the cylinder and loosen the main bolts (arrows) evenly, in a criss-cross pattern - note the location of the IN mark on the piston; it must face the same way on installation

13.4 Lift the cylinder off the crankcase; if you're experienced and very careful, the cylinder can be installed over the rings without a ring compressor, but a compressor is recommended

3   If the cylinder head dowels stayed in the cylinder, remove them. Loosen the main cylinder attaching bolts in two or three stages in a criss-cross pattern **(see illustration)**.

4   Lift the cylinder straight up, off the piston (and the front cam chain guide on XR400R models) **(see illustration)**. If it's stuck, tap around its perimeter with a soft-faced hammer (but don't tap on the cooling fins or they may break). Don't attempt to pry between the cylinder and the crankcase, as you'll ruin the sealing surfaces.

5   Locate the dowel pins (they may have come off with the cylinder or still be in the crankcase) **(see illustration)**. Be careful not to let these drop into the engine. Stuff rags around the piston and remove the gasket and all traces of old gasket material from the surfaces of the cylinder and the crankcase.

Inspection

Refer to illustrations 13.6 and 13.8

Caution: *Don't attempt to separate the liner from the cylinder.*

6   Check the top surface of the cylinder for warpage, using the same method as for the cylinder head (see Section 12). Measure along the sides and diagonally across the stud holes **(see illustration)**.

7   Check the cylinder walls carefully for scratches and score marks.

8   Using the appropriate precision measuring tools, check the cylinder's diameter at the top, center and bottom of the cylinder bore, parallel to the crankshaft axis **(see illustration)**. Next, measure the cylinder's diameter at the same three locations across the crankshaft axis. Compare the results to this Chapter's Specifications. If the cylinder

13.5 Locate the dowels and remove the base gasket

walls are tapered, out-of-round, worn beyond the specified limits, or badly scuffed or scored, have the cylinder rebored and honed by a dealer service department or a motorcycle repair shop. If a rebore is done, oversize pistons and rings will be required as well. **Note:** *Honda supplies pistons in two oversizes.*

9   As an alternative, if the precision measuring tools are not avail-

13.6 Check the cylinder top surface for warpage in the directions shown

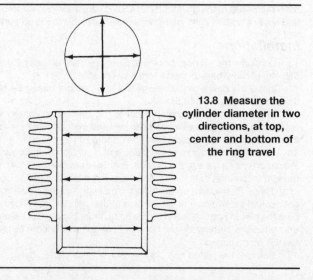

13.8 Measure the cylinder diameter in two directions, at top, center and bottom of the ring travel

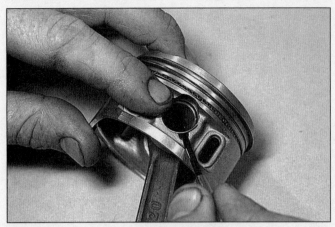

14.3   Wear eye protection and pry the circlip out of its groove with a pointed tool

14.4a   Push the piston pin partway out, then pull it the rest of the way

able, a dealer service department or other repair shop will make the measurements and offer advice concerning servicing of the cylinder.

10   If it's in reasonably good condition and not worn to the outside of the limits, and if the piston-to-cylinder clearance can be maintained properly, then the cylinder does not have to be rebored; honing is all that is necessary.

11   To perform the honing operation you will need the proper size flexible hone with fine stones as shown in *Maintenance techniques, tools and working facilities* at the front of this book, or a "bottle brush" type hone, plenty of light oil or honing oil, some shop towels and an electric drill motor. Hold the cylinder in a vise (cushioned with soft jaws or wood blocks) when performing the honing operation. Mount the hone in the drill motor, compress the stones and slip the hone into the cylinder. Lubricate the cylinder thoroughly, turn on the drill and move the hone up and down in the cylinder at a pace which will produce a fine crosshatch pattern on the cylinder wall with the crosshatch lines intersecting at approximately a 60-degree angle. Be sure to use plenty of lubricant and do not take off any more material than is absolutely necessary to produce the desired effect. Do not withdraw the hone from the cylinder while it is running. Instead, shut off the drill and continue moving the hone up and down in the cylinder until it comes to a complete stop, then compress the stones and withdraw the hone. Wipe the oil out of the cylinder. Remember, do not remove too much material from the cylinder wall. If you do not have the tools, or do not desire to perform the honing operation, a dealer service department or vehicle repair shop will generally do it for a reasonable fee.

12   Next, the cylinder must be thoroughly washed with warm soapy water to remove all traces of the abrasive grit produced during the honing operation. Be sure to run a brush through the bolt holes and flush them with running water. After rinsing, dry the cylinder thoroughly and apply a coat of light, rust-preventative oil to all machined surfaces.

Installation

13   Lubricate the cylinder bore with plenty of clean engine oil. Apply a thin film of moly-based grease to the piston skirt.

14   Install the dowel pins, then lower a new cylinder base gasket over them **(see illustration 13.5)**.

15   Attach a piston ring compressor to the piston and compress the piston rings. A large hose clamp can be used instead - just make sure it doesn't scratch the piston, and don't tighten it too much.

16   Install the cylinder over the studs and carefully lower it down until the piston crown fits into the cylinder liner **(see illustration 13.4)**. While doing this, pull the camshaft chain up, using a hooked tool or a piece of stiff wire. Push down on the cylinder, making sure the piston doesn't get cocked sideways, until the bottom of the cylinder liner slides down past the piston rings. A wood or plastic hammer handle can be used to gently tap the cylinder down, but don't use too much force or the piston will be damaged.

17   Remove the piston ring compressor or hose clamp, being careful

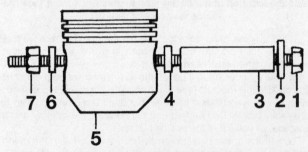

14.4b   The piston pin should come out with hand pressure - if it doesn't, this removal tool can be fabricated from readily available parts

1	Bolt	7	Nut (B)
2	Washer	A	Large enough for piston
3	Pipe (A)		pin to fit inside
4	Padding (A)	B	Small enough to fit
5	Piston		through piston pin bore
6	Washer (B)		

not to scratch the piston.

18   The remainder of installation is the reverse of the removal steps.

14   Piston - removal, inspection and installation

1   The piston is attached to the connecting rod with a piston pin that is a slip fit in the piston and rod.

2   Before removing the piston from the rod, stuff a clean shop towel into the crankcase hole, around the connecting rod. This will prevent the circlips from falling into the crankcase if they are inadvertently dropped.

Removal

Refer to illustrations 14.3, 14.4a and 14.4b

3   The piston should have an IN mark on its crown that goes toward the intake (rear) side of the engine **(see illustration 13.3)**. If this mark is not visible due to carbon buildup, scribe an arrow into the piston crown before removal. Support the piston and pry the circlip out with a pointed tool **(see illustration)**.

4   Push the piston pin out from the opposite end to free the piston from the rod **(see illustration)**. You may have to deburr the area around the groove to enable the pin to slide out (use a triangular file for this procedure). If the pin won't come out, you can fabricate a piston pin removal tool from a long bolt, a nut, a piece of tubing and washers **(see illustration)**.

14.6 Remove the piston rings with a ring removal and installation tool

14.13 Measure the piston ring-to-groove clearance with a feeler gauge

14.14 Measure the piston diameter with a micrometer

Inspection

Refer to illustrations 14.6, 14.13, 14.14, 14.15 and 14.16

5   Before the inspection process can be carried out, the pistons must be cleaned and the old piston rings removed.

6   Using a piston ring removal and installation tool, carefully remove the rings from the pistons **(see illustration)**. Do not nick or gouge the pistons in the process.

7   Scrape all traces of carbon from the tops of the pistons. A hand-held wire brush or a piece of fine emery cloth can be used once the majority of the deposits have been scraped away. Do not, under any circumstances, use a wire brush mounted in a drill motor to remove deposits from the pistons; the piston material is soft and will be eroded away by the wire brush.

8   Use a piston ring groove cleaning tool to remove any carbon deposits from the ring grooves. If a tool is not available, a piece broken off the old ring will do the job. Be very careful to remove only the carbon deposits. Do not remove any metal and do not nick or gouge the sides of the ring grooves.

9   Once the deposits have been removed, clean the pistons with solvent and dry them thoroughly. Make sure the oil return holes below the oil ring grooves are clear.

10   If the pistons are not damaged or worn excessively and if the cylinders are not rebored, new pistons will not be necessary. Normal piston wear appears as even, vertical wear on the thrust surfaces of the piston and slight looseness of the top ring in its groove. New piston rings, on the other hand, should always be used when an engine is rebuilt.

11   Carefully inspect each piston for cracks around the skirt, at the pin bosses and at the ring lands.

12   Look for scoring and scuffing on the thrust faces of the skirt, holes in the piston crown and burned areas at the edge of the crown. If the skirt is scored or scuffed, the engine may have been suffering from overheating and/or abnormal combustion, which caused excessively high operating temperatures. The oil pump should be checked thoroughly. A hole in the piston crown, an extreme to be sure, is an indication that abnormal combustion (pre-ignition) was occurring. Burned areas at the edge of the piston crown are usually evidence of spark knock (detonation). If any of the above problems exist, the causes must be corrected or the damage will occur again.

13   Measure the piston ring-to-groove clearance (side clearance) by laying a new piston ring in the ring groove and slipping a feeler gauge in beside it **(see illustration)**. Check the clearance at three or four locations around the groove. Be sure to use the correct ring for each groove; they are different. If the clearance is greater than specified, a new piston will have to be used when the engine is reassembled.

14   Check the piston-to-bore clearance by measuring the bore (see Section 13) and the piston diameter **(see illustration)**. Measure the piston across the skirt on the thrust faces at a 90-degree angle to the piston pin, at the specified distance up from the bottom of the skirt. Subtract the piston diameter from the bore diameter to obtain the clearance. If it is greater than specified, the cylinder will have to be rebored and a new oversized piston and rings installed. If the appropriate precision measuring tools are not available, the piston-to-cylinder clearance can be obtained, though not quite as accurately, using feeler gauge stock. Feeler gauge stock comes in 12-inch lengths and various thicknesses and is generally available at auto parts stores. To check the clearance, slip a piece of feeler gauge stock of the same thickness as the specified piston clearance into the cylinder along with appropriate piston. The cylinder should be upside down and the piston must be positioned exactly as it normally would be. Place the feeler gauge between the piston and cylinder on one of the thrust faces (90-degrees to the piston pin bore). The piston should slip through the cylinder (with the feeler gauge in place) with moderate pressure. If it falls through, or slides through easily, the clearance is excessive and a new piston will be required. If the piston binds at the lower end of the cylinder and is loose toward the top, the cylinder is tapered, and if tight spots are encountered as the piston/feeler gauge is rotated in the cylinder, the cylinder is out-of-round. Be sure to have the cylinder and piston checked by a dealer service department or other repair shop to confirm your findings before purchasing new parts.

15   Apply clean engine oil to the pin, insert it into the piston and check for freeplay by rocking the pin back-and-forth **(see illustration)**. If the pin is loose, a new piston and possibly new pin must be installed.

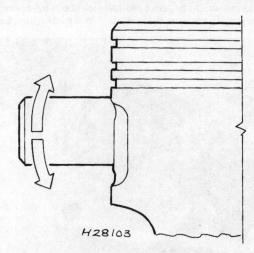

H28103

14.15 Slip the pin into the piston and try to wiggle it back-and-forth; if it's loose, replace the piston and pin

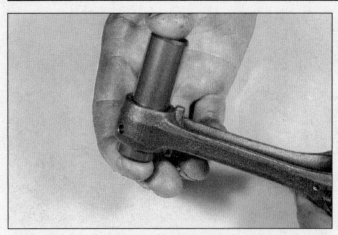

14.16 Slip the piston pin into the rod and try to rock it back-and-forth to check for looseness

14.18 Make sure both piston pin circlips are securely seated in the piston grooves

16   Repeat Step 15, this time inserting the piston pin into the connecting rod **(see illustration)**. If the pin is loose, measure the pin diameter and the pin bore in the rod (or have this done by a dealer or repair shop). A worn pin can be replaced separately; if the rod bore is worn, the rod and crankshaft must be replaced as an assembly.

17   Refer to Section 15 and install the rings on the pistons.

Installation

Refer to illustration 14.18

18   Install the piston with its IN mark toward the intake side (rear) of the engine. Lubricate the pin and the rod bore with moly-based grease. Install a new circlip in the groove in one side of the piston (don't reuse the old circlips). Push the pin into position from the opposite side and install another new circlip. Compress the circlips only enough for them to fit in the piston. Make sure the circlips are properly seated in the grooves **(see illustration)**.

15   Piston rings - installation

Refer to illustrations 15.2, 15.4, 15.7a, 15.7b and 15.7c

1   Before installing the new piston rings, the ring end gaps must be checked.

2   Insert the top (No. 1) ring into the bottom of the cylinder and square it up with the cylinder walls by pushing it in with the top of the piston. The ring should be about one-half inch above the bottom edge of the cylinder. To measure the end gap, slip a feeler gauge between

the ends of the ring **(see illustration)** and compare the measurement to the Specifications.

3   If the gap is larger or smaller than specified, double check to make sure that you have the correct rings before proceeding.

4   If the gap is too small, it must be enlarged or the ring ends may come in contact with each other during engine operation, which can cause serious damage. The end gap can be increased by filing the ring ends very carefully with a fine file **(see illustration)**. When performing this operation, file only from the outside in.

5   Repeat the procedure for the second compression ring and oil ring.

6   Once the ring end gaps have been checked/corrected, the rings can be installed on the piston.

7   The oil control ring (lowest on the piston) is installed first. It is composed of three separate components. Slip the spacer into the groove, then install the upper side rail **(see illustrations)**. Do not use a piston ring installation tool on the oil ring side rails as they may be damaged. Instead, place one end of the side rail into the groove between the spacer expander and the ring land. Hold it firmly in place and slide a finger around the piston while pushing the rail into the groove (taking care not to cut your fingers on the sharp edges). Next, install the lower side rail in the same manner.

8   After the three oil ring components have been installed, check to make sure that both the upper and lower side rails can be turned smoothly in the ring groove.

9   Install the no. 2 (middle) ring next. It can be readily distinguished from the top ring by its cross-section shape **(see illustration 15.7c)**. Do not mix the top and middle rings.

15.2 Check the piston ring end gap with a feeler gauge at the bottom of the cylinder

15.4 If the end gap is too small, clamp a file in a vise and file the ring ends (from the outside in only) to enlarge the gap slightly

15.7a Installing the oil ring expander - make sure the ends don't overlap

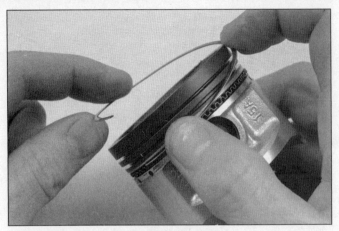

15.7b Installing an oil ring side rail - don't use a ring installation tool to do this

10　To avoid breaking the ring, use a piston ring installation tool and make sure that the identification mark is facing up **(see illustration 15.7c)**. Fit the ring into the middle groove on the piston. Do not expand the ring any more than is necessary to slide it into place.

11　Finally, install the no. 1 (top) ring in the same manner. Make sure the identifying mark is facing up. Be very careful not to confuse the top and second rings.

12　Once the rings have been properly installed, stagger the end gaps, including those of the oil ring side rails **(see illustration 15.7c)**.

16　Clutch - removal, inspection and installation

Cable

Removal

Refer to illustrations 16.2 and 16.3

1　Loosen the cable adjuster at the handlebar grip all the way (see Chapter 1). Rotate the cable so the inner cable aligns with the slot in the lever, then slip the cable end fitting out of the lever.

2　If you're working on an XR250L or XR250R, loosen the locknut and adjusting nut at the engine bracket **(see illustration)**. Disengage the cable from the lifter lever in the right engine cover, then pull it out of the bracket.

3　If you're working on an XR400R, you can loosen the locknut and adjusting nut or unbolt the bracket from the engine **(see illustration)**. Slip the cable end out of the lifter lever.

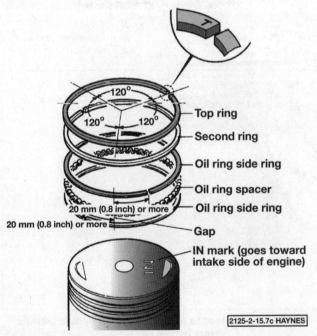

15.7c Piston ring details

- Top ring
- Second ring
- Oil ring side ring
- Oil ring spacer
- Oil ring side ring
- Gap
- IN mark (goes toward intake side of engine)

120°　120°　120°

20 mm (0.8 inch) or more

20 mm (0.8 inch) or more

2125-2-15.7c HAYNES

16.2 The XR250L and XR250R clutch cable runs down the back of the engine; loosen the locknut and adjusting nut (upper arrow) and slip the cable out of the bracket, then slip it out of the lifter lever (lower arrow)

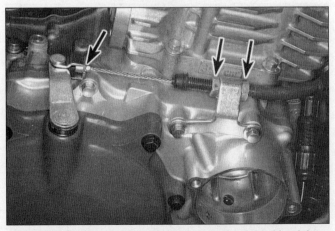

16.3 The XR400R clutch cable runs along the right side of the engine; loosen the locknut and adjusting nut (right arrows) and slip the cable out of the bracket, then slip it out of the lifter lever (left arrow)

**16.9 Right engine cover details - later XR250R
(XR250L and early XR250R similar)**

A	Dowels	D	Spring
B	Push piece	E	Crankshaft end seal
C	Lifter lever	F	Kickstarter shaft seal

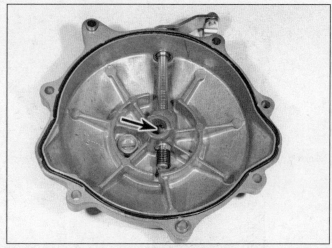

**16.10b . . . you'll need to turn the lifter lever to disengage its
center portion (arrow) . . .**

**16.10c . . . from the push piece (A); the pressure plate is secured
by five bolts (B)**

**16.10a Remove the bolts (arrows) to detach the XR400R clutch
cover; before you can take the cover off . . .**

Inspection

4   Slide the inner cable back and forth in the housing and make sure
it moves freely. If it doesn't, try lubricating it as described in Chapter 1.
If that doesn't help, replace the cable.

Installation

5   Installation is the reverse of the removal steps. Refer to Chapter 1
and adjust clutch freeplay.

Right engine cover

XR250L and XR250R

Refer to illustration 16.9

6   Drain the engine oil (see Chapter 1). Remove the oil pipe (see
Section 22) and the kickstarter pedal (see Section 21).
7   If you're working on an XR250L or a 1986 through 1995 XR250R,
refer to Section 20 and disconnect the kickstarter decompressor cable
at the engine.
8   Remove the brake pedal (see Chapter 6).
9   Remove the cover bolts and pull the cover off the engine **(see
illustration)**. Tap gently with a rubber mallet if necessary to break the
O-ring seal. Don't pry against the mating surfaces of the cover and
crankcase. Once the cover is off, locate the dowels; they may have
stayed in the crankcase or come off with the cover.

**16.12a To remove the entire engine cover from an XR400R,
remove the bolts (arrows) . . .**

16.12b . . . and pull the cover off; note the locations of the dowels (arrows) . . .

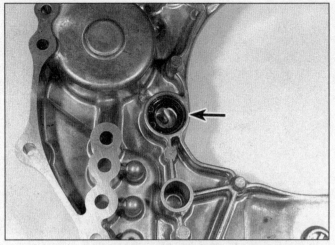

16.12c . . . the crankshaft end seal is held in the cover by a snap-ring

XR400R

Refer to illustrations 16.10a, 16.10b, 16.10c, 16.12a, 16.12b and 16.12c

10   If you're planning to work on just the clutch, it's only necessary to remove the outer cover **(see illustration)**. Disconnect the cable from the lifter lever as described above. Turn the lifter lever to disengage its shaft from the push piece inside the cover **(see illustrations)**, then remove the cover bolts and pull it off. Don't pry against the mating surfaces of the cover and crankcase. Once the cover is off, locate the dowels; they may have stayed in the crankcase or come off with the cover.

11   If you need to remove the entire right engine cover, remove the brake pedal and the right footpeg (see Chapters 6 and 7). Remove the kickstarter pedal (Section 21) and disconnect the oil hoses (Section 22).

12   Remove the cover bolts and nut and pull the cover off the engine **(see illustration)**. Tap gently with a rubber mallet if necessary to break the O-ring seal. Don't pry against the mating surfaces of the cover and crankcase. Once the cover is off, locate the dowels; they may have stayed in the crankcase or come off with the cover **(see illustration)**. The seal for the end of the crankshaft that supports the primary drive gear is held in the cover by a snap-ring **(see illustration)**.

Lifter lever

Removal

13   Remove the right engine cover as described above.
14   If you're working on an XR250L or XR250R, lift the push piece out of the cover **(see illustration 16.9)**.
15   Note how the spring is installed, then pull the lifter lever shaft out of the cover **(see illustration 16.9 or 16.10b)**.

Inspection

16   Check for visible wear or damage at the contact points of the lifter lever and push piece. Replace any parts that show problems. Replace the lifter shaft seal in the engine cover whenever it's removed.

Installation

17   Installation is the reverse of the removal steps. Refill the engine oil and adjust the clutch (see Chapter 1).

Clutch

Removal (XR250L and XR250R)

Refer to illustration 16.19

18   Remove the right engine cover as described above.
19   Remove the spring bolts and take off the lifter plate, together with the release bearing **(see illustration)**. Take the springs off the posts.

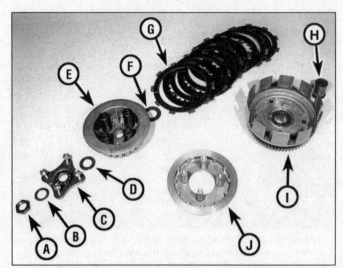

16.19 Clutch details - XR250L and XR250R

A	Locknut	F	Thrust washer
B	Lockwasher	G	Friction and metal plates
C	Lifter plate, bolts and bearing	H	Bushing
D	Thrust washer	I	Clutch housing
E	Clutch center and springs	J	Pressure plate

20   Bend back the edge of the locknut where it's been staked into the groove on the transmission mainshaft, using a hammer and sharp punch. Honda suggests drilling or grinding away the staked portion of the nut, but if you use this method, you'll need to be very careful not to damage the mainshaft.

21   Wedge a rag between the primary drive gear and the driven gear on the clutch housing to prevent the clutch housing from turning counterclockwise. Unscrew the locknut and remove the lockwasher. If you're working on an XR250L or a 1986 through 1995 XR250R, you'll need a four-pronged locknut wrench (Honda tool no. 07716-0020100 or equivalent). If you're working on a 1996 or later XR250R, remove the thrust washer. Note the OUT SIDE mark on the lockwasher; this faces away from the engine on installation.

22   Pull off the clutch center, together with the clutch plates (friction plates and metal plates).

23   Remove the remaining thrust washer and the pressure plate. Pull the clutch housing off the bushing, then remove the bushing from the mainshaft.

16.25a The tabs of the outermost friction plate fit in the clutch housing's short grooves (arrow); all other friction and metal plate tabs fit in the long grooves

16.25b With the bolts and springs removed, pull off the pressure plate together with the metal and friction plates

16.25c Wedge a rag or a copper penny into the primary and driven gears to prevent the clutch housing from turning; bend back the staked portion of the locknut (arrow) and unscrew it (don't forget to stake the new locknut on installation)

16.25d Pull off the lockwasher (its OUT SIDE mark faces away from the engine on installation)

Inspection

Refer to illustrations 16.26a, 16.26b, 16.28, 16.29, 16.31, 16.32 and 16.33

26   Rotate the release bearing and check it for rough, loose or noisy operation. If the bearing's condition is in doubt, push it out of the lifter

Removal (XR400R)

Refer to illustrations 16.25a through 16.25g

24   Remove the clutch cover as described in Steps 10 through 12.
25   Refer to the accompanying illustrations to remove the clutch components **(see illustrations)**.

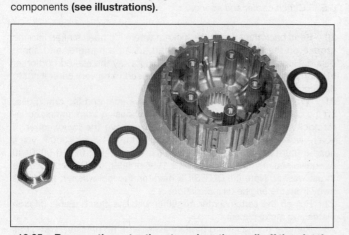

16.25e Remove the outer thrust washer, then pull off the clutch center and remove the inner thrust washer

16.25f Pull the clutch housing off the bushing . . .

16.25g . . . and remove the bushing from the crankshaft

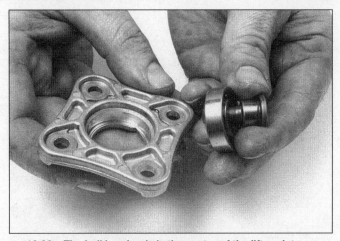

16.26a The ball bearing is in the center of the lifter plate on XR250L and XR250R models . . .

16.26b . . . and in the pressure plate on XR400R models; check the bearing for roughness, looseness or noise; check the pressure plate friction surface (arrow) for scoring

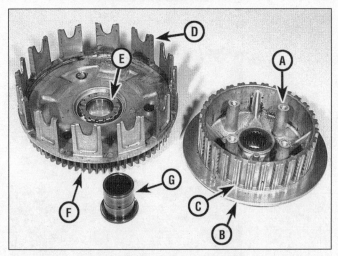

16.28 Clutch inspection points

A	Clutch center posts	E	Clutch housing bushing
B	Clutch center friction		surface
	surface	F	Driven gear
C	Clutch center splines	G	Clutch housing bushing
D	Clutch housing slots		

plate (XR250L and XR250R) or pressure plate (XR400R) and push in a new one **(see illustrations)**.

27   Check the friction surface on the pressure plate for scoring or wear. Replace the pressure plate if any defects are found.

28   Check the edges of the slots in the clutch housing for indentations made by the friction plate tabs **(see illustration)**. If the indentations are deep they can prevent clutch release, so the housing should be replaced with a new one. If the indentations can be removed easily with a file, the life of the housing can be prolonged to an extent. Also, check the driven gear teeth for cracks, chips and excessive wear and the springs on the back side (if equipped) for breakage. If the gear is worn or damaged or the springs are broken, the clutch housing must be replaced with a new one.

29   Check the bearing surface in the center of the clutch housing for score marks, scratches and excessive wear **(see illustration)**. Measure the inside diameter of the bearing surface, the inside and outside diameters of the clutch housing bushing and the bushing's mounting surface on the transmission mainshaft. Compare these to the values listed in this Chapter's Specifications. Replace any parts worn beyond the service limits. If the bushing mounting surface on the mainshaft is worn excessively, the mainshaft will have to be replaced.

30   Check the clutch center's friction surface and slots for scoring, wear and indentations **(see illustration 16.28)**. Also check the splines in the middle of the clutch center. Replace the clutch center if problems are found.

16.29 Check the clutch housing bearing surface (arrow) for wear

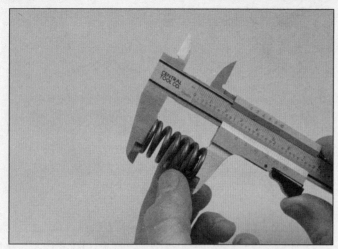

16.31 Measure the clutch spring free length

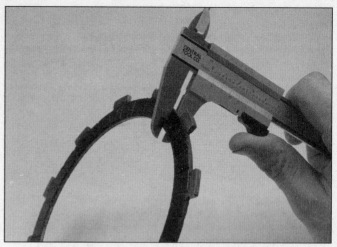

16.32 Measure the thickness of the friction plates

16.33 Check the metal plates for warpage

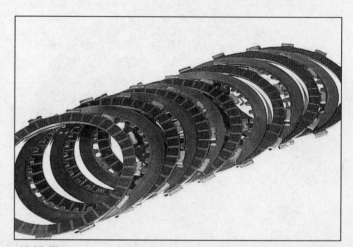

16.35 The number of plates varies according to model, but on all models, there's a metal plate between each pair of friction plates; friction plates go on first and last

31   Measure the free length of the clutch springs **(see illustration)** and compare the results to this Chapter's Specifications. If the springs have sagged, or if cracks are noted, replace them with new ones as a set.

32   If the lining material of the friction plates smells burnt or if it is glazed, new parts are required. If the metal clutch plates are scored or discolored, they must be replaced with new ones. Measure the thickness of the friction plates **(see illustration)** and replace with new parts any friction plates that are worn.

33   Lay the metal plates, one at a time, on a perfectly flat surface (such as a piece of plate glass) and check for warpage by trying to slip a feeler gauge between the flat surface and the plate **(see illustration)**. The feeler gauge should be the same thickness as the maximum warp listed in this Chapter's Specifications. Do this at several places around the plate's circumference. If the feeler gauge can be slipped under the plate, it is warped and should be replaced with a new one.

34   Check the tabs on the friction plates for excessive wear and mushroomed edges. They can be cleaned up with a file if the deformation is not severe. Check the friction plates for warpage as described in Step 33.

Installation

Refer to illustration 16.35

35   Installation is the reverse of the removal steps, with the following additions:

a) *Install the lockwasher with its OUT SIDE mark facing away from*

the engine, then install the clutch nut and tighten it to the torque listed in this Chapter's Specifications.

b) *Stake the nut into the notch on the mainshaft.*

c) *Coat the friction plates with clean engine oil before you install them.*

d) *Install a friction plate, then alternate the remaining metal and friction plates until they're all installed. Friction plates go on first and last, so the friction material contacts the metal surfaces of the clutch center and the pressure plate* **(see illustration)**.

17 Oil pump - removal, inspection and installation

Note: *The oil pump can be removed with the engine in the frame.*

Removal

Refer to illustrations 17.3, 17.4a, 17.4b, 17.4c and 17.4d

1   Remove the right engine cover and clutch (see Section 16).

2   If you're working on a XR250L or an early XR250R, remove two bolts and lift off the stamped sheet metal oil pump cover. Pull the dowel and O-ring off the outer side of the oil pump.

3   Pull the driven gear off the oil pump shaft **(see illustration)**.

4   Remove the oil pump mounting bolts and take the pump off the engine, together with the mounting shim **(see illustrations)**. Note the locations of the two dowels.

17.3 Remove the oil pump driven gear; the flat on the shaft aligns with the flat in the gear (arrow)

17.4a Remove the three-port O-ring (1996 and later) and the oil pump mounting bolts (arrows); on later XR250R models, the lower left bolt also secures the retainer for the crankcase oil screen

17.4b The XR400R crankcase oil screen has its own bolt; the O-ring is offset, so it won't fit upside down

17.4c Locate the dowels (arrows); they may come off with the pump or stay in the crankcase - don't forget the shim behind the pump; this is an XR250R shim

17.4d The XR400R pump shim surrounds an oil passage

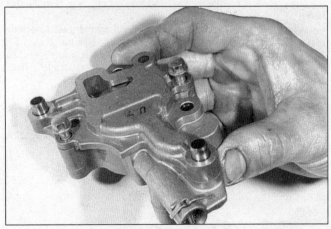

17.6a Remove the oil pump cover screws or bolts . . .

Inspection

Refer to illustrations 17.6a, 17.6b, 17.7a, 17.7b, 17.7c, 17.7d, 17.9a, 17.9b, 17.10 and 17.12

5   Construction details differ slightly between models, but all of the oil pumps used on these machines have an outer housing, an outer pair of rotors, a central spacer, an inner pair of rotors and an inner housing. The rotors on early models are driven by flats on the oil pump shaft. Later rotors are driven by a drive pin that passes through a hole in the shaft and fits in notches in the inner rotors. There's a separate drive pin for each set of rotors. The pump is held together by screws (early models) or bolts (later models).

6   Remove the screws or bolts and lift off the pump cover with its rotors **(see illustrations)**.

17.6b . . . then lift off the housing to expose one set of rotors

17.7a On later models, push out the drive pin (arrow) . . .

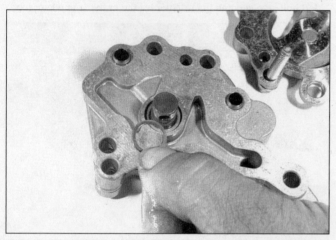

17.7b . . . and remove the washer . . .

17.7c . . . then remove the remaining housing and rotors

7   Pull the drive pins and remove the washer (later models). Pull out the pump shaft, then remove the remaining set of rotors **(see illustrations)**.

8   Wash all the components in solvent, then dry them off. Check the pump body, the rotors, the drive gear and the covers for scoring and wear. If any damage or uneven or excessive wear is evident, replace the pump. If you are rebuilding the engine, it's a good idea to install a new oil pump.

9   Place the rotors in the pump body. Measure the clearance between the outer rotor and body, and between the inner and outer rotors, with a feeler gauge **(see illustrations)**. If any of the clearances are beyond the limits listed in this Chapter's Specifications, replace the pump.

10   Place a straightedge across the outer pump body and rotors and measure the gap with a feeler gauge **(see illustration)**. If the clearance is beyond the limits listed in this Chapter's Specifications, replace

17.7d Oil pump details (later type shown)

17.9a Measure the clearance between the outer rotor and body . . .

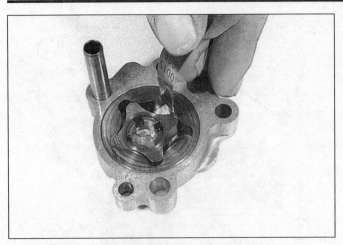

17.9b . . . between the inner and outer rotors . . .

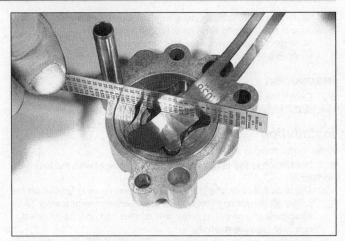

17.10 . . . and between the thin rotors and a straightedge laid
across the pump body

the pump.

11   To check the end clearance of the inner rotors and pump, you'll
need some Plastigage. Place the rotors in the pump. Cut a strip of
Plastigage, lay it across the rotors, then install the pump cover and
tighten the screws or bolts. Remove the screws or bolts, lift off the
cover, and measure the width of the crushed Plastigage with the scale
on the envelope it comes in. If the end clearance is beyond the limit
listed in this Chapter's Specifications, replace the pump.

12   Remove the cotter pin, washer, spring and relief valve **(see illustration)**. If any of the parts are damaged or if the relief valve or its bore
are scored, replace the pump. If you're planning to reuse the pump,
use a new cotter pin when you install the relief valve.

13   Reassemble the pump by reversing the disassembly steps, with
the following additions:

a) *Before installing the covers, pack the cavities between the rotors
with petroleum jelly - this will ensure the pump develops suction
quickly and begins oil circulation as soon as the engine is started.*

b) *Tighten the cover screws or bolts securely.*

Installation

14   Installation is the reverse of removal, with the following additions:

a) *Be sure you don't forget the shim and pump dowels.*

b) *Install new O-rings on the pump sleeve (early models) or outer
body (later models).*

c) *Tighten the oil pump mounting screws or bolts securely, but don't
overtighten them.*

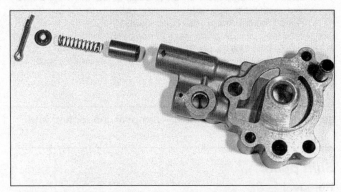

17.12 Remove the cotter pin, washer, spring and check valve

18 Primary drive gear and camshaft sprocket - removal, inspection and installation

Removal

Refer to illustrations 18.2a, 18.2b and 18.2c

1   Remove the oil pump (Section 17).

2   Wedge a rag between the teeth of the primary drive gear and the
primary driven gear on the clutch housing. Remove the clutch (Sec-

18.2a Wedge a rag between the primary drive and driven gears
(arrow) and loosen the locknut, then remove the clutch . . .

18.2b . . . unscrew the nut and slide off the lockwasher, the pulse
generator rotor (XR250L and early XR250R, not shown) and the oil
pump drive gear; on installation, the OUT SIDE mark on the
lockwasher (and pulse generator rotor, if equipped) faces away
from the engine

tion 16). Unscrew the primary drive gear locknut, then remove the lock-washer and the oil pump drive gear **(see illustrations)**.
3   Slide the primary drive gear off the crankshaft.
4   If necessary, slide the camshaft sprocket off as well.

Inspection

5   Check the drive gear for obvious damage such as chipped or broken teeth. Replace it if any of these problems are found.

Installation

Refer to illustrations 18.6a and 18.6b

6   Installation is the reverse of the removal steps, with the following additions:
   a) *The wide spline on the crankshaft aligns with a wide groove on the camshaft sprocket, primary drive gear, pulse generator rotor (if equipped) and oil pump drive gear so they can only be installed one way* **(see illustration)**.
   b) *If you're working on a 1996 or 1997 XR250R, align the wide grooves in the oil pump drive gear and primary drive gear with each other. Install them on the crankshaft and align the primary drive gear tooth opposite the wide spline with the positioning mark on the crankcase* **(see illustration)**.
   c) *Install the pulse generator rotor (if equipped) and lockwasher with its OUT SIDE mark away from the engine.*
   d) *Tighten the locknut to the torque listed in this Chapter's Specifications.*

19 External shift mechanism - removal, inspection and installation

Shift pedal

Removal

Refer to illustration 19.1

1   Look for alignment marks on the end of the shift pedal and shift shaft **(see illustration)**. If they aren't visible, make your own marks with a sharp punch.
2   Remove the shift pedal pinch bolt and slide the pedal off the shaft.

Inspection

Refer to illustration 19.4

3   Check the shift pedal for wear or damage such as bending.

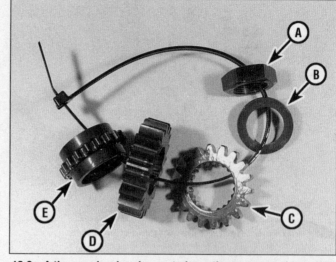

18.2c A tie wrap is a handy way to keep the parts together and in order (on XR250L and 1986 through 1995 XR250R models, there's a pulse generator rotor between the lockwasher and oil pump drive gear)

Check the splines on the shift pedal and shaft for stripping or step wear. Replace the pedal or shaft if these problems are found.
4   Check the shift shaft seal for signs of oil leakage **(see illustration)**. If it has been leaking, refer to Chapter 4 and remove the left engine cover. Pry the seal out of the cover and install a new one. You may be able to push the seal in with your thumbs; if not, tap it in with a hammer and block of wood or a socket the same diameter as the seal.

Installation

5   Line up the punch marks, install the shift pedal and tighten the pinch bolt.

External shift linkage

6   Shift linkage components accessible without splitting the crankcase include the stopper plate and cam plate.

Removal

Refer to illustrations 19.9a, 19.9b and 19.10

7   Remove the shift pedal as described above.

18.6a The wide grooves (arrows) in the cam sprocket, primary drive gear, oil pump drive gear and signal generator rotor (if equipped) align with a wide spline on the crankshaft . . .

18.6b . . . on 1996 and 1997 XR250R models, align the primary drive gear tooth opposite the wide groove with the mark on the crankcase (arrow)

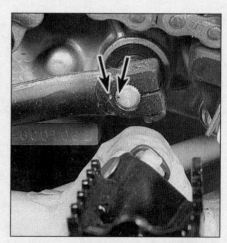

19.1 If you don't see a punch mark on the pedal and the end of the spindle, make your own (arrows)

19.4 The smaller seal in the left engine cover is for the shift shaft; the other is for the transmission countershaft

19.9a Note how the ends of the spring are positioned, then loosen the stopper arm bolt; the XR400 stopper arm (shown) pivots upward from below, while the XR250 stopper arm pivots downward from above . . .

8 Remove the clutch (Section 16).

9 Note how the stopper arm spring presses against the case and hooks around the stopper arm **(see illustration)**. Pull the stopper arm away from the shift drum cam, then loosen the stopper arm bolt and release the spring tension **(see illustration)**. Remove the bolt and take the stopper arm and spring off the crankcase.

10 Remove the bolt from the shift drum cam and take the cam off the drum **(see illustration)**.

Inspection

11 Check all parts for visible wear or damage and replace any parts that show problems.

Installation

12 Position the shift drum cam on the shift drum, aligning the hole in the back of the cam with the pin on the shift drum. Apply non-permanent thread locking agent to the threads of the bolt, then tighten it to the torque listed in this Chapter's Specifications.

13 Position the spring on the stopper arm, then install the stopper arm on the engine and tighten its bolt loosely **(see illustration 19.9b)**. Pull up the stopper arm and engage its roller end with the neutral notch in the shift drum cam **(see illustration 19.9a)**. Tighten the bolt to the torque listed in this Chapter's Specifications.

14 The remainder of installation is the reverse of the removal steps.

15 Check the engine oil level and add some, if necessary (see Chapter 1).

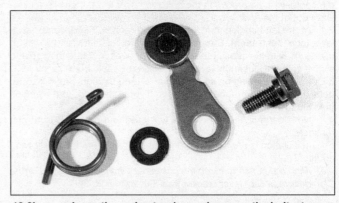

19.9b . . . release the spring tension and remove the bolt, stopper arm, washer and spring

20 Decompressor lever and cable - removal and installation

Refer to illustrations 20.1, 20.2 and 20.3

1 At the top of the engine, loosen the cable locknuts and slip the cable out of the bracket **(see illustration)**. Turn the cable end to align

19.10 The hole in the shift drum cam (lower arrow) aligns with the pin in the shift drum (upper arrow) on installation

20.1 Loosen the locknuts and slip the cable out of the bracket (right arrow), then rotate the cable to align it with the slot in the lever (left arrow) and slide it sideways out of the lever

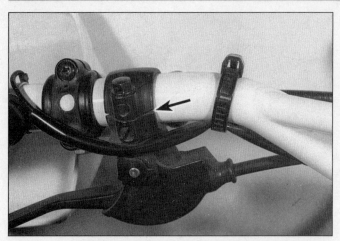

20.2 The decompressor lever is secured to the handlebar by a clamp; on installation, align the split in the clamp with the punch mark on the handlebar (arrow)

20.3 The kickstarter decompressor cable is secured in a bracket behind the engine (upper arrow); detach it from the bracket, then rotate the cable to align it with the slot in the lever (lower arrow) and slide it sideways out of the lever

the cable with the groove in the decompressor lever, then slip it sideways out of the lever.

2   At the left handlebar, loosen the pinch bolt on the decompressor lever **(see illustration)**. Slide the lever toward the center of the bike to create slack in the cable. Pull back the rubber boot, rotate the cable to align it with the slot in the lever and detach the cable from the lever.

3   If you're working on an XR250L or a 1986 through 1995 XR250R, detach the cable from the bracket and lever at the back of the engine **(see illustration)**.

4   Note carefully how the cable is routed and detach it from any retainers.

5   Installation is the reverse of the removal steps, with the following additions:

   a) *Align the punch mark on the handlebar with the parting line of the decompressor lever bracket* **(see illustration 20.2)**.

   b) *Adjust decompressor lever freeplay* (see Chapter 1).

---

21   Kickstarter - removal, inspection and installation

Removal

Pedal

Refer to illustrations 21.2 and 21.3

1   The kickstarter pedal is accessible from outside the engine. The

kickstarter mechanism can be reached by removing the right engine cover (Section 16).

2   To remove the pedal from the shaft, remove its mounting screw and slip the pedal off **(see illustration)**.

3   Look for a punch mark on the end of the kickstarter spindle **(see illustration)**. If you can't see one, make your own to align with the slit in the pedal shaft. Loosen the pinch bolt and slide the pedal off the spindle.

Kickstarter mechanism

Refer to illustrations 21.6a, 21.6b, 21.6c, 21.6d, 21.7, 21.8a, 21.8b and 21.9

4   Remove the kickstarter pedal (see Step 3 above) and the right engine cover (see Section 16). If you're planning to remove the kickstarter idler gear, you'll need to remove the clutch (Section 16).

5   If you're working on an XR250L or a 1986 through 1995 XR250R, remove the thrust washer, decompressor cam, cam spring and spring seat.

6   Slip the kickstarter pedal back onto the shaft. Turn the pedal counterclockwise until the ratchet pawl clears the guide, then pull the kickstarter partway out of the engine **(see illustrations)**. Slowly release the spring tension, so the tab is on the outer side of the guide. Unhook

21.2 The pedal is secured to the lever by a screw

21.3 Look for alignment marks on the pedal and shaft; if you don't see them, make a punch mark on the end of the shaft that aligns with the slit in the pedal

21.6a Turn the kickstarter so the tab (arrow) . . .

21.6b . . . clears the guide on the crankcase (kickstarter removed for clarity)

21.6c Unhook the spring from the hole in the crankcase . . .

21.6d . . . and pull the kickstarter out of the engine (XR400R shown)

the spring and pull the kickstarter the rest of the way out **(see illustration)**.

7   Unbolt the guide from the engine. Slide the kickstarter idler gear off its shaft, then remove its bushing **(see illustration)**.

8   Disengage the return spring from the hole in the shaft **(see illustrations)**. Slide off the return spring and collar, spring seat, ratchet

21.7 With the guide removed, the idler gear and its bushing can be taken off

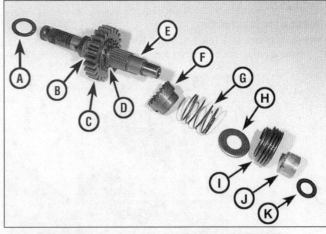

21.8a Kickstarter details (XR250L and XR250R)

A	Thrust washer	F	Ratchet
B	Washer	G	Spring
C	Pinion gear (with bushing inside on 1996 and later models)	H	Spring seat
		I	Return spring
D	Washer and snap-ring	J	Bushing
E	Kickstarter spindle	K	Washer

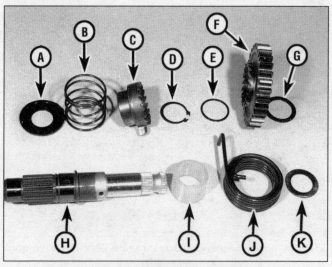

21.8b Kickstarter details (XR400R)

A	Spring seat	F	Pinion gear	I	Bushing
B	Spring	G	Washer	J	Return
C	Ratchet	H	Kickstarter		spring
D	Snap-ring		spindle	K	Washer
E	Washer				

21.9 Remove the snap-ring with snap-ring pliers - use a new one on installation

spring and ratchet.

9   Remove the snap-ring **(see illustration)**. Slide off the washer, the pinion gear and second washer. On 1996 and later XR250R models, slide off the bushing that fits inside the pinion gear.

Inspection

10   Check all parts for wear or damage, paying special attention to the teeth on the ratchet and the matching teeth on the pinion gear. Replace worn or damaged parts.

11   Measure the inside diameter of the pinion gear (all except 1996 and later XR250R) or the bushing (1996 and later XR250R) and the outside diameter of the shaft where the pinion gear or bushing rides. Replace any parts that are worn beyond the limit listed in this Chapter's Specifications.

Installation

Kickstarter mechanism

Refer to illustrations 21.12a through 21.12e

12   Installation is the reverse of the removal steps, with the follow-

21.12a Align the ratchet punch mark with the mark on the spindle; on XR250 models, the spindle mark is in the smooth area on the end . . .

ing additions:

a) *Use a new snap-ring.*
b) *Align the punch marks on the ratchet and shaft* **(see illustrations)**.
c) *Place the end of the return spring in the notch of the collar* **(see illustrations)**.

21.12b . . . the spindle punch mark on XR400R models is in the splined area

21.12c On XR250 models, the inner end of the return spring fits into the hole in the spindle . . .

21.12d . . . and into the hole in the bushing; the end of the bushing with the spring hole goes on the spindle first

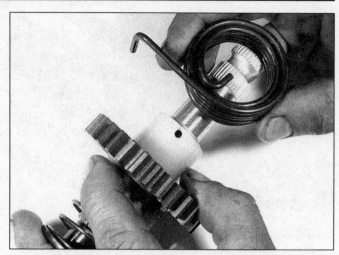

21.12e On XR400R models, the bushing fits up against the pinion gear so its spring hole aligns with the hole in the spindle; the inner end of the return spring fits through both holes

Pedal

13   Slip the pedal onto the kickstarter spindle, aligning the marks. Install the pinch bolt and tighten it securely.

---

22   Oil cooler and lines - removal and installation

Oil pipe (XR250L and 1986 through 1995 XR250R)

Refer to illustrations 22.2a and 22.2b

1   Remove the exhaust system (see Chapter 3).
2   Unscrew the union bolts at the upper rear corner of the cylinder head and on each side of the crankcase **(see illustrations)**. Remove the oil pipe and the union bolt sealing washers (two per fitting).
3   Lift the oil pipe off the engine, together with the rubber damper.
4   Installation is the reverse of the removal steps, with the following additions:
   a) *Use a new sealing washer on each side of the union bolt fittings.*
   b) *Tighten the union bolts to the torque listed in this Chapter's Specifications.*
   c) *Make sure the rubber damper is in place so the oil pipe won't be damaged by vibration* **(see illustration 22.2a)**.

Oil hoses (XR250R, XR400R)

5   There are two oil hoses connected to the lower front of the engine.

1986 through 1995 XR250R

6   The lower hose is the outlet from the engine to the oil cooler and the upper hose is the inlet from the oil cooler to the engine. The oil cooler is mounted in front of the steering head on the frame.
7   Drain the engine oil (see Chapter 1).
8   Remove the bolt and retaining plate from the upper hose, then pull the hose and its seal out of the engine.
9   Remove the bolt that secures the lower hose fitting to the engine. Pull the fitting out of the engine and remove its O-ring.
10   At the oil cooler, remove the union bolts and sealing washers. Take the hoses off the engine.
11   Installation is the reverse of the removal steps, with the following additions:
   a) *Use a new O-ring, seal and sealing washers.*
   b) *Tighten the oil cooler union bolts to the torque listed in this Chapter's Specifications.*
   c) *Be sure to install the rubber dampers on the metal tube portions of the hoses where they run up to the oil cooler.*

1996 and later XR250R, all XR400R

Refer to illustrations 22.14a, 22.14b, 22.15, 22.16a and 22.16b

12   The shorter hose is the inlet from the oil tank (in the upper frame member) to the engine. The longer hose returns oil from the engine to the oil tank (through the external oil cooler on XR400R models).

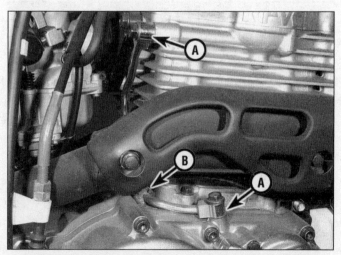

22.2a On the right side of the bike, unscrew the upper and lower union bolts (A); be sure to reinstall the rubber damper (B)

22.2b There's another union bolt on the left side of the bike

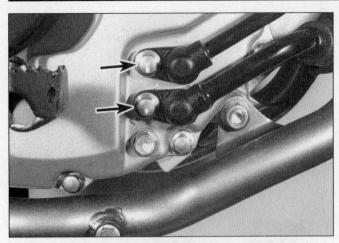

22.14a Remove the hose mounting plate bolts (arrows) . . .

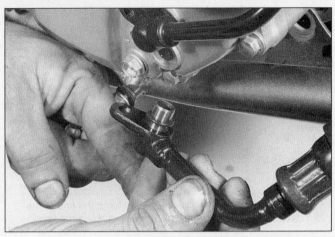

22.14b . . . and pull the hose ends and their O-rings
out of the engine

13   Drain the engine oil (see Chapter 1).
14   Unbolt the hose mounting plates at the crankcase **(see illustration)**. Pull out the two hoses and their O-rings **(see illustration)**.
15   Unscrew the union bolt that secures the forward end of the lower hose to the frame **(see illustration)**.
16   At the oil cooler, unscrew the flare nut and detach the hose from

the left side of the cooler **(see illustration)**. At the other end of this hose, unbolt the retaining plate and pull the hose and O-ring out of the frame **(see illustration)**.
17   Unscrew the remaining flare nut from the oil cooler **(see illustration 22.16b)**.
18   Installation is the reverse of the removal steps, with the following addition:
   a) Use new O-rings at the ends of the hoses.
   b) Tighten the flare nuts securely.
   c) Tighten the mounting plate bolts securely, but don't overtighten them and strip the threads.
   d) Be sure to install the rubber damper on the tubing portion of the long hose where it runs up the frame.

Oil cooler (1986 through 1995 XR250R, all XR400R)

19   To remove the oil cooler, disconnect its hoses as described above. Remove the mounting bolt and grommet on each side and take the cooler off **(see illustration 22.16b)**.
20   Check the grommets for wear and deterioration and replace as needed.
21   Install the grommets and position the cooler on the frame. If you're working on an XR400R, place the oil cooler stopper against the stay on the steering head. Tighten the bolts securely, but don't overtighten them and strip the threads.

22.15 Place a pan beneath the lower front hose fitting to catch
dripping oil and unscrew the union bolt

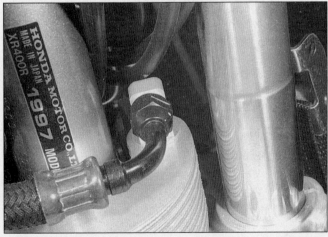

22.16a Unscrew the flare nut on the left side of the oil cooler . . .

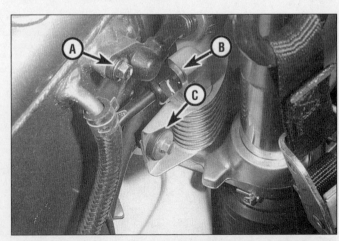

22.16b . . . remove the mounting plate bolt on the right side and
pull the hose end out of the frame

A   Mounting plate bolt   C   Oil cooler mounting bolt
B   Flare nut

23.11a Remove the bolts from the left side of the crankcase (arrows) . . .

23.11b . . . on XR400R models, remove one bolt from the right side of the case near the rear of the engine . . .

23 Crankcase - disassembly and reassembly

1   To examine and repair or replace the crankshaft, connecting rod, balancer, bearings and transmission components, the crankcase must be split into two parts.

Disassembly

Refer to illustrations 23.11a, 23.11b, 23.11c and 23.12

2   Remove the engine from the motorcycle (see Section 5).
3   Remove the carburetor (see Chapter 3).
4   Remove the alternator rotor (see Chapter 4).
5   Remove the clutch (see Section 16).
6   Remove the external shift mechanism (see Section 19).
7   Remove the oil pump (see Section 17).
8   Remove the cylinder head cover, cam chain tensioner, camshaft, cylinder head, cylinder, cam chain, chain guides and piston (see Sections 7, 8, 9, 10, 13 and 14).
9   Remove the kickstarter (see Section 21).
10   Check carefully to make sure there aren't any remaining components that attach the halves of the crankcase together.
11   Loosen the crankcase bolts in the left side of the crankcase evenly in two or three stages, then remove them **(see illustration)**. Remove the bolt(s) from the other side of the crankcase **(see illustrations)**.

12   Place the crankcase with its left side down on a pair of wood blocks so the shift pedal shaft and transmission countershaft shaft can extend downward. Carefully tap the crankcase apart and lift the right half off the left half **(see illustration)**. Don't pry against the mating surfaces or they'll develop leaks.
13   Locate the two crankcase dowels **(see illustration 23.12)**.
14   Refer to Sections 24 through 27 for information on the internal components of the crankcase.

Reassembly

15   Remove all traces of old gasket and sealant from the crankcase mating surfaces with a sharpening stone or similar tool. Be careful not to let any fall into the case as this is done and be careful not to damage the mating surfaces.
16   Check to make sure the two dowel pins are in place in their holes in the mating surface of the left crankcase half **(see illustration 23.12)**.
17   Pour some engine oil over the transmission and balancer gears, the right crankshaft bearing and the shift drum. Don't get any oil on the crankcase mating surface.
18   Coat the crankcase mating surface with Gaskacinch or equivalent sealant, then install a new gasket on the crankcase mating surface **(see illustration 23.12)**. Cut out the portion of the gasket that crosses the cylinder opening.
19   Carefully place the right crankcase half onto the left crankcase half. While doing this, make sure the transmission shafts, shift drum,

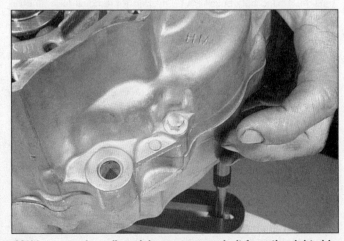

23.11c . . . and on all models, remove one bolt from the right side near the front

23.12 Support the crankcase on wood blocks so it isn't resting on the shift or transmission shafts, then lift the right case half off the left half; the two dowels may stay in either side of the case (arrows)

24.1 On XR250L and XR250R models, remove the bolt (arrow) and take off the baffle plate

24.3a Check the case bearings for roughness, looseness or noise; don't forget the shift drum needle bearing (right arrow) on XR400R models - the return spring pin (right arrow) should be tight

24.3b One transmission bearing in the XR400R right case half is secured by a retainer

24.3c A blind hole puller like this one is needed to remove bearings which are only accessible from one side

crankshaft and balancer fit into their bearings in the right crankcase half.

20   Install the crankcase bolts and tighten them so they are just snug. Then tighten them evenly in two or three stages to the torque listed in this Chapter's Specifications.

21   Turn the transmission mainshaft to make sure it turns freely. Also make sure the crankshaft turns freely.

22   The remainder of assembly is the reverse of disassembly.

24   Crankcase components - inspection and servicing

Refer to illustrations 24.1, 24.3a, 24.3b and 24.3c

1   Separate the crankcase and remove the following:
a) *Balancer*
b) *Transmission shafts and gears*
c) *Crankshaft*
d) *Shift drum and forks*
e) *Oil baffle (XR250L and XR250R)* **(see illustration)**.

2   Clean the crankcase halves thoroughly with new solvent and dry them with compressed air. All oil passages should be blown out with compressed air and all traces of old gasket should be removed from the mating surfaces. **Caution:** *Be very careful not to nick or gouge the crankcase mating surfaces or leaks will result.* Check both crankcase halves very carefully for cracks and other damage.

3   Check the bearings in the case halves **(see illustrations)**. For details of the transmission and balancer bearings in the left side of the crankcase, see Sections 26 and 27. If the bearings don't turn smoothly, replace them. For bearings which aren't accessible from the outside, a blind hole puller will be needed for removal **(see illustration)**. Drive the remaining bearing out with a bearing driver or a socket having an outside diameter slightly smaller than that of the bearing outer race. Before installing the bearings, allow them to sit in the freezer overnight, and about fifteen-minutes before installation, place the case half in an oven, set to about 200-degrees F, and allow it to heat up. The bearings are an interference fit, and this will ease installation. **Warning:** *Before heating the case, wash it thoroughly with soap and water so no explosive fumes are present. Also, don't use a flame to heat the case.* Install the ball bearings with a socket or bearing driver that contacts the bearing outer race.

4   If any damage is found that can't be repaired, replace the crankcase halves as a set.

5   Assemble the case halves (see Section 23) and check to make sure the crankshaft and the transmission shafts turn freely.

25   Internal shift mechanism - removal, inspection and installation

1   Refer to Section 23 and separate the crankcase halves.

25.2 Pull the shift shaft pawls clear of the shift drum and pull the shift shaft out of the crankcase

A *Shift pawls*   C *Shift drum*
B *Shift shaft*   D *Shift fork pins*

25.4 The shift forks are labeled R, C and L (right, center and left) - the letters face the right side of the crankcase when the forks are installed

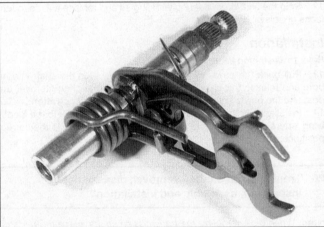

25.6a The return spring is installed like this . . .

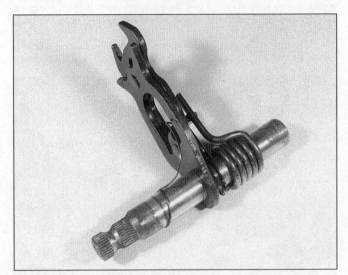

25.6b . . . and the pawl spring is installed like this

Removal

Refer to illustration 25.2

2   Pull the pawls of the gearshift plate back against spring pressure until they clear the shift drum, then lift the shift shaft out of the crankcase **(see illustration)**.
3   Lift the shift drum out of the case, disengaging it from the pins on the shift forks.
4   Pull up on the shift rod until it clears the case, then move the rod and forks away from the gears **(see illustration)**.

Inspection

Refer to illustrations 25.6a, 25.6b, 25.9a, 25.9b and 25.11

5   Wash all of the components in clean solvent and dry them off.
6   Check the shift shaft for bends and damage to the splines **(see illustration)**. If the shaft is bent, you can attempt to straighten it, but if the splines are damaged it will have to be replaced. Check the condition of the gearshift plate and the pawl spring **(see illustration)**. Replace them if they're worn, cracked or distorted.
7   Make sure the return spring pin isn't loose **(see illustration 24.3a)**. If it is, unscrew it, apply a non-hardening locking compound to the threads, reinstall it and tighten it securely.
8   Inspect the shift fork grooves in the gears. If a groove is worn or scored, replace the affected gear (see Section 27) and inspect its corresponding shift fork.
9   Check the shift forks for distortion and wear, especially at the fork ears **(see illustrations)**. Measure the thickness of the fork ears and

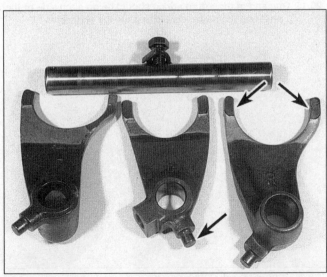

25.9a The fork ears and pins (arrows) are common wear points

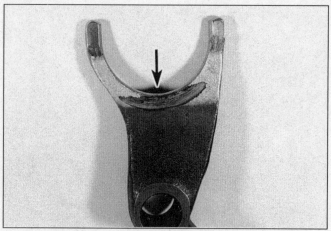

25.9b An arc-shaped burn mark like this means the fork was
rubbing against a gear, probably due to bending or worn fork ears

compare your findings with this Chapter's Specifications. If they are
discolored or severely worn they are probably bent. Inspect the guide
pins for excessive wear and distortion and replace any defective parts
with new ones.
10   Measure the inside diameter of the forks and the outside diameter
of the fork shaft and compare to the values listed in this Chapter's

25.13 One end of the return spring should be on each side of the
post and the pawls should engage the shift drum

26.4a On the right side, the countershaft has a
thrust washer (arrow) . . .

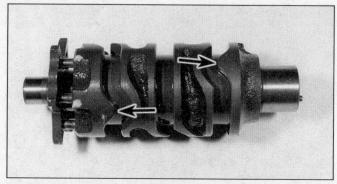

25.11 Check the shift drum grooves for wear, especially
at the points

Specifications. Replace any parts that are worn beyond the limits.
Check the shift fork shaft for evidence of wear, galling and other damage. Make sure the shift forks move smoothly on the shaft. If the shaft
is worn or bent, replace it with a new one.
11   Check the edges of the grooves in the drum for signs of excessive
wear (see illustration).
12   Spin the shift drum bearing with fingers and replace it if it's rough,
loose or noisy.

Installation

Refer to illustration 25.13
13   Pull back the pawls of the gearshift plate, slide the shaft into its
bore and release the claws. Make sure the return spring fits over the
post and the pawls engage the shift drum pins (see illustration).
14   Installation is the reverse of the removal steps. Refer to the identifying letters on the forks and make sure they're installed in the correct
positions.

26   Transmission shafts - removal, disassembly, inspection, assembly and installation

Note: When disassembling the transmission shafts, place the parts on
a long rod or thread a wire through them to keep them in order and facing the proper direction.

Removal

Refer to illustrations 26.4a and 26.4b
1   Remove the engine, then separate the case halves (see Sections 5 and 23).

26.4b . . . and both shafts have a thrust washer on the left side

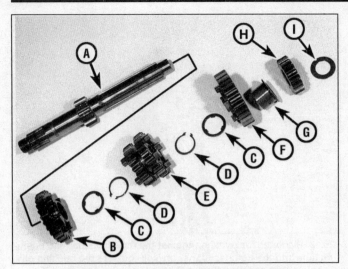

26.6a Mainshaft details (XR250L and XR250R)

A	Mainshaft	F	Sixth gear
B	Fifth gear	G	Flanged bushing
C	Splined washer	H	Second gear
D	Snap-ring	I	Thrust washer
E	Third-fourth gear		

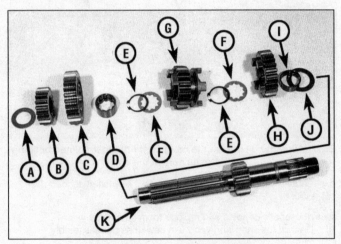

26.6c Mainshaft details (XR400R)

A	Thrust washer	F	Splined washer
B	Second gear	G	Third gear
C	Fifth gear	H	Fourth gear
D	Splined bushing	I	Bushing
E	Snap-ring	J	Thrust washer

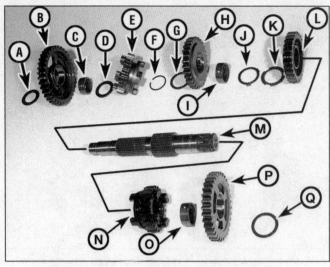

26.6b Countershaft details (XR250L and XR250R)

A	Thrust washer	J	Lockwasher
B	First gear	K	Splined thrust washer
C	Bushing - 1996 and later XR250R (flanged bushing on XR250L and 1986 through 1995 XR250R)	L	Fourth gear
		M	Countershaft
D	Thrust washer - 1996 and later XR250R (integral with flanged bushing on XR250L and 1986 through 1995 XR250R)	N	Sixth gear
		O	Bushing - 1996 and later XR250R (flanged bushing on XR250L and 1986 through 1995 XR250R)
E	Fifth gear		
F	Snap-ring	P	Second gear
G	Splined washer	Q	Thrust washer - 1996 and later XR250R (integral with flanged bushing on XR250L and 1986 through 1995 XR250R)
H	Third gear		
I	Bushing (1996 and later XR250R only)		

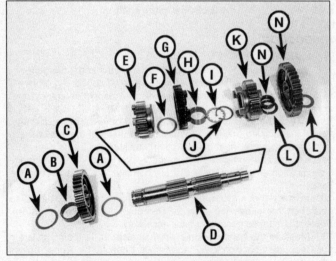

26.6d Countershaft details (XR400R)

A	Thrust washer	H	Bushing
B	Bushing	I	Splined washer
C	Second gear	J	Snap-ring
D	Countershaft	K	Fourth gear
E	Fifth gear	L	Thrust washer
F	Thrust washer	M	Bushing
G	Third gear	N	First gear

2   The transmission components remain in the left case half when the case is separated.

3   Refer to Section 25 and remove the shift shaft, shift drum and forks.

4   Take the thrust washer off the countershaft **(see illustration)**. Lift the transmission shafts out of the case together, then remove the thrust washers from the case **(see illustration)**.

5   Separate the shafts once they're lifted out. If you're not planning to disassemble them right away, reinstall the removed components and place a large rubber band over both ends of each shaft so the gears won't slide off.

Disassembly

Refer to illustrations 26.6a, 26.6b, 26.6c and 26.6d

6   To disassemble the shafts, remove the snap-rings and slide the gears, bushings and thrust washers off **(see illustrations)**.

26.10 Check the slots (left arrow) and dogs (right arrow) for wear, especially at the edges; rounded corners cause the transmission to jump out of gear - new gears (bottom) have sharp corners

26.18 Place the lockwasher against the thrust washer and push its tabs into the notches (upper arrow) - be sure the bushing oil hole aligns exactly with the shaft oil hole (lower arrow); if it doesn't, try aligning the bushing hole with the oil hole on the opposite side of the shaft

26.19 Align the oil hole in the mainshaft sixth gear bushing with the oil hole in the shaft

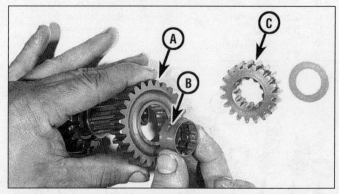

26.20 Align the oil hole in the mainshaft fifth gear splined bushing with the oil hole in the shaft

A   Mainshaft fifth gear   C   Mainshaft second gear
B   Bushing

Inspection

Refer to illustration 26.10

7   Wash all of the components in clean solvent and dry them off.

8   Inspect the shift fork grooves in gears so equipped. If a groove is worn or scored, replace the affected gear and inspect its corresponding shift fork.

9   Check the gear teeth for cracking and other obvious damage. Check the bushing or surface in the inner diameter of the freewheeling gears for scoring or heat discoloration. Measure the inside diameters of the gears and compare them to the values listed in this Chapter's Specifications. Replace parts that are damaged or worn beyond the limits.

10   Inspect the engagement dogs and dog holes on gears so equipped for excessive wear or rounding off **(see illustration)**. Replace the paired gears as a set if necessary.

11   Measure the transmission shaft diameters at the points listed in this Chapter's Specifications. If they're worn beyond the limits, replace the shaft(s).

12   Measure the inner and outer diameters of the gear bushings and replace any that are worn beyond the limit listed in this Chapter's Specifications.

13   Inspect the thrust washers. Honda doesn't specify wear limits, but they should be replaced if they show any visible wear or scoring. It's a good idea to replace them whenever the transmission is disassembled.

14   Check the transmission shaft bearings in the crankcase for rough-

ness, looseness or noise and replace them if necessary.

15   Discard the snap-rings and use new ones on reassembly.

Assembly and installation

16   Assembly and installation are the reverse of the removal procedure, but take note of the following points:

XR250L and XR250R

Refer to illustrations 26.18 and 26.19

17   Countershaft third and fourth gear look similar to each other, but countershaft third gear has more teeth than countershaft fourth gear.

18   Align the lockwasher tabs with the three notches in countershaft fourth gear. If you're working on a 1996 or later XR250R, align the oil hole in the countershaft third gear bushing with the oil hole in the shaft **(see illustration)**.

19   Align the oil hole in the mainshaft sixth gear bushing with the oil hole in the shaft **(see illustration)**.

XR400R

Refer to illustration 26.20

20   Align the oil hole in the mainshaft fifth gear splined bushing with the oil hole in the shaft **(see illustration)**.

All models

Refer to illustrations 26.21, 26.23a and 26.23b

21   Make sure the snap-rings are securely seated in their grooves, with their sharp sides facing away from the direction of the thrust

26.21 Install the snap-rings with their rounded sides away from the gears they retain - after installation, rotate them to make sure they're secure in their grooves, then center the snap-ring gap on a spline groove (arrow)

(gears they hold on the shafts). The ends of the snap-rings must align with a spline groove **(see illustration)**.
22   Lubricate the components with engine oil before assembling them.
23   After assembly, check the gears to make sure they're installed correctly **(see illustrations)**.

27   Crankshaft and balancer - removal, inspection and installation

Balancer

Removal

Refer to illustration 27.2
1   Remove the engine and separate the crankcase halves (Sections 5 and 23).
2   Turn the crankshaft so the punch marks on the balancer and crankshaft are aligned **(see illustration)**. The marks must be aligned like this on installation to prevent severe engine vibration.
3   The balancer gear on XR250L models is made in two parts, with the teeth of each part held slightly offset from each other by springs.

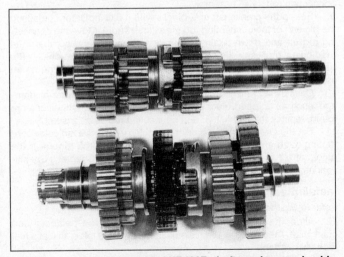

26.23b . . . and the assembled XR400R shafts and gears should look like this

26.23a The assembled XR250L and XR250R shafts and gears should look like this . . .

This spring-loaded offset eliminates backlash between the balancer and crankshaft gears. If you're working on an XR250L, pry the two parts of the gear into alignment with each other and insert a paper clip through the small hole in both parts of the gear to keep them in alignment.
4   Lift the balancer shaft out of its bearing.

Inspection
5   Check the balancer gear teeth and its bearing surface for wear or damage. Replace the balancer if problems can be seen in these areas.
6   To check the springs on XR250L models, remove the snap-ring and washer from the balancer gear and lift the outer portion of the gear off. Check the springs for wear or damage, replacing them if their condition is in doubt.

Crankshaft

Removal

Refer to illustrations 27.7a, 27.7b and 27.7c
Note: *Removal and installation of the crankshaft require a press and some special tools. If you don't have the necessary equipment or suitable substitutes, have the crankshaft removed and installed by a Honda dealer.*
7   Place the left crankcase half in a press and push the crankshaft

27.2 The timing marks (arrows) on the balancer and crankshaft must be aligned to prevent severe engine vibration

27.7a Press the crankshaft out of the crankcase . . .

27.7b . . . you can also use a puller if you have the correct adapters

27.7c If the bearing stays on the crankshaft, remove it with a puller attached to a bearing splitter

27.8 Check the connecting rod side clearance with a feeler gauge

out **(see illustration)**, or remove it with a three-legged puller **(see illustration)**. The ball bearing may remain in the crankcase or come out with the crankshaft. If it stays on the crankshaft, remove it with a bearing splitter **(see illustration)**. Discard the bearing, no matter what its apparent condition, and use a new one on installation.

27.9 Check the connecting rod radial clearance with a dial indicator

Inspection
Refer to illustrations 27.8 and 27.9

8   Measure the side clearance between connecting rod and crankshaft with a feeler gauge **(see illustration)**. If it's more than the limit listed in this Chapter's Specifications, replace the crankshaft and connecting rod as an assembly.

9   Set up the crankshaft in V-blocks with a dial indicator contacting the big end of the connecting rod **(see Illustration)**. Move the connecting rod up-and-down against the indicator pointer and compare the reading to the value listed in this Chapter's Specifications. If it's beyond the limit, replace the crankshaft and connecting rod as an assembly.

10   Check the crankshaft, gear and splines for visible wear or damage, such as chipped teeth or scoring. If any of these conditions are found, replace the crankshaft and connecting rod as an assembly.

11   Set the crankshaft in a pair of V-blocks, with a dial indicator contacting each end. Rotate the crankshaft and note the runout. If the runout at either end is beyond the limit listed in this Chapter's Specifications, replace the crankshaft and connecting rod as an assembly.

Installation
Refer to illustrations 27.12, 27.14 and 27.15

12   Align the index marks on the left end of the balancer and crankshaft, then position them simultaneously in the left crankcase half **(see illustration)**.

13   Verify that the alignment marks on the right end of the balancer and crankshaft are still aligned **(see illustration 27.2)**. If you're working

27.12 Align the crankshaft and balancer marks on the left end before installing them; on XR250L models, align the crankshaft line with the single line on the balancer

27.14 Thread the adapter into the end of the crankshaft . . .

on an XR250L, pull the alignment pin out of the balancer gear.

14   Thread a puller adapter (part of Honda tool part no. 07965-VM00000) into the end of the crankshaft (see illustration).

15   Install the crankshaft puller and collar on the end of the crankshaft (see illustration).

16   Hold the puller shaft with one wrench and turn the nut with another wrench to pull the crankshaft into the center race of the ball bearing.

17   Remove the special tools from the crankshaft.

18   Make sure the crankshaft and balancer timing marks are still aligned (see illustration 27.2). Note: *It's important to align the timing marks exactly throughout this procedure. Severe engine vibration will occur if the crankshaft and balancer are out of time.*

19   Installation is the reverse of the removal steps.

28   Initial start-up after overhaul

1   Make sure the engine oil level is correct, then remove the spark plug from the engine. Unplug the primary wires from the coil.

2   Crank the engine over with the kickstarter several times to build up oil pressure. Reinstall the spark plug and connect the wires.

3   Make sure there is fuel in the tank, then operate the choke.

4   Start the engine and allow it to run at a moderately fast idle. Let the engine continue running until it reaches operating temperature.

5   Check carefully for oil leaks and make sure the transmission and controls, especially the brakes, function properly before road testing the machine. Refer to Section 29 for the recommended break-in procedure.

6   Upon completion of the road test, and after the engine has cooled down completely, recheck the oil level and valve clearances (see Chapter 1).

29   Recommended break-in procedure

1   Any rebuilt engine needs time to break-in, even if parts have been

27.15 . . . and attach the puller to the adapter

installed in their original locations. For this reason, treat the machine gently for the first few miles to make sure oil has circulated throughout the engine and any new parts installed have started to seat.

2   Even greater care is necessary if the cylinder has been rebored or a new crankshaft has been installed. In the case of a rebore, the engine will have to be broken in as if the machine were new. This means greater use of the transmission and a restraining hand on the throttle for the first few operating days. There's no point in keeping to any set speed limit - the main idea is to vary the engine speed, keep from lugging the engine and to avoid full-throttle operation. These recommendations can be lessened to an extent when only a new crankshaft is installed. Experience is the best guide, since it's easy to tell when an engine is running freely.

3   If a lubrication failure is suspected, stop the engine immediately and try to find the cause. If an engine is run without oil, even for a short period of time, irreparable damage will occur.

Notes

Chapter 3
Fuel and exhaust systems

Contents

Specifications

General

Fuel type	Unleaded or low lead gasoline subject to local regulations; minimum octane 91 RON (87 pump octane)

Carburetor (XR250L)

Identification mark
1991
49 states ... PD 79E
California ... PD 79F
1992 on
49 states ... PD 79G
California ... PD79H

Jet sizes and settings
Standard main jet ... 122
High altitude main ... 120
Slow jet ... 38
Jet needle clip position ... 3rd groove
Mixture screw setting (turns out from lightly seated position)
Standard setting
1991 ... 1-7/8
1992 on ... 2-1/4
High altitude setting ... 1/2-turn in from standard
Float level ... 14.0 mm (0.55 inch)
Accelerator pump rod clearance ... 1.0 mm (0.4 inch)

Carburetor (1986 through 1995 XR250R)

Identification mark
1986 through 1991 ... PD 05A
1992 through 1995 ... PD 05B
Jet sizes and settings
Standard main jet ... 125
Slow jet ... 40
Jet needle clip position ... 3rd groove
Mixture screw setting (turns out from lightly seated position)
Standard ... 2-1/4
High altitude ... 1/2-turn in from standard
Float level ... 12.5 mm (0.49 inch)

Carburetor (1996 and later XR250R)

Identification mark
All 1996 and 1997; 1998 and later non-California ... PDG1A
1998 and later California ... PDG1C

Carburetor (1996 and later XR250R) (continued)

Jet sizes and settings
Standard main jet (sea level to 5000 ft)
All 1996 and 1997; 1998 and later non-California 132
1998 and later California.. 122
Slow jet.. 45
Jet needle clip position... 3rd groove
Mixture screw initial setting (turns out from lightly seated position)
All 1996 and 1997; 1998 and later non-California
Standard 1-3/8
High altitude... 1/2-turn in from standard
1998 and later California 1-3/8
Float level... 12.5 mm (0.49 inch)

Carburetor (XR400R)

Identification mark
1996 and 1997 .... PDK1A
1998 and later non-California... PDK1C
1998 and later California PDK1E
Jet sizes and settings
1996 and 1997
Standard main jet.. 162
Trail riding main jet.. 158
Standard slow jet.. 62
Trail riding slow jet.. 60
1998 and later
Main jet 142
Slow jet 52
Jet needle clip position
Standard.. 3rd groove
Trail riding... 2nd groove
Mixture screw initial setting (turns out from lightly seated position)
1996 and 1997 .... 2-1/4
1998 and later
Non-California.. 1-1/2
California.. 1-5/8
Float level... 14.5 mm (0.57 inch)

Torque settings

Exhaust pipe to cylinder head nuts
XR250L .... 10 Nm (86 inch-lbs)
XR250R
1986 through 1995 .... 8 to 12 Nm (72 to 108 inch-lbs)
1996 on .... 10 Nm (86 inch-lbs)
XR400R .... 18 Nm (13 ft-lbs)
Exhaust heat shield bolts
XR250L .... 12 Nm (108 inch-lbs)
XR250R
1986 through 1991... 10 to 14 Nm (86 to 120 inch-lbs) (1)
1992 through 1995... 15 to 21 Nm (11 to 15 ft-lbs) (1)
1996 on .... 12 Nm (108 inch-lbs)
XR400R .... Not specified
Muffler clamp bolts
XR250L .... 20 Nm (14 ft-lbs)
XR250R
1986 through 1989.. Not specified
1990 through 1995.. 15 to 25 Nm (11 to 18 ft-lbs)
1996 on .... 20 Nm (14 ft-lbs)
XR400R .... 20 Nm (14 ft-lbs)
Muffler mounting bolts
XR250L
Front... 32 Nm (24 ft-lbs)
Rear .... 65 Nm (47 ft-lbs)
XR250R (1986 through 1995)
Front... 30 to 35 Nm (22 to 26 ft-lbs)
Rear
1986 through 1989 .... 35 to 45 Nm (25 to 33 ft-lbs)
1990 through 1995 .... 60 to 70 Nm (43 to 51 ft-lbs)
XR250R (1996 on) .... 32 Nm (24 ft-lbs)
XR400R .... 32 Nm (24 ft-lbs)

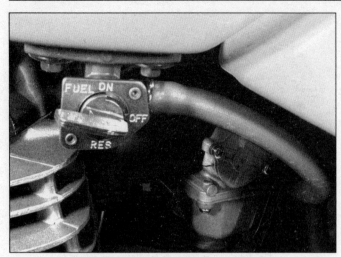

2.2 Disconnect the fuel line from the tap

2.3a The XR250L fuel tank is secured by bolts that fit through these grommets at the rear . . .

1 General information

The fuel system consists of the fuel tank, fuel tap, filter screen, carburetor and connecting lines, hoses and control cables.

All models use the slide carburetor design, in which the slide acts as the throttle valve. Basic design is the same for all models, except that the XR250L is equipped with an accelerator pump. For cold starting on all models, a choke valve is actuated by a lever. The lever is mounted on the left handlebar and connected to the carburetor by a cable on XR250L models; on all others, the lever is mounted on the carburetor. The XR250L models are equipped with an accelerator pump.

The exhaust system consists of a pipe and muffler/silencer with a spark arrester function.

XR250L models sold in California use an evaporative emission control system that routes fuel tank vapors to the engine for burning.

Many of the fuel system service procedures are considered routine maintenance items and for that reason are included in Chapter 1.

2 Fuel tank - removal and installation

Warning: *Gasoline is extremely flammable, so take extra precautions when you work on any part of the fuel system. Don't smoke or allow open flames or bare light bulbs near the work area, and don't work in a garage where a natural gas-type appliance (such as a water heater or clothes dryer) with a pilot light is present. Since gasoline is carcinogenic,* wear latex gloves when there's a possibility of being exposed to fuel, and, if you spill any fuel on your skin, rinse it off immediately with soap and water. Mop up any spills immediately and do not store fuel-soaked rags where they could ignite. When you perform any kind of work on the fuel system, wear safety glasses and have a Class B type fire extinguisher on hand.*

Removal
Refer to illustration 2.2

1   Remove the seat (see Chapter 7).
2   Turn the fuel tap to Off and disconnect the fuel line **(see illustration)**.

XR250L
Refer to illustrations 2.3a and 2.3b

3   Remove the mounting bolts at the rear of the tank **(see illustration)**. Pull the tank backward so the cups clear the rubber mounts, then lift the tank off the machine together with the fuel tap **(see illustration)**.

XR250R and XR400R
Refer to illustrations 2.5 and 2.6

4   Remove the seat (see Chapter 7).
5   Pull the fuel tank vent hose out of the steering stem nut. Unhook the strap from the rear of the tank **(see illustration)**.
6   Remove the fuel tank mounting bolts **(see illustration)**.
7   Lift the fuel tank off the bike together with the fuel tap.

2.3b . . . at the front, the tank fits over these insulators (there's one on each side)

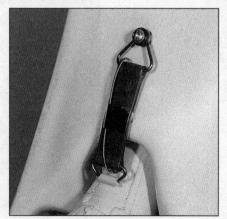

2.5 The XR250R and XR400R fuel tank is secured at the rear by this retaining strap . . .

2.6 . . . and at the front by mounting bolts (there's one on each side)

Installation

Refer to illustration 2.8

8   Before installing the tank, check the condition of the rubber mounting bushings at the front, the insulator on the frame and the rubber mount or strap at the rear - if they're hardened, cracked, or show any other signs of deterioration, replace them **(see illustration 2.3b and the accompanying illustration)**.

9   When installing the tank, reverse the removal procedure. Make sure the tank does not pinch any wires. Tighten the tank mounting bolts securely, but don't overtighten them and strip the threads.

3   Fuel tank - cleaning and repair

1   All repairs to the fuel tank should be carried out by a professional who has experience in this critical and potentially dangerous work. Even after cleaning and flushing of the fuel system, explosive fumes can remain and ignite during repair of the tank.

2   If the fuel tank is removed from the vehicle, it should not be placed in an area where sparks or open flames could ignite the fumes coming out of the tank. Be especially careful inside garages where a natural gas-type appliance is located, because the pilot light could cause an explosion.

4   Idle fuel/air mixture adjustment

Refer to illustrations 4.2a and 4.2b

Normal adjustment

1   Idle fuel/air mixture on these vehicles is preset at the factory and should not need adjustment unless the carburetor is overhauled or the mixture adjustment screw is replaced.

2   Mixture is controlled by a pilot screw mounted in the underside of the carburetor. On street-legal bikes (XR250L), the screw is covered by a limiter cap **(see illustration)**. The cap has a tab that rests against a stop cast into the float chamber, which prevents the screw from being turned to enrich the mixture. Honda specifies that the pilot screw should not be adjusted except when a new one is installed. On off-road models (XR250R, XR400R) there is no limiter cap **(see illustration)**.

3   The engine must be properly tuned up before making the adjustment (valve clearances set to specifications, spark plug in good condition and properly gapped). You'll also need a tune-up tachometer that can accurately indicate changes as small as 100 rpm.

XR250L

4   Remove the carburetor from the motorcycle, then remove the float chamber from the carburetor (see Sections 6 and 7).

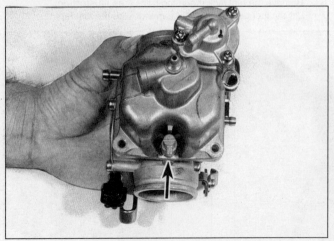

4.2a The pilot screw limiter cap on XR250L models has a tab (arrow) that contacts a stop to prevent over-rich mixture adjustments

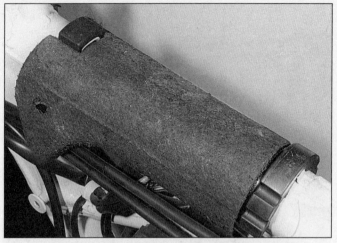

2.8 Replace the mounting insulator on top of the frame if it's deteriorated

5   Remove the old pilot screw from the carburetor **(see illustration 4.2a)**. Install the new one without the limiter cap for now. Reinstall the float chamber, then reinstall the carburetor on the motorcycle.

6   Turn the pilot screw clockwise until it seats lightly, then back it out the number of turns listed in this Chapter's Specifications. **Caution:** *Turn the screw just far enough to seat it lightly. If it's bottomed hard, the screw or its seat may be damaged, which will make accurate mixture adjustments impossible.*

7   Warm up the engine to normal operating temperature (10 minutes of stop-and-go riding will do). Shut it off and connect a tune-up tachometer, following the tachometer manufacturer's instructions.

8   Restart the engine and compare idle speed to the value listed in the Chapter 1 Specifications. Adjust it if necessary with the throttle stop screw (don't turn the pilot screw).

9   Back out the pilot screw 1/2-turn. If idle speed increases by less than 50 rpm, don't adjust it further. If it increases by 50 rpm or more, keep backing the pilot screw out, 1/2-turn at a time, until idle speed stops increasing.

10   Turn the pilot screw back in until idle speed drops 50 rpm, then turn it in 1/2-turn more.

11   Reset idle speed to the Chapter 1 specification with the throttle stop screw.

12   Coat the inside of a new limiter cap with Loctite 601 or equivalent, then install it so its tab will rest against the stop on the float chamber (after the float chamber is installed) so the screw can be turned clockwise but not counterclockwise.

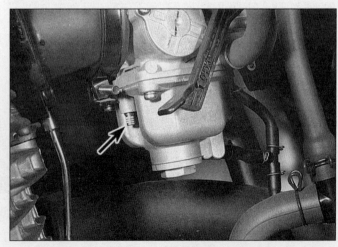

4.2b The XR250R and XR400 pilot screw (arrow) doesn't have a limiter cap

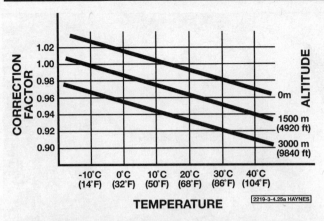

4.25a Correction factor chart (1986 through 1995 XR250R)

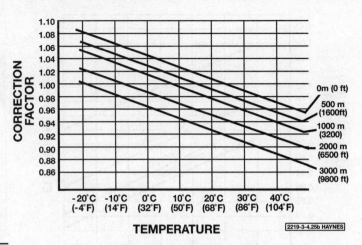

4.25b Correction factor chart (1996 and later XR250R, XR400R with standard jetting)

XR250R and XR400R

13   Turn the pilot screw clockwise until it seats lightly, then back it out the number of turns listed in this Chapter's Specifications **(see illustration 4.2b)**. **Caution:** *Turn the screw just far enough to seat it lightly. If it's bottomed hard, the screw or its seat may be damaged, which will make accurate mixture adjustments impossible.*

14   Warm up the engine to normal operating temperature (10 minutes of stop-and-go riding will do). Shut it off and connect a tune-up tachometer, following the tachometer manufacturer's instructions.

15   Restart the engine and compare idle speed to the value listed in the Chapter 1 Specifications. Adjust it if necessary.

16   Slowly turn the pilot screw in or out to obtain the highest idle speed. Recheck idle speed on the tachometer and adjust it if necessary with the throttle stop screw.

17   If you're working on a 1997 or earlier model, rev the engine and make sure it doesn't miss or hesitate. If it does, repeat the adjustment.

18   If you're working on a 1998 or later model, lightly rev the engine two or three times, then recheck idle speed on the tachometer and reset it if necessary, using the throttle stop screw. Slowly turn the pilot screw clockwise until engine speed drops 100 rpm. Then turn the pilot screw counterclockwise, 3/4-turn on non-California models or 1/4-turn on California models.

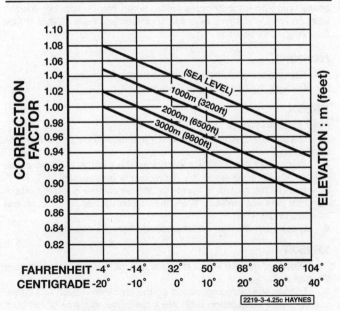

4.25c Main jet correction factor chart (1996 and 1997 XR400R jetted for trail riding)

High altitude adjustment (XR250L)

19   If the motorcycle is normally used below 6500 feet, use the normal main jets and mixture screw setting. If it's used regularly above 6500 feet, the mixture screw setting and main jet must be changed to compensate for the thinner air. **Caution:** *Don't use the bike for sustained operation below 5000 feet with the main jet and mixture screw at the high altitude settings or the engine may overheat and be damaged.*

20   Remove the carburetor (see Section 6). Replace the main jet with the high altitude jet listed in this Chapter's Specifications, then reinstall the carburetor.

21   Turn the pilot screw to the high altitude setting listed in this Chapter's Specifications.

22   Warm up the engine to normal operating temperature (10 minutes of stop-and-go riding will do). Shut it off and connect a tune-up tachometer, following the tachometer manufacturer's instructions.

23   Restart the engine and compare idle speed to the value listed in the Chapter 1 Specifications. Adjust it if necessary with the throttle stop screw.

Trail riding adjustment (1996 and 1997 XR400R)

24   These models come from the factory with the carburetor set up for closed-course racing (which assumes that the exhaust diffuser and noise suppressor have been removed). This means the bike may be jetted too rich for trail riding with the exhaust diffuser and noise suppressor installed. If this is the type of riding you plan to do, you may need to change the slow jet, main jet and needle clip position. In addition, the pilot screw setting has a specified range, rather than just one position. Refer to this Chapter's Specifications for the appropriate information. To change jets and needle clip position, refer to Section 7.

Altitude and temperature adjustment (XR250R and XR400R)

Refer to illustrations 4.25a, 4.25b, 4.25c and 4.25d

25   These models should be re-jetted to compensate for changes in temperature as well as altitude. This means you'll need a thermometer to determine the air temperature. To figure out whether you need to make any changes, find your altitude and the local air temperature on the accompanying charts **(see illustrations)**. Draw a line up from the temperature setting to the altitude line. From where the two lines meet, read across to the correction factor. **Note:** *1996 and 1997 XR400R models use different correction factor charts, depending on whether they are at the standard or trail riding settings. Be sure to refer to the correct illustration(s).*

26   If the correction factor is above 0.95, leave the carburetor at the standard settings. If it's 0.95 or less, make changes as described below.

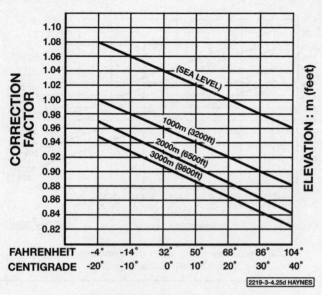

**4.25d Slow jet correction factor chart
(1996 and 1997 XR400R jetted for trail riding)**

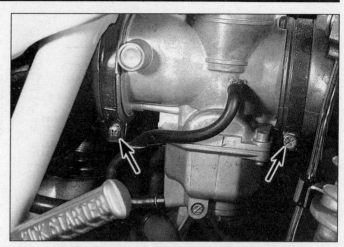

6.5 Loosen the clamping band screws (arrows)

XR250R

27   Turn the pilot screw in 1/2-turn from the standard setting. Raise the jet needle clip by one groove from the standard setting.

XR400R

28   If the bike is at the standard jet settings, turn the pilot screw in 1/4-turn. If it's been re-jetted for trail riding, leave the pilot screw at the specified setting.

All models

29   Multiply the standard main jet number by the correction factor to determine the proper size of main jet. For example, if your main jet is a no. 165 and the correction factor is 0.92, multiply 165 X 0.92 to get 151.8. Rounded off, the correct size main jet is 152.
30   Refer to Section 7 for procedures to change the jet(s) and needle clip position.
31   Refer to Chapter 1 and adjust the idle speed.

5   Carburetor overhaul - general information

1   Poor engine performance, hesitation, hard starting, stalling, flooding and backfiring are all signs that major carburetor maintenance may be required.
2   Keep in mind that many so-called carburetor problems are really not carburetor problems at all, but mechanical problems within the engine or ignition system malfunctions. Try to establish for certain that the carburetor is in need of maintenance before beginning a major overhaul.
3   Check the fuel tap and its strainer screen, the fuel lines, the intake manifold clamps, the O-ring between the intake manifold and cylinder head, the vacuum hoses, the air filter element, the cylinder compression, the spark plug and the ignition timing before assuming that a carburetor overhaul is required. If the bike has been unused for more than a month, refer to Chapter 1, drain the float chamber and refill the tank with fresh fuel.
4   Most carburetor problems are caused by dirt particles, varnish and other deposits which build up in and block the fuel and air passages. Also, in time, gaskets and O-rings shrink or deteriorate and cause fuel and air leaks which lead to poor performance.
5   When the carburetor is overhauled, it is generally disassembled completely and the parts are cleaned thoroughly with a carburetor

cleaning solvent and dried with filtered, unlubricated compressed air. The fuel and air passages are also blown through with compressed air to force out any dirt that may have been loosened but not removed by the solvent. Once the cleaning process is complete, the carburetor is reassembled using new gaskets, O-rings and, generally, a new inlet needle valve and seat.
6   Before disassembling the carburetor, make sure you have a carburetor rebuild kit (which will include all necessary O-rings and other parts), some carburetor cleaner, a supply of rags, some means of blowing out the carburetor passages and a clean place to work.

6   Carburetor - removal and installation

Warning: *Gasoline is extremely flammable, so take extra precautions when you work on any part of the fuel system. Don't smoke or allow open flames or bare light bulbs near the work area, and don't work in a garage where a natural gas-type appliance (such as a water heater or clothes dryer) with a pilot light is present. Since gasoline is carcinogenic, wear latex gloves when there's a possibility of being exposed to fuel, and, if you spill any fuel on your skin, rinse it off immediately with soap and water. Mop up any spills immediately and do not store fuel-soaked rags where they could ignite. When you perform any kind of work on the fuel system, wear safety glasses and have a Class B type fire extinguisher on hand.*

Removal

1   Remove the seat and both side covers (see Chapter 7).
2   Remove the fuel tank (see Section 2).

XR250L

Refer to illustration 6.5
3   Dismount the rear shock reservoir and move it out of the way (see Chapter 5).
4   Disconnect the throttle and choke cables at the carburetor (see Section 10). Remove the air cleaner resonator (see Section 9).
5   Loosen the clamping bands on the air cleaner duct and intake manifold **(see illustration)**. Work the carburetor free of the duct and manifold and lift it off.
6   Disconnect the vent and drain hoses from the carburetor.

XR250R

7   Dismount the rear shock reservoir and move it out of the way (see Chapter 5).
8   Loosen the clamping bands on the air cleaner duct and intake manifold **(see illustration 6.5)**. Work the carburetor free of the duct and manifold and lift it off to the left side of the motorcycle.
9   Disconnect the throttle cables, vent and drain hoses from the carburetor.

6.12 Remove the cable bracket screw (arrow)

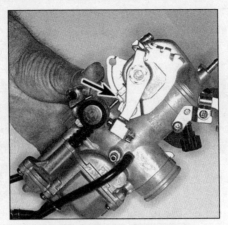

6.17 Check the gap between the accelerator pump rod and throttle lever (arrow)

7.2a To remove the XR250L accelerator pump, remove three screws (arrows) . . .

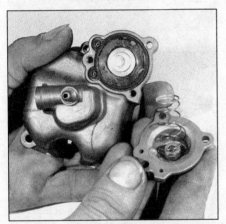

7.2b . . . lift off the cover and spring; note how the diaphragm protrusions fit into notches in the carburetor body . . .

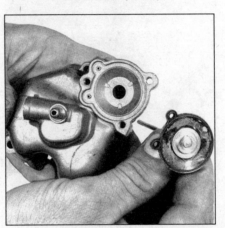

7.2c . . . and pull out the pump rod, taking care not to tear the diaphragm

7.3a Remove the two screws . . .

XR400R

Refer to illustration 6.12

10   Remove the sub-frame from the motorcycle (see Chapter 7).

11   Drain the fuel from the float chamber (see Chapter 1). Disconnect the drain and vent hoses from the carburetor.

12   Remove the screw and detach the cable bracket from the carburetor **(see illustration)**.

13   Loosen the clamping bands on the air cleaner duct and intake manifold **(see illustration 6.5)**. Work the carburetor free of the duct and manifold and lift it off.

14   Disconnect the throttle cables from the carburetor.

All models

15   Check the intake manifold tube for cracks, deterioration or other damage. If it has visible defects, or if there's reason to suspect its O-ring is leaking, remove it from the engine and inspect the O-ring.

16   After the carburetor has been removed, stuff clean rags into the intake manifold (or the intake port in the cylinder head, if the manifold has been removed) to prevent the entry of dirt or other objects.

Installation

Refer to illustration 6.17

17   Installation is the reverse of the removal steps, with the following additions:

a) *Adjust the throttle freeplay (see Chapter 1).*

b) *Adjust the idle speed (see Chapter 1).*

c) *If you're working on an XR250L, check the clearance between the throttle lever and the tip of the accelerator pump rod* **(see illustration)**. *If it's not at the value listed in this Chapter's Specifications, bend the lever to adjust it.*

7   Carburetor - disassembly, cleaning and inspection

Warning: *Gasoline is extremely flammable, so take extra precautions when you work on any part of the fuel system. Don't smoke or allow open flames or bare light bulbs near the work area, and don't work in a garage where a natural gas-type appliance (such as a water heater or clothes dryer) with a pilot light is present. Since gasoline is carcinogenic, wear latex gloves when there's a possibility of being exposed to fuel, and, if you spill any fuel on your skin, rinse it off immediately with soap and water. Mop up any spills immediately and do not store fuel-soaked rags where they could ignite. When you perform any kind of work on the fuel system, wear safety glasses and have a Class B type fire extinguisher on hand.*

Disassembly

Refer to illustrations 7.2a, 7.2b, 7.2c and 7.3a through 7.3m

1   Remove the carburetor from the machine as described in Section 6. Set it on a clean working surface.

2   If you're working on an XR250L, remove the accelerator pump **(see illustrations)**.

3   To disassemble the carburetor, refer to the accompanying illustrations **(see illustrations)**.

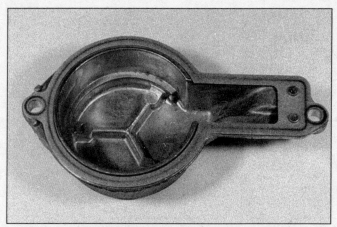

7.3b . . . and lift the top and gasket off the carburetor

7.3c Remove the screw from the link arm

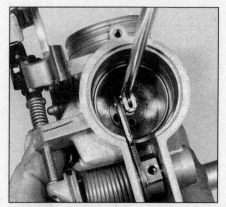

7.3d Remove the screws and lift out the link arm, link and jet needle retainer

7.3e Lift the jet needle out of the throttle valve and lift the throttle valve out of the carburetor

7.3f Remove the air cutoff valve cover screws; note the location of the air passage (arrow)

7.3g Remove the O-ring (arrow), spring and diaphragm

7.3h Remove the float chamber screws (arrows); the plug in the bottom of the float chamber allows the main jet to be changed without removing the carburetor from the engine

Cleaning

Caution: *Use only a carburetor cleaning solution that is safe for use with plastic parts (be sure to read the label on the container).*

4   Submerge the metal components in the carburetor cleaner for approximately thirty minutes (or longer, if the directions recommend it).

5   After the carburetor has soaked long enough for the cleaner to loosen and dissolve most of the varnish and other deposits, use a brush to remove the stubborn deposits. Rinse it again, then dry it with compressed air. Blow out all of the fuel and air passages in the carburetor body. **Caution:** *Never clean the jets or passages with a piece of wire or a drill bit, as they will be enlarged, causing the fuel and air metering rates to be upset.*

Inspection

6   Check the operation of the choke valve (XR250L) or choke lever (XR250R and XR400R). If it doesn't move smoothly, replace it.

7   Check the tapered portion of the pilot screw for wear or damage. Replace the screw if necessary.

8   Check the carburetor body, float chamber and carburetor top for

7.3i Lift the float chamber and O-ring off the carburetor body

7.3j Note the location of the notch in the baffle (arrow); push out the float pivot pin and remove the floats

7.3k Remove the clip and detach the needle valve from the floats

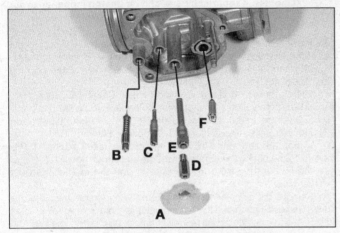

7.3l Float chamber component details

A   Baffle
B   Pilot screw (if equipped)
C   Slow jet
D   Main jet
E   Needle jet holder
F   Needle valve and clip

7.3m If necessary, remove the throttle stop screw and spring

cracks, distorted sealing surfaces and other damage. If any defects are found, replace the faulty component, although replacement of the entire carburetor will probably be necessary (check with your parts supplier for the availability of separate components).

9   Check the jet needle for straightness by rolling it on a flat surface (such as a piece of glass). Replace it if it's bent or if the tip is worn.

10   Check the tip of the fuel inlet valve needle. If it has grooves or scratches in it, it must be replaced. Push in on the rod in the other end of the needle, then release it - if it doesn't spring back, replace the valve needle.

11   Check the O-rings on the float chamber and the drain plug (in the float chamber). Replace them if they're damaged.

12   Check the floats for damage. This will usually be apparent by the presence of fuel inside one of the floats. If the floats are damaged, they must be replaced.

13   Insert the throttle valve in the carburetor body and see that it moves up-and-down smoothly. Check the surface of the throttle valve for wear. If it's worn excessively or doesn't move smoothly in the bore, replace the carburetor.

8   Carburetor - reassembly and float height check

Caution: *When installing the jets, be careful not to over-tighten them - they're made of soft material and can strip or shear easily.*
Note: *When reassembling the carburetor, be sure to use the new O-rings, gaskets and other parts supplied in the rebuild kit.*

1   Install the clip on the jet needle if it was removed. Place it in the needle groove listed in this Chapter's Specifications. Install the needle and clip in the throttle valve.

2   Install the pilot screw along with its spring, washer and O-ring, turning it in until it seats lightly. Now, turn the screw out the number of turns listed in this Chapter's Specifications.

3   Reverse the disassembly steps to install the jets.

4   Invert the carburetor. Attach the fuel inlet valve needle to the float. Set the float into position in the carburetor, making sure the valve needle seats correctly. Install the float pivot pin. To check the float height, hold the carburetor so the float hangs down, then tilt it back until the valve needle is just seated. Measure the distance from the float chamber gasket surface to the top of the float and compare your measurement to the float height listed in this Chapter's Specifications. Bend the float tang as necessary to change the adjustment.

5   Install the O-ring into the groove in the float chamber. Place the float chamber on the carburetor and install the screws, tightening them securely.

9   Air cleaner housing - removal and installation

XR250L

Refer to illustration 9.5

1   Remove the seat and both side covers and the inner fender (see Chapter 7).

2   Remove the retainers for the wiring harness that runs across the top of the air cleaner case, then unplug the harness at the connector and position it out of the way.

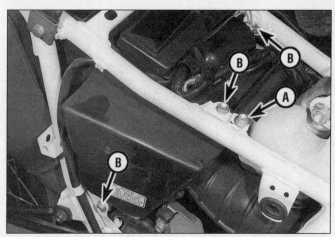

9.5 On XR250L models, unbolt the resonator (A) and remove the air cleaner housing bolts (B)

9.17 The air cleaner housing on 1996 and later XR250R and all XR400 models is secured by one bolt on the top (upper arrow) and one on each side (lower arrow)

3   Unbolt the rear brake fluid reservoir (see Chapter 6). Be sure to support the reservoir in a level position so brake fluid doesn't leak out.
4   Remove the crankcase breather separator (see Section 12). Detach the separator tube and the breather tube from the front of the air cleaner housing.
5   Unbolt the resonator. Loosen its clamp and detach it from the air cleaner intake tube **(see illustration)**.
6   Remove the air cleaner housing bolts **(see illustration 9.5)**. Loosen the connecting tube clamp **(see illustration 6.5)**. Pull the housing back to separate the intake tube from the carburetor, then remove the housing from the left side of the motorcycle.
7   Installation is the reverse of the removal steps.

1986 through 1995 XR250R

8   Remove the seat and both side covers and the inner fender (see Chapter 7).
9   Remove the retainers for the wiring harness that runs across the top of the air cleaner case, then unplug the harness at the connector and position it out of the way.
10   Remove the air cleaner housing bolts, two from the top and one from the right side. Loosen the connecting tube clamp **(see illustration 6.5)**. Pull the housing back to separate the intake tube from the carburetor, then remove the housing from the left side of the motorcycle.
11   Installation is the reverse of the removal steps.

1996 and later XR250R, all XR400R

Refer to illustration 9.17
12   Remove the seat and both side covers (see Chapter 7).

13   Remove the retainer for the wiring harnesses that run across the top of the air cleaner case, then unplug the harnesses (alternator, AC regulator and ignition pulse generator) at the connector and position them out of the way.
14   Unbolt the rear brake fluid reservoir (see Chapter 6). Be sure to support the reservoir in a level position so brake fluid doesn't leak out.
15   Loosen the carburetor connecting tube clamp **(see illustration 6.5)** and the muffler-to-exhaust pipe clamp (see Section 11).
16   Unbolt the sub-frame from the motorcycle (see Chapter 7). Pull the sub-frame backward together with the air cleaner housing to separate the intake tube from the carburetor and the muffler from the exhaust pipe.
17   Remove the air cleaner housing from the sub-frame **(see illustration)**. If necessary, remove the AC regulator and brake reservoir bracket (XR250R) and inner fender (all models) from the air cleaner housing.
18   Installation is the reverse of the removal steps.

---

10   Throttle cables - removal and installation

1   Remove the fuel tank (see Section 2).
2   At the handlebar, loosen the throttle cable adjuster all the way (see Chapter 1).

XR250L, 1986 through 1995 XR250R

Refer to illustrations 10.3 and 10.4
3   On the forward side of the handlebar, remove the screws that

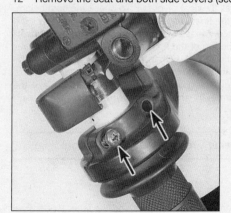

10.3 Remove the two screws (arrows) and separate the halves of the XR250L throttle housing . . .

10.4 . . . remove the cable guide (arrow) and separate the cable ends from the throttle pulley

10.5 Loosen the screw that secures the throttle roller cover (upper arrow) and remove the throttle housing screws (lower arrows)

10.6a Slide the throttle grip off the handlebar, then remove the throttle roller cover, gasket and throttle roller

10.6b Free the ends of the throttle cables from the throttle grip pulley

10.7 At the carburetor, loosen the cable locknuts, detach the cables from the bracket and free the ends from the throttle pulley

hold the throttle housing together (see illustration).

4   Remove the cable guide from the throttle housing (see illustration). Rotate the cables to align them with the slots in the throttle pulley, then slide the cables out of the pulley.

1996 and later XR250R, all XR400R

Refer to illustrations 10.5, 10.6a and 10.6b

5   Loosen the screw that secures the cover on the throttle cable roller (see illustration). Separate the halves of the throttle cable housing, then slide the housing and throttle grip off the handlebar.

6   Remove the cover, gasket and throttle cable roller (see illustration). Rotate the cable ends to align them with the slots in the throttle grip pulley, then slip the ends out of the pulley (see illustration).

All models

Refer to illustrations 10.7 and 10.10

7   At the carburetor, loosen the cable locknuts and slip the cables out of the bracket (see illustration). Rotate the cables to align with the slots in the throttle pulley and slide the cable ends sideways to detach them from the pulley.

8   Route the cables into place. Make sure they don't interfere with any other components and aren't kinked or bent sharply.

9   Lubricate the throttle pulley ends of the cables with multi-purpose grease. Reverse the disconnection steps to connect the throttle cables to the throttle grip pulley. If the bike has a throttle roller, install the roller, gasket and cover.

10   Coat the handlebar with silicone grease and slide the throttle

housing and throttle grip on. Position the throttle housing so the parting line of the throttle housing and clamp is aligned with the punch mark on the handlebar, then install the clamp (see illustration). Tighten the clamp screws securely, then tighten the throttle roller screw (if equipped) to the torque listed in this Chapter's Specifications.

11   Attach the cables to the throttle pulley at the carburetor and position them in the bracket.

12   Operate the throttle and make sure it returns to the idle position by itself under spring pressure. **Warning:** *If the throttle doesn't return by itself, find and solve the problem before continuing with installation. A stuck throttle can lead to loss of control of the motorcycle.*

13   Follow the procedure outlined in Chapter 1, *Throttle operation/grip freeplay - check and adjustment*, to adjust the cables.

14   Turn the handlebars back and forth to make sure the cables don't cause the steering to bind.

15   Once you're sure the cables operate properly, install the fuel tank.

16   With the engine idling, turn the handlebars through their full travel (full left lock to full right lock) and see if the idle speed increases. If it does, the cables are routed incorrectly. Correct this dangerous condition before riding the bike.

---

11   Exhaust system - removal and installation

Refer to illustrations 11.1, 11.2a, 11.2b and 11.4

1   Remove the exhaust pipe holder nuts and slide the holders off the mounting studs (see illustration).

10.10 The punch mark in the handlebar (arrow) aligns with the parting line of the throttle housing halves on installation

11.1 Remove the holder nuts (arrows) and slide the holders off the studs

11.2a Remove the muffler clamp bolt (right arrow) and the forward mounting bolt (left arrow)

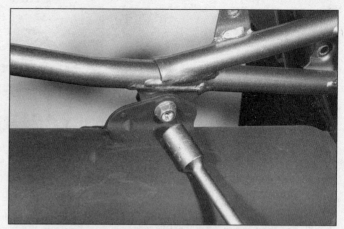

11.2b Remove the rear mounting bolt to detach the muffler from the frame

11.4 Install new gaskets in the exhaust ports

12.1 The crankcase breather separator is mounted forward of the air cleaner housing (XR250L shown)

2   Remove the muffler mounting bolts **(see illustrations)**.
3   Pull the exhaust system forward, separate the pipe from the cylinder head and remove the system from the machine. To detach the muffler, loosen the clamp and pull the pipes out of it **(see illustration 11.2a)**.
4   Installation is the reverse of removal, with the following additions:
 a) *Be sure to install new gaskets at the cylinder head* **(see illustration)**.
 b) *Tighten the muffler mounting bolts and holder nuts securely.*

12 Emission controls

Crankcase breather

Refer to illustration 12.1
1   All XR250L models, as well as 1998 and later XR250R and XR400R California models, are equipped with a breather that recirculates crankcase vapors to the air cleaner so they can be drawn into the engine and burned. A separator prevents the breather from pulling liquid oil into the engine **(see illustration)**.
2   Periodic maintenance consists of checking the hoses and cleaning the drain tube (see Chapter 1).
3   To remove the separator, disconnect the hoses from the fittings and unbolt the separator bracket from the engine **(see illustration 12.1)**. Installation is the reverse of the removal steps.

Evaporative emission control system

Refer to illustration 12.6
4   This system is used on XR250L California models. It routes fuel vapors into the engine so they can be burned. While the engine is off, the vapors are stored in a canister. When the engine starts, a vacuum

signal opens the purge control valve, which allows vapors to be pulled from the canister and fuel tank into the carburetor.
5   Periodic maintenance consists of checking the hoses (see Chapter 1).
6   To remove the purge control valve, disconnect the hoses from the fittings and pull the valve's rubber mount off the engine bracket **(see illustration)**.
7   To remove the canister, disconnect the hoses and unbolt the canister from the engine.
8   Installation is the reverse of the removal steps.

12.6 XR250L California models have a purge control valve (upper arrow) and canister (lower arrow) mounted on the left side of the engine

Chapter 4
Ignition and electrical systems

Contents

Specifications

General

Battery (XR250L)
Type ... 12V, 3Ah (amp-hours); maintenance free
Charging rate (normal) ... 0.4 amps, 5 to 10 hours
Charging rate (quick charge) ... 4 amps, 30 minutes
Terminal voltage (fully charged) ... 13.0 to 13.2 volts
Needs recharge at ... 12.3 volts or less
Charging system (XR250L)
Maximum current drain ... 1 mA (milliamp)
Charging system voltage ... 14.7 to 15.1 volts
Stator coil resistance ... 0.1 to 1.0 ohms
Alternator (1986 through 1995 XR250R)
Exciter coil resistance ... 50 to 200 ohms
Lighting coil resistance ... 0.2 to 1.2 ohms
Regulated voltage (engine running) ... 12.0 to 14.0 volts at 3000 rpm
Alternator (1996 and later XR250R)
Regulated voltage ... 12.0 to 14.0 volts at 3000 rpm
Alternator (XR400R)
Regulated voltage ... 12.5 to 13.5 volts at 3000 rpm

Ignition system

XR250L

Coil primary resistance...	0.1 to 0.3 ohms
Coil secondary resistance	
With spark plug cap..	6500 to 10,000 ohms
Without spark plug cap...	2500 to 3500 ohms
Pulse generator resistance..	460 to 580 ohms

XR250R (1986 through 1995)

Coil primary resistance...	0.1 to 0.3 ohms
Coil secondary resistance	
With spark plug gap...	7400 to 11000 ohms
Without spark plug cap...	3700 to 4500 ohms
Pulse generator resistance..	460 to 580 ohms
Pulse generator rotor air gap	0.7 mm (0.03 inch)

XR250R (1996 on) and XR400R

Ignition coil primary peak voltage (minimum)...............................	100 volts
Pulse generator peak voltage (minimum).....................................	0.7 volts
Exciter coil peak voltage (minimum)..	100 volts
Lighting coil resistance..	0.2 to 1.2 ohms

Light bulbs

XR250L

Headlight	60/55 watts
Tail/brake light	8/27 watts
Turn signals	23 watts
Instrument lights...	3.4 watts

XR250R

Headlight	35 watts
Tail light	
1986 through 1991..	3.4 watts
1992 through 1995..	3.8 watts
1996 on..	5 watts

XR400R

Headlight...	35 watts
Tail light..	5 watts

Torque specifications

Sidestand switch (XR250L)...	10 Nm (84 inch-lbs)*
Alternator rotor bolt	
XR250L, XR250R	105 Nm (76 ft-lbs)
XR400R	127 Nm (94 ft-lbs)

Use a new bolt on installation.

1   General information

All of the machines covered by this manual are equipped with a capacitive discharge ignition system (CDI), a headlight and a tail light.

XR250R and XR400R models, which are intended for off-road use, do not have a battery, a fuse, turn signals or brake lights. Current generated by the alternator operates the ignition system and powers the headlight and tail light.

XR250L models, which are street-legal, use a 12-volt electrical system with a battery. The components include a crankshaft-mounted permanent-magnet alternator and a solid state voltage regulator/rectifier unit. The alternator consists of a multi-coil stator mounted inside the left engine cover and a permanent magnet rotor mounted on the end of the crankshaft. The regulator maintains the charging system output within the specified range to prevent overcharging. The rectifier converts the AC output of the alternator to DC current to power the lights and other components and to charge the battery. Fuses protect the electrical system.

Note: *Keep in mind that electrical parts, once purchased, can't be returned. To avoid unnecessary expense, make very sure the faulty component has been positively identified before buying a replacement part.*

2   Electrical troubleshooting

A typical electrical circuit consists of an electrical component, the switches, relays, etc. related to that component and the wiring and connectors that hook the component to both the battery (if equipped) and the frame. To aid in locating a problem in any electrical circuit, complete wiring diagrams of each model are included at the end of this manual.

Before tackling any troublesome electrical circuit, first study the appropriate diagrams thoroughly to get a complete picture of what makes up that individual circuit. Trouble spots, for instance, can often be narrowed down by noting if other components related to that circuit are operating properly or not. If several components or circuits fail at one time, chances are the fault lies in the fuse (if equipped) or ground connection, as several circuits often are routed through the same fuse and ground connections.

Electrical problems often stem from simple causes, such as loose or corroded connections or a blown fuse. Prior to any electrical troubleshooting, always visually check the condition of the fuse (if equipped), wires and connections in the problem circuit.

If testing instruments are going to be utilized, use the diagrams to plan where you will make the necessary connections in order to accurately pinpoint the trouble spot.

The basic tools needed for electrical troubleshooting include a test light or voltmeter, an ohmmeter or a continuity tester (which includes a bulb, battery and set of test leads) and a jumper wire, preferably with a circuit breaker incorporated, which can be used to bypass electrical components. Specific checks described later in this Chapter may also require an ammeter.

On XR250L models (which have a battery), voltage checks should be performed if a circuit is not functioning properly. Connect one lead of a test light or voltmeter to either the negative battery terminal or a known good ground. Connect the other lead to a connector in the circuit being tested, preferably nearest to the battery or fuse. If the bulb lights, voltage is reaching that point, which means the part of the circuit between that connector and the battery is problem-free. Continue checking the remainder of the circuit in the same manner. When you reach a point where no voltage is present, the problem lies between there and the last good test point. Most of the time the problem is due to a loose connection. Keep in mind that some circuits only receive voltage when the ignition key is in the On position.

One method of finding short circuits on XR250L models is to remove the fuse and connect a test light or voltmeter in its place to the fuse terminals. There should be no load in the circuit. Move the wiring harness from side-to-side while watching the test light. If the bulb lights, there is a short to ground somewhere in that area, probably where insulation has rubbed off a wire. The same test can be performed on other components in the circuit, including the switch.

A ground check should be done on XR250L models to see if a component is grounded properly. Disconnect the battery and connect one lead of a self-powered test light (such as a continuity tester) to a known good ground. Connect the other lead to the wire or ground connection being tested. If the bulb lights, the ground is good. If the bulb does not light, the ground is not good.

A continuity check is performed to see if a circuit, section of circuit or individual component is capable of passing electricity through it. Disconnect the battery and connect one lead of a self-powered test light (such as a continuity tester) to one end of the circuit being tested and the other lead to the other end of the circuit. If the bulb lights, there is continuity, which means the circuit is passing electricity through it properly. Switches can be checked in the same way.

Remember that all electrical circuits are designed to conduct electricity from the battery (if equipped), through the wires, switches, etc. to the electrical component (light bulb, etc.). From there it is directed to the frame (ground) where it is passed back to the battery or alternator. Electrical problems are basically an interruption in the flow of electricity from the battery or back to it.

3 Battery (XR250L models) - inspection and maintenance

Refer to illustration 3.4

1 Most battery damage is caused by heat, vibration, and/or low electrolyte levels, so keep the battery securely mounted, check the electrolyte level frequently and make sure the charging system is functioning properly.
2 These models are equipped with a sealed maintenance-free battery. Scheduled maintenance isn't required, but it's still a good idea to inspect the battery regularly.
3 Check around the base inside of the battery for sediment, which is the result of sulfation caused by low electrolyte levels. These deposits will cause internal short circuits, which can quickly discharge the battery. Look for cracks in the case and replace the battery if either of these conditions is found.
4 Check the battery terminals and cable ends for tightness and corrosion. If corrosion is evident, remove the cables from the battery and clean the terminals and cable ends with a wire brush or knife and emery paper **(see illustration)**. Reconnect the cables and apply a thin coat of petroleum jelly to the connections to slow further corrosion.
5 The battery case should be kept clean to prevent current leakage, which can discharge the battery over a period of time (especially when

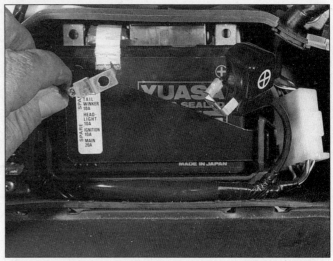

3.4 Disconnect the cables from the battery; the positive cable is covered by a rubber shield to prevent accidental shorts

it sits unused). Wash the outside of the case with a solution of baking soda and water. Do not get any baking soda solution in the battery cells. Rinse the battery thoroughly, then dry it.
6 If acid has been spilled on the frame or battery box, neutralize it with the baking soda and water solution, dry it thoroughly, then touch up any damaged paint. Make sure the battery vent tube is directed away from the frame and is not kinked or pinched.
7 If the motorcycle sits unused for long periods of time, disconnect the cables from the battery terminals. Refer to Section 4 and charge the battery approximately once every month.

4 Battery (XR250L models) - charging

1 If the machine sits idle for extended periods or if the charging system malfunctions, the battery can be charged from an external source.
2 To properly charge the battery, you will need a charger of the correct rating, a hydrometer, a clean rag and a syringe for adding distilled water to the battery cells.
3 The maximum charging rate for any battery is 1/10 of the rated amp/hour capacity. As an example, the maximum charging rate for the 14 amp/hour battery would be 1.4 amps. If the battery is charged at a higher rate, it could be damaged.
4 Do not allow the battery to be subjected to a so-called quick charge (high rate of charge over a short period of time) unless you are prepared to buy a new battery. Battery charge rates and times are listed in this Chapter's Specifications.
5 When charging the battery, always remove it from the machine and be sure to check the electrolyte level before hooking up the charger. The battery supplied with these models is a maintenance free type, to which water can't be added. Replace the battery if any cells are low.
6 Hook up the battery charger leads (red to positive, black to negative), then, and only then, plug in the battery charger. **Warning:** *Remember, the gas escaping from a charging battery is explosive, so keep open flames and sparks well away from the area. Also, the electrolyte is extremely corrosive and will damage anything it comes in contact with.*
7 Allow the battery to charge at the rate and time listed in this Chapter's Specifications.
8 If voltage across the battery terminals doesn't reach the specified minimum after a long slow charge, or if the battery as a whole does not seem to want to take a charge, it is time for a new battery.
9 When the battery is fully charged, unplug the charger first, then disconnect the leads from the battery.

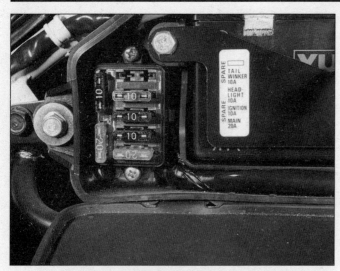

5.1 The fuse block contains four fuses and two spares; fuse functions are printed inside the cover

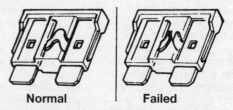

5.2 A blown fuse can be identified by its broken element - be sure to replace a blown fuse with one of the same amperage rating

5 Fuses (XR250L) - check and replacement

Refer to illustrations 5.1 and 5.2

1   The fuses are located under the seat, next to the battery **(see illustration)**. The fuse is protected by a plastic cover.

2   Fuses can be removed and checked visually **(see illustration)**, but the quickest way to check the fuses is with the use of a test light. Probe the exposed terminals of each fuse with the ignition On - if a fuse has power available on one side of the exposed terminals but not the other, it's blown. To remove a fuse, carefully pull it out of the fuse block. A fuse puller tool will make this easier.

3   If a fuse blows, be sure to check the wiring harnesses very carefully for evidence of a short circuit. Look for bare wires and chafed, melted or burned insulation. If a fuse is replaced before the cause is located, the new fuse will blow immediately.

4   Never, under any circumstances, use a higher rated fuse or bridge the fuse holder terminals, as damage to the electrical system or a fire could result.

5   Occasionally a fuse will blow or cause an open circuit for no obvious reason. Corrosion of the fuse ends and fuse holder terminals may occur and cause poor fuse contact. If this happens, remove the corrosion with a wire brush or emery paper, then spray the fuse end and terminals with electrical contact cleaner.

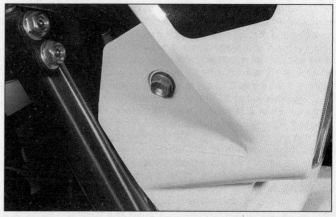

6.2a Remove the bolt from each side of the XR250L headlight housing . . .

6 Bulbs - replacement

1   Since these bikes are used off-road, it's a good idea to check the lens and bulb housing for built-up dirt and clean them thoroughly whenever a bulb is changed.

Headlight bulbs

Warning: *To avoid burning your fingers, let the bulb cool before replacing it.*

XR250L models

Refer to illustrations 6.2a, 6.2b, 6.2c, 6.3a, 6.3b and 6.4

2   Remove the two mounting bolts and lift the headlight case off the motorcycle **(see illustrations)**. Detach the headlight housing from its frame **(see illustration)**.

3   Unplug the electrical connector and pull off the rubber cover on

6.2b . . . and lift the grommets off the pins (arrows) . . .

6.2c . . . remove the frame bolts (there's one on each side) and the screw (arrows) . . .

6.3a . . . unplug the connector . . .

6.3b . . . pull off the dust cap (note the TOP mark) . . .

6.4 . . . and lift the retainer ring to free the bulb

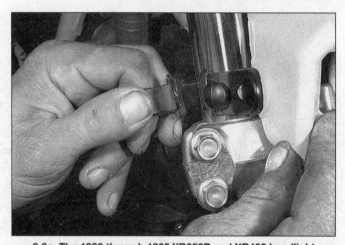

6.6a The 1986 through 1995 XR250R and XR400 headlight housing is secured by four rubber retainers

the back of the headlight assembly (see illustrations).

4   Disengage the bulb retaining clip and pull the bulb out (see illustration).

5   Installation is the reverse of the removal steps, with the following additions:

a) *Don't touch the bulb glass with your fingers; the oil from your skin will form a hot spot and shorten bulb life. If you touch the glass accidentally, clean it with rubbing alcohol.*

b) *Make sure the Top mark on the rubber cover is up.*

XR250R and XR400R models

Refer to illustrations 6.6a, 6.6b, 6.7 and 6.8

6   If you're working on a 1986 through 1995 XR250R, unhook the four rubber mounting bands and take the headlight case off (see illustration). If you're working on a 1996 or later XR250R or an XR400R, unhook the two rubber mounting bands and lift the headlight housing out of the mounting grommets (see illustration).

7   Twist the bulb socket counterclockwise and remove it from the headlight assembly (see illustration).

6.6b Later XR250R and all XR400R models use two rubber retainers, pins and grommets

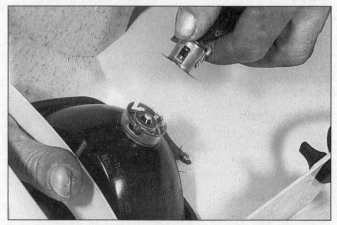

6.7 Press in the bulb socket and turn it counterclockwise, then pull it out

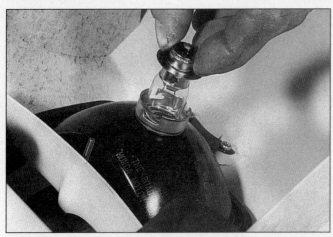

6.8 Rotate the bulb to align its tabs with the slots and pull it out

6.11 Remove the lens screws to detach the XR250L tail light lens

6.14a The 1986 through 1995 XR250R tail light lens screws (arrows) are accessible from beneath the fender

6.14b Later XR250R and all XR400R tail light lens screws are on top of the lens

6.17a For access to an XR250L turn signal bulb, remove the screw from the back of the housing . . .

8   Twist the bulb counterclockwise and remove it **(see illustration)**.
9   Installation is the reverse of the removal steps.

All models
10   Refer to Section 7 and adjust headlight aim.

Tail/brake/license plate light bulb (XR250L models)
Refer to illustration 6.11
11   Remove the lens screws and take the lens off the tail light housing **(see illustration)**.
12   Press the bulb into its socket, turn it counterclockwise to align the bulb retaining pins with their grooves and pull the bulb out.
13   Installation is the reverse of the removal steps. The bulb pins are offset so the bulb can only go in one way.

Tail light bulb
Refer to illustrations 6.14a and 6.14b
14   Remove the lens screws **(see illustrations)**.
15   Take the lens off, remove the bulb and install a new one.
16   Installation is the reverse of the removal steps.

Turn signals (XR250L)
Bulb replacement
Refer to illustrations 6.17a and 6.17b
17   Remove the lens screw from the turn signal housing **(see illustra-**

tion). Rotate the lens out to disengage its tab from the housing and take the lens and gasket off the housing **(see illustration)**.
18   Press the bulb into its socket, turn it counterclockwise to align the bulb retaining pins with their grooves and pull the bulb out.
19   Installation is the reverse of the removal steps.

6.17b . . . and pull out the lens to detach the lens tab from its slot (right arrow) - remove the nut (left arrow) to detach the rear turn signal stalk from the bike, if necessary

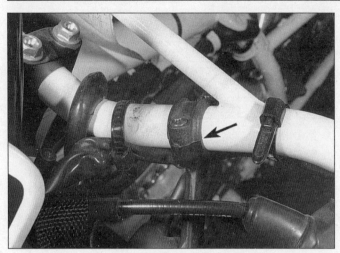

6.20 Align the split in the front turn signal clamp with the punch mark on the handlebar (arrow)

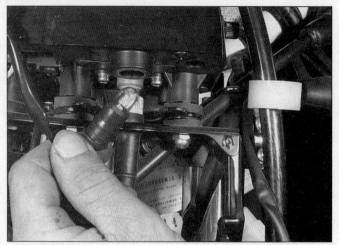

6.22 Pull the bulb socket out of the cluster, then pull the bulb out of the socket

Turn signal housing replacement

Refer to illustration 6.20

20   To replace a front housing, unplug its electrical connector and free the harness from the retainer on the handlebar. Remove the mounting screws and separate the clamp halves. On installation, align the split in the clamp with the punch mark on the handlebar **(see illustration)**.

21   Follow the wires from the housing to the connector and unplug them. Remove the housing nut, pull the wires through it and separate the housing from the bike **(see illustration 6.17b)**.

Instrument light bulbs

Refer to illustration 6.22

22   Pull the bulb socket out of the underside of the instrument housing **(see illustration)**. Pull the bulb out of the socket, push in a new one and push the socket back into the housing.

7   Headlight aim - check and adjustment

1   An improperly adjusted headlight may cause problems for oncoming traffic or provide poor, unsafe illumination of the terrain ahead. Before adjusting the headlight, be sure to consult with local traffic laws and regulations. Honda doesn't provide specifications for headlight adjustment.

7.3 The horizontal headlight adjuster is located beneath the lens (arrow) (XR250L shown)

XR250L models

Refer to illustration 7.3

2   Adjust the headlight vertically by loosening the headlight housing bolts, swiveling the housing and tightening the bolts.

3   Adjust the headlight horizontally by turning the screw in the underside of the headlight housing, to the right of center **(see illustration)**.

XR250R and XR400R

4   These bikes don't have a horizontal adjustment. Adjust the beam vertically by turning the screw in the lower front edge of the headlight housing.

8   Brake light switches (XR250L) - check and replacement

1   Before checking any electrical circuit on an XR250L, check the fuse (see Section 5).

2   The front brake light switch is mounted under the master cylinder. The rear brake light switch is mounted in a bracket behind the brake pedal.

Test light check

3   Turn the ignition switch On. Using a test light connected to a good ground, check for voltage to the black wire at the front brake light switch or the black wire in the harness side of the connector at the rear brake light switch. Leave the connector at the rear brake light switch connected and insert the test light probe into the back of the terminal. If there's no voltage, check the wiring from the brake light switch to the ignition switch (see the wiring diagrams at the end of the book).

4   If voltage is available, connect the test light to the other terminal at the brake light switch, then pull the lever or push the pedal. If the test light comes on, the switch is good. If not, replace the switch.

Ohmmeter check

5   This test can also be made with a self-powered test light (one that has its own battery).

6   Disconnect the wires from the switch. Connect the ohmmeter or test light between the switch terminals (if you're testing a rear switch, connect the tester between the terminals in the switch side of the wiring harness).

7   Pull the lever or press the pedal. The ohmmeter should show zero or near-zero; the test light should illuminate. If not, replace the switch.

9.7 The ignition switch bolts are accessible from beneath the switch (arrows)

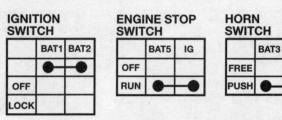

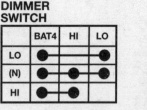

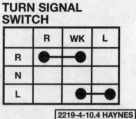

10.4 Handlebar switch continuity chart - continuity should exist between the terminals connected by a solid line when the switch is in the indicated position

Replacement

8   To remove a front brake light switch, disconnect its wires, remove the switch mounting screw and take the switch off the master cylinder.
9   To remove a rear brake light switch, unhook the spring and disconnect the electrical connector. Loosen the adjusting nut until it comes off the switch threads, then pull the switch out of the bracket (don't turn the switch body).
10   Installation is the reverse of the removal steps. Refer to Chapter 1 to adjust the rear brake light switch. The front switch isn't adjustable.

9   Ignition switch (XR250L) - check and replacement

Check

1   Follow the wiring harness from the ignition switch to the connector and unplug the connector.
2   Using an ohmmeter, check the continuity between the terminals of the switch. Continuity should exist when the switch is in the On position.
3   If the switch fails any of the tests, replace it.

Replacement

Refer to illustration 9.7

4   Refer to Section 6 and remove the headlight housing.
5   Follow the switch wires to the connector and unplug it.
6   Place the key in the lock and turn it to On.
7   Remove the switch mounting bolts and take it off the bike **(see illustration)**.
8   Installation is the reverse of the removal steps.

10   Handlebar switches - check and replacement

Check

Refer to illustration 10.4

1   Generally speaking, the switches are reliable and trouble-free. Most troubles, when they do occur, are caused by dirty or corroded contacts, but wear and breakage of internal parts is a possibility that should not be overlooked. If breakage does occur, the entire switch and related wiring harness will have to be replaced with a new one, since individual parts are not usually available.
2   The switches can be checked for continuity with an ohmmeter or a continuity test light. If you're working on an XR250L, always disconnect the battery negative cable, which will prevent the possibility of a short circuit, before making the checks.
3   Trace the wiring harness of the switch in question and unplug the electrical connectors.
4   Using the ohmmeter or test light, check for continuity between the terminals of the switch harness with the switch in the various positions **(see illustration)**.
5   If the continuity check indicates a problem exists, disassemble the switch and spray the switch contacts with electrical contact cleaner. If they are accessible, the contacts can be scraped clean with a knife or polished with crocus cloth. If switch components are damaged or broken, it will be obvious when the switch is disassembled.

Replacement

Refer to illustrations 10.6, 10.8a and 10.8b

6   The handlebar switches, with the exception of the kill switch on off-road models, are composed of two halves that clamp around the bars. The kill switch on off-road models (XR250R and XR400R) is a button that is secured to the left handlebar by a clamp. They are easily removed for cleaning or inspection by taking out the clamp screws and pulling the switch halves away from the handlebars **(see illustration)**.
7   To completely remove the switches, the electrical connectors in the wiring harness must be unplugged and the harness separated from the tie wraps and retainers.

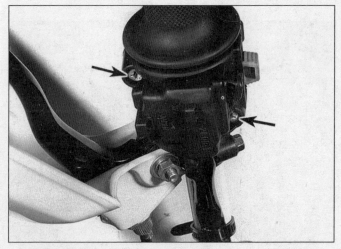

10.6 The XR250L handlebar switch screws are accessible from below (arrows)

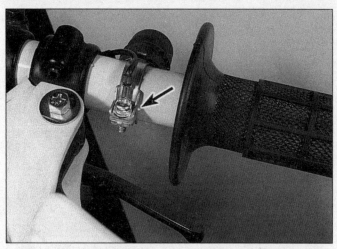

10.8a Align the split in the switch housing or clamp with the punch mark in the handlebar (arrow) (off-road kill button shown)

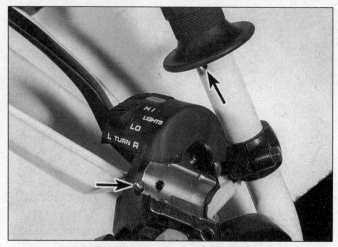

10.8b Align the button on the XR250L handlebar switch (left arrow) with the hole in the handlebar (right arrow)

8   Installation is the reverse of the removal steps, with the following additions:

a) Make sure the wiring harness is properly routed to avoid pinching or stretching the wires.
b) Where there's a punch mark on the handlebar, align the split in the switch housing or clamp with the punch mark **(see illustration)**.
c) Where there's a hole In the handlebar, position the switch alignment in the hole **(see illustration)**.
d) If you're installing the left handlebar switches on an XR250L, tighten the front screw first, then the rear screw. Be careful not to overtighten them and crack the housing.

11   Sidestand switch (XR250L) - check and replacement

Check

Refer to illustration 11.1
1   Follow the wiring harness from the sidestand switch to the electrical connector and unplug it **(see illustration)**.
2   Connect an ohmmeter between the switch terminals. Have an assistant support the bike while you raise and lower the sidestand.
3   With the sidestand up, there should be continuity between the green-white and green terminals. With the sidestand down, there should be continuity between the yellow-black and green terminals. If

there's no continuity, or continuity between the wrong terminals, replace the switch.

Replacement

4   If you haven't already done so, follow the switch harness to the connector and unplug it. Detach the harness from the retainer on the frame.
5   Remove two bolts and take the cover off the switch. Remove and discard the switch mounting bolt (it screws into the head of the sidestand pivot bolt). Take the switch off.
6   Installation is the reverse of the removal steps, with the following addition: Use a new switch bolt and tighten it to the torque listed in this Chapter's Specifications.

12   Speedometer/odometer and cable - removal and installation

Refer to illustrations 12.2, 12.3, 12.4, 12.5a and 12.5b
1   XR250L models use a speedometer. XR250R and XR400R models are equipped with a trip odometer.
2   Unscrew the cable retaining bolt and pull the lower end of the cable out of the gear at the front wheel **(see illustration)**.
3   Remove the retainer that secures the cable to the right fork leg **(see illustration)**.

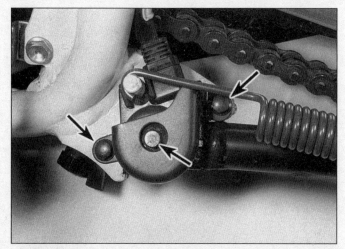

11.1 Remove the cover bolts (left and right arrows) and the mounting bolt (center arrow)

12.2 Remove the bolt and pull the cable out of the gear

12.3 Detach the cable retainer from the fork leg

12.4 Unscrew the knurled nut (center arrow) and pull the cable out of the meter (XR250L shown); remove the mounting nuts (outer arrows) to detach the gauge

12.5a On the XR250L, unplug the electrical connectors (arrows) . . .

12.5b . . . and take the bracket out of its mount (arrow)

4   Unscrew the knurled nut and detach the cable from the instrument housing and remove the mounting nuts **(see illustration)**.
5   If you're working on an XR250L, unplug the electrical connectors at the cluster bracket and detach the bracket from the insulator on the right side **(see illustrations)**. Take the speedometer or odometer off the triple clamp.
6   Installation is the reverse of the removal steps.

13   Horn (XR250L) - removal and installation

Refer to illustration 13.1
1   The horn is mounted in front of the lower triple clamp **(see illustration)**.
2   To remove the horn, disconnect its wires and remove the mounting nut. Installation is the reverse of the removal steps.

14   Charging system testing (XR250L) - general information and precautions

1   If the performance of the charging system is suspect, the system as a whole should be checked first, followed by testing of the individual components (the alternator and the regulator/rectifier). **Note:** *Before beginning the checks, make sure the battery is fully charged and that all system connections are clean and tight.*

2   Checking the output of the charging system and the performance of the various components within the charging system requires the use of a voltmeter, ammeter and ohmmeter or the equivalent multimeter.
3   When making the checks, follow the procedures carefully to prevent incorrect connections or short circuits, as irreparable damage to

13.1 Disconnect the wires and remove the mounting nut to detach the horn

electrical system components may result if short circuits occur.

4   If the necessary test equipment is not available, it is recommended that charging system tests be left to a dealer service department or a reputable motorcycle repair shop.

15 Charging system (XR250L) - leakage and output test

1   If a charging system problem is suspected, perform the following checks. Start by removing the right side cover for access to the battery (see Chapter 7).

Leakage test

Refer to illustration 15.3

Caution: *Don't turn the ignition switch on during this test or a current surge may ruin the ammeter.*

2   Turn the ignition switch Off and disconnect the cable from the battery negative terminal.

3   Set the multimeter to the mA (milliamps) function and connect its negative probe to the battery negative terminal, and the positive probe to the disconnected negative cable **(see illustration)**. Compare the reading to the value listed in this Chapter's Specifications.

4   If the reading is too high there is probably a short circuit in the wiring. Thoroughly check the wiring between the various components (see the wiring diagrams at the end of the book).

5   If the reading is satisfactory, disconnect the meter and connect the negative cable to the battery, tightening it securely. Check the alternator output as described below.

Output test

6   Make sure the battery is fully charged, with a voltmeter reading between the terminals of at least 13 volts. If it's too low, charge the battery before making the test.

7   Start the engine and let it warm up to normal operating temperature.

8   With the engine idling, attach the positive (red) voltmeter lead to the positive (+) battery terminal and the negative (black) lead to the battery negative (-) terminal. The voltmeter selector switch (if equipped) must be in the 0 to 20 volt DC range.

9   Slowly increase the engine speed until voltage reaches its maximum (don't exceed 8000 rpm) and compare the voltmeter reading to the value listed in this Chapter's Specifications.

10   If the output is as specified, the alternator is functioning properly.

11   Low voltage output may be the result of damaged windings in the alternator charging coil or wiring problems between the alternator and battery. Make sure all electrical connections are clean and tight, then refer to the following Section to check the alternator charging coil. If the wiring and the charging coil are good, the problem may be a defec-

tive regulator/rectifier.

12   High voltage output (above the specified range) indicates a defective voltage regulator/rectifier.

16 Alternator - check and replacement

XR250L and 1986 through 1995 XR250R

1   Locate and disconnect the alternator coil connector on the left side of the vehicle frame.

2   To check the coils, connect an ohmmeter between the specified terminals in the side of the connector that runs back to the stator coils on the left side of the engine (in cases where ground is specified, connect the ohmmeter negative terminal to bare metal on the engine or frame). Wire colors and connections are as follows:

a) *XR250L - between each of the three yellow wires, then between each yellow wire and ground*

b) *1986 through 1995 XR250R blue and ground (lighting coil), black/red and ground (ignition executor coil)*

If the readings are much outside the value listed in this Chapter's Specifications, replace the stator coils as described below.

1996 and later XR250R and all XR400R

Lighting coil

3   Remove the seat (see Chapter 7). Locate the lighting coil connectors (yellow and pink wires) on top of the air cleaner housing and disconnect them.

4   Connect an ohmmeter between the connectors and measure the resistance. If it's not within the value listed in this Chapter's Specifications, replace the stator coils as described below.

Executor coil

Refer to illustration 16.7

5   The executor coil on these models is checked by measuring its peak voltage. This requires special test equipment not normally possessed by do-it-yourselfers. If you don't already have one of the necessary testers, it's best to have this procedure done by a Honda dealer.

6   To test the coil, you'll need one of the following:

a) *Imrie diagnostic tester model 625*

b) *Digital multimeter (minimum impedance 10 meg-ohms per DC volt) and peak voltage adapter (Honda part no. 07HGJ-0020100)*

7   Locate the ignition control module (ICM) on the frame **(see illustration)**. Unplug both of its electrical connectors, then connect the tester between the black/red terminal of the two-pin connector and ground (bare metal on the frame).

15.3 Checking the charging system leakage rate with an ammeter

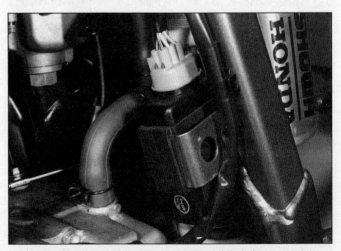

16.7 The XR400R ignition control module is in a mount on the frame

16.12a Remove the cover bolts (and nut if equipped)
(XR400R shown) . . .

16.12b . . . remove the cover and gasket and locate the dowels
(arrows) (XR400R shown)

16.13a Remove three bolts (A) to detach the stator coils; on later
XR250R models, the ignition pulse generator is inside the cover
(B), and the harness retainer is held by a bolt (C)

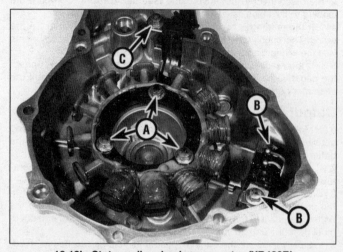

16.13b Stator coil and pulse generator (XR400R)

A Stator coil bolts   C Harness retainer bolt
B Pulse generator bolts

8   Crank the engine with the kickstarter and note the peak voltage
reading. **Warning:** *Do not touch the spark plug or the tester probes
while cranking or you may get an electric shock.*
9   If peak voltage is less than the minimum listed in this Chapter's
Specifications, refer to Chapter 7 and remove the seat. Locate the
executor coil connector (black) on top of the air cleaner housing.
Unplug it and repeat the peak voltage test.
10   If peak voltage is okay at the executor coil connector but not at
the ICM connector, check the wiring for breaks or poor connections. If
it's not okay at either point, the problem may be a bad executor coil, a
bad ICM or even a problem within the tester itself. For these reasons,
further testing should be done by a Honda dealer or other repair shop.

Stator coil replacement

Refer to illustrations 16.12a, 16.12b, 16.13a and 16.13b

11   Remove the engine sprocket cover (see Chapter 5).
12   Remove the left engine cover and clean away the gasket **(see
illustrations)**.
13   Peel the sealant away from the wiring harness grommet **(see
illustration)**. Remove the stator coil bolts and take the stator coils out
of the cover **(see illustration)**. If you're working on a 1996 or later
XR250R or an XR400R, unbolt the ignition pulse generator as well (it's
replaced as a unit with the coils).
14   Installation is the reverse of the removal steps. Tighten the stator
coil bolts to the torque listed in this Chapter's Specifications.

Rotor replacement

Removal

Refer to illustrations 16.16, 16.17 and 16.19

Note: *To remove the alternator rotor, the special Honda puller (part no.
07733-0020001) or an aftermarket equivalent will be required. Don't try
to remove the rotor without the proper puller, as it's almost sure to be
damaged. Pullers are readily available from motorcycle dealers and
aftermarket tool suppliers.*

15   Remove the left engine cover as described above.
16   Hold the alternator rotor with a strap wrench. If you don't have
one and the engine is in the frame, the rotor can be locked by placing
the transmission in gear and holding the rear brake on. Unscrew the
rotor bolt **(see illustration)**.
17   Thread an alternator puller into the center of the rotor and use it to
remove the rotor **(see illustration)**. If the rotor doesn't come off easily,
tap sharply on the end of the puller to release the rotor's grip on the
tapered crankshaft end.
18   Pull the rotor off.
19   Check the Woodruff key **(see illustration)**; if it's not secure in its
slot, pull it out and set it aside for safekeeping. A convenient method is
to stick the Woodruff key to the magnets inside the rotor, but be certain not to forget it's there, as serious damage to the rotor and stator
coils will occur if the engine is run with anything stuck to the magnets.

16.16 Hold the rotor and unscrew the bolt

16.17 Remove the rotor with a puller like this one

16.19 Look for the Woodruff key - if it isn't secure in its slot, set it aside for safekeeping

16.20 Be sure there aren't any small metal objects stuck to the rotor magnets; an inconspicuous item like this Woodruff key (arrow) can ruin the rotor and stator if the engine is run

17.9 The XR400R AC regulator (left arrow) and ignition coil (right arrow) are mounted under the seat

Installation

Refer to illustration 16.20

20   Take a look to make sure there isn't anything stuck to the inside of the rotor **(see illustration)**.

21   Degrease the center of the rotor and the end of the crankshaft.

22   Make sure the Woodruff key is positioned securely in its slot **(see illustration 16.19)**.

23   Align the rotor slot with the Woodruff key. Place the rotor on the crankshaft.

24   Install the rotor bolt. Hold the rotor from turning with one of the methods described in Step 16 and tighten the bolt to the torque listed in this Chapter's Specifications.

25   The remainder of installation is the reverse of the removal steps.

17 AC regulator - check and replacement

1   The AC regulator is used on off-road models (XR250R and XR400R).

Check

2   Refer to Section 6 and remove the headlight assembly. Leave the headlight wires connected.

3   Connect a voltmeter between the headlight wires (insert probes into the terminals without disconnecting the wires). Set the voltmeter to

measure alternating current.

4   Connect a tune-up tachometer to the motorcycle, following the manufacturer's instructions.

5   Start the engine. Slowly increase engine speed and compare the voltmeter reading to the value listed in this Chapter's Specifications.

6   If voltage is within the specified range, the A/C regulator is okay.

7   If the voltage isn't within the specified range, check the AC regulator wiring for breaks or bad connections and make any necessary repairs.

8   If the wiring is good, or if repairing it doesn't produce AC regulator voltage within the Specifications, the regulator itself may be defective. It's a good idea to have it tested by a Honda dealer or substitute a known good unit before condemning it as trash.

Replacement

Refer to illustration 17.9

9   Follow the wiring harness from the AC regulator to the connector and unplug the connector **(see illustration)**. Remove the regulator from its rubber mount and take it off the motorcycle.

10   Installation is the reverse of the removal steps.

18 Regulator/rectifier (XR250L) - replacement

Refer to illustration 18.1

1   The regulator/rectifier is mounted on the frame next to the air

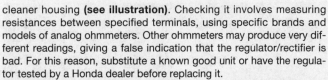

18.1 The XR250L regulator/rectifier is mounted on the frame, in front of the air cleaner housing

20.5 Unscrew the spark plug cap from the plug wire and measure its resistance with an ohmmeter

cleaner housing **(see illustration)**. Checking it involves measuring resistances between specified terminals, using specific brands and models of analog ohmmeters. Other ohmmeters may produce very different readings, giving a false indication that the regulator/rectifier is bad. For this reason, substitute a known good unit or have the regulator tested by a Honda dealer before replacing it.

2   Follow the wiring harnesses from the regulator/rectifier to the electrical connector and unplug it. Remove the regulator/rectifier mounting bolts and lift it off the bike.

3   Installation is the reverse of the removal steps.

19 Ignition system - general information

These motorcycles are equipped with a breakerless (CDI) ignition system. The CDI ignition system functions on the same principle as a breaker point ignition system with the pulse generator and CDI unit performing the tasks previously associated with the breaker points and mechanical advance system. As a result, adjustment and maintenance of breakerless ignition components is eliminated (with the exception of spark plug replacement).

Because of their nature, the individual ignition system components can be checked but not repaired. If ignition system troubles occur, and the faulty component can be isolated, the only cure for the problem is to replace the part with a new one. Keep in mind that most electrical parts, once purchased, can't be returned. To avoid unnecessary expense, make very sure the faulty component has been positively identified before buying a replacement part.

20 Ignition system - check

Refer to illustrations 20.5 and 20.12
Warning: *Because of the very high voltage generated by the ignition system, extreme care should be taken when these checks are performed.*

1   If the ignition system is the suspected cause of poor engine performance or failure to start, a number of checks can be made to isolate the problem.

2   Make sure the ignition kill switch is in the Run or On position.

Engine will not start

3   Refer to Chapter 4 and disconnect the spark plug wire. Connect the wire to a spare spark plug and lay the plug on the engine with the threads contacting the engine. If necessary, hold the spark plug with an insulated tool. Crank the engine over and make sure a well-defined, blue spark occurs between the spark plug electrodes. **Warning:** *Don't*

remove the spark plug from the engine to perform this check - atomized fuel being pumped out of the open spark plug hole could ignite, causing severe injury!

4   If no spark occurs, the following checks should be made:

5   Unscrew the spark plug cap from the plug wire and check the cap resistance with an ohmmeter **(see illustration)**. If the resistance is infinite, replace it with a new one.

6   Make sure all electrical connectors are clean and tight. Check all wires for shorts, opens and correct installation.

7   If you're working on an XR250L, check the battery voltage with a voltmeter. If the voltage is less than 13-volts, recharge the battery.

8   On all models, check the pulse generator and executor coil (see Sections 16 and 22).

9   Refer to Section 21 and check the ignition coil primary and secondary resistance.

10   If the preceding checks produce positive results but there is still no spark at the plug, refer to Section 23 and check the CDI unit.

Engine starts but misfires

11   If the engine starts but misfires, make the following checks before deciding that the ignition system is at fault.

12   The ignition system must be able to produce a spark across a seven millimeter (1/4-inch) gap (minimum). A simple test fixture **(see illustration)** can be constructed to make sure the minimum spark gap can be jumped. Make sure the fixture electrodes are positioned seven millimeters apart.

20.12 A simple spark gap testing fixture can be made from a block of wood, two nails, a large alligator clip, a screw and a piece of wire

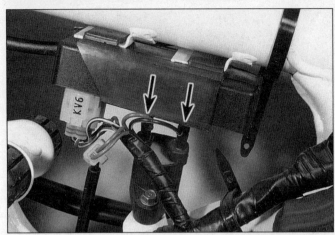

21.4 The XR250L ignition coil is mounted beneath the ICM, under the frame top tube; unplug the primary terminals (arrows) to test resistance

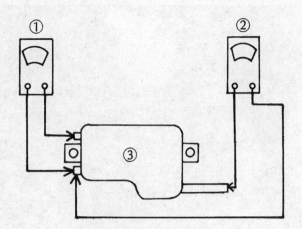

21.5 Ignition coil test

1   *Measure primary winding resistance*
2   *Measure secondary winding resistance*
3   *Ignition coil*

13   Connect the spark plug wire to the protruding test fixture electrode, then attach the fixture's alligator clip to a good engine ground.
14   Crank the engine over with the kill switch in the Run position and see if well-defined, blue sparks occur between the test fixture electrodes. If the minimum spark gap test is positive, the ignition coil is functioning properly. If the spark will not jump the gap, or if it is weak (orange colored), refer to Steps 5 through 10 of this Section and perform the component checks described.

21   Ignition coil - check, removal and installation

Check

XR250L and 1986 through 1995 XR250R

Refer to illustrations 21.4 and 21.5
1   In order to determine conclusively that the ignition coil is defective, it should be tested by an authorized Honda dealer service department which is equipped with the special electrical tester required for this check.
2   However, the coil can be checked visually (for cracks and other damage) and the primary and secondary coil resistances can be measured with an ohmmeter. If the coil is undamaged, and if the resistances are as specified, it is probably capable of proper operation.
3   To check the coil for physical damage, it must be removed (see Steps 8 and 9). To check the resistance, remove the fuel tank (see Chapter 3), unplug the primary circuit electrical connector(s) from the coil and remove the spark plug wire from the spark plug. Mark the locations of all wires before disconnecting them.
4   Label the primary terminal wires, then disconnect them from the ignition coil primary terminals **(see illustration)**.
5   Connect an ohmmeter between the primary terminals. Set the ohmmeter selector switch in the R x 100 position and compare the measured resistance to the value listed in this Chapter's Specifications **(see illustration)**.
6   Connect the ohmmeter between the green wire's primary terminal and the spark plug cap. Set the ohmmeter selector switch in the R x 100 position and compare the measured resistance to the values listed in this Chapter's Specifications.
7   If the resistances are not as specified, unscrew the spark plug cap from the plug wire and check the resistance between the green wire's primary terminal and the end of the spark plug wire. If it's now within specifications, the spark plug cap is bad. If it's still not as specified, the coil is probably defective and should be replaced with a new one.

1996 and later XR250R and all XR400R models

8   Honda doesn't provide resistance specifications for these models. Instead, they recommend testing the coil peak primary voltage with the same special equipment used to test peak voltage of the executor coil (see Section 16). To test, connect the tester between the ignition coil primary terminal and ground (bare metal on the engine).
9   If peak voltage is low or there isn't any at all, check the wiring for breaks or poor connections. Also check the executor coil (see Section 16). If these are good, the ICM may be defective, but substitute a known good unit or have it tested by a Honda dealer before replacing it.
10   If peak voltage is within the Specifications but there is no spark at the plug, the plug or its wire may be defective. If they're good, the ignition coil may be defective, but substitute a known good unit or have it tested by a Honda dealer before replacing it.

Removal and installation

11   To remove the coil, refer to Chapter 3 and remove the fuel tank, then disconnect the spark plug wire from the plug. After labeling them with tape to aid in reinstallation, unplug the coil primary circuit electrical connector(s) **(see illustrations 17.9 and 21.4)**. Some models have a single primary circuit connector and another wire that connects to one of the coil mounting bolts to provide ground.
12   Remove the coil mounting bolt(s), then lift the coil out.
13   Installation is the reverse of removal.

22   Pulse generator - check, removal and installation

Check

XR250L and 1986 through 1995 XR250R

1   Locate the pulse generator harness on the right side of the engine. Follow the harness to the connector and unplug it.
2   Connect an ohmmeter between the wire terminals in the pulse generator side of the connector. Compare the reading to the value listed in this Chapter's Specifications. If it's outside the specified range, replace the pulse generator.

1996 and later XR250R and all XR400R models

Refer to illustration 22.4
3   Testing the pulse generator on these models requires the same special equipment used for the executor coil (see Section 16).

22.4 The XR400R ICM is mounted on the frame

22.8 The pulse generator is bolted to the right side of the engine, inside the cover (arrows); coat the wiring harness grommet in the crankcase with a thin layer of sealant

4   Unplug the connector from the ICM **(see illustration)**. Connect the tester between the blue-yellow and green terminals in the connector, then crank the engine with the kickstarter.
5   If voltage is less than the peak voltage listed in this Chapter's Specifications, locate the pulse generator connector (the white two-pin connector above the ICM). Unplug the connector and connect the tester to the terminals in the pulse generator side of the connector.
6   Crank the engine with the kickstarter. If peak voltage is now within the Specifications, look for a break or poor connection in the wiring. If it's still too low, the pulse generator may be defective, but substitute a known good unit or have it tested by a Honda dealer before replacing it.

Removal and installation

XR250L and 1986 through 1995 XR250R models

Refer to illustration 22.8
7   Remove the right engine cover (see Chapter 2). Disconnect the pulse generator wire at the connector above the engine.
8   Remove the pulse generator mounting bolts and take it off the engine **(see illustration)**.
9   Installation is the reverse of the removal steps. Tighten the bolts securely, but don't overtighten them and strip the threads.

1996 and later XR250R and all XR400R models

10   The pulse generator is mounted in the alternator cover and is replaced together with the stator coils (see Section 16).

---

23   CDI unit - harness check, removal and installation

1   The CDI unit is tested by process of elimination (when all other possible causes of ignition problems have been checked and eliminated, the CDI unit is at fault).

Harness check (XR250L)

2   Remove the fuel tank (see Chapter 3).
3   Follow the harness from the CDI unit to the two-pin and four-pin connectors and unplug them **(see illustration 21.4)**.
4   Set an ohmmeter at R x 1 and connect it between the black/yellow and green wire terminals in the harness. It should give the same reading as for ignition coil primary resistance, listed in this Chapter's Specifications.

5   Set the ohmmeter at R x 100 and connect it between the green and blue/yellow wire terminals in the harness. It should give the same reading as for the pulse generator resistance, listed in this Chapter's Specifications.
6   Connect a voltmeter between the battery terminals and measure the voltage. Connect the voltmeter between the black/white and green terminals in the harness. The reading should be the same as between the battery terminals.
7   With the sidestand up, connect the ohmmeter between the green/white and green wires. It should indicate continuity (little or no resistance).
8   Leave the ohmmeter connected to the green/white and green wires and put the sidestand down. The ohmmeter should now indicate no continuity (infinite resistance).
9   If the harness failed any of the preceding tests, check the affected wires for breaks or poor connections.
10   If the harness and all other system components tested good, the CDI unit may be defective. Before buying a new one, it's a good idea to substitute a known good CDI unit.

Removal and installation

11   If you're working on an XR250L or XR250R, remove the fuel tank if you haven't already done so (see Chapter 3).
12   Locate the CDI unit **(see illustration 21.4 or 22.4)**. Unplug its connector and work the unit out of its mounting band.
13   Installation is the reverse of the removal steps.

---

24   Wiring diagrams - general information

Prior to troubleshooting a circuit, check the fuse (XR250L only) to make sure it's in good condition. Make sure the battery (XR250L only) is fully charged and check the cable connections.
When checking a circuit, make sure all connectors are clean, with no broken or loose terminals or wires. When unplugging a connector, don't pull on the wires - pull only on the connector housings themselves.
The wiring diagrams are located at the end of this manual.

Chapter 5
Steering, suspension and final drive

Contents

Specifications

Front forks

Oil type
- XR250L .... Pro-Honda SS-8 suspension fluid or equivalent
- XR250R, XR400R .... Pro-Honda SS7 suspension fluid or equivalent

Oil capacity
- XR250L .... 550 cc (18.6 fl oz)
- XR250R
  - 1986 through 1989 (standard) .... 535 cc (18.1 fl oz)
  - 1986 through 1989 (limit) .... 531 to 539 cc (17.9 to 18.2 fl oz)
  - 1990 through 1995 (standard) .... 492 cc (16.6 fl oz)
  - 1990 and 1995 (limit) .... 472 to 496 cc (16.0 to 16.8 fl oz)
  - 1996 on .... 477 cc (16.13 fl oz)
- XR400R
  - 1996 and 1997 .... 570 cc (19.2 fl oz)
  - 1998 and later .... 559 cc (18.9 fl oz)

Oil level (fork fully compressed and spring removed)
- XR250L .... 139 mm (5.5 inches)
- XR250R
  - 1986 through 1989 (standard) .... 135 mm (5.3 inches)
  - 1986 through 1989 (limit) .... 125 to 165 mm (4.9 to 6.5 inches)
  - 1990 through 1995 (standard) .... 128 mm (5.0 inches)
  - 1990 through 1995 (limit) .... 124 to 150 mm (4.9 to 5.9 inches)
  - 1996 on (standard) .... 82 mm (3.2 inches)
  - 1996 on (limit) .... 77 to 108 mm (3.0 to 4.2 inches)
- XR400R
  - 1996 and 1997 .... 100 mm (3.9 inches)
  - 1998 and later .... 116 mm (4.6 inches)

Fork spring free length limit (minimum)
- XR250L
  - Short spring .... 87.2 mm (3.43 inches)
  - Long spring .... 539.2 mm (21.23 inches)
- XR250R
  - 1986 through 1989 .... 598.4 mm (23.56 inches)
  - 1990 through 1995 (short spring) .... 78.2 mm (3.08 inches)
  - 1990 through 1995 (long spring) .... 438.6 mm (17.27 inches)
  - 1996 on .... 438.1 mm (17.25 inches)
- XR400R .... 505.3 mm (19.89 inches)

Fork tube bend limit .... 0.2 mm (0.008 inch)

Rear suspension

Rear shock absorber spring free length
   XR250L
      Standard .... 213.0 mm (8.4 inches)
      Limit .... 210.9 mm (8.30 inches)
   XR250R
      1986 through 1989
         Standard.. 215.0 mm (8.46 inches)
         Limit .... 212.0 mm (8.35 inches)
      1990 through 1995
         Standard.. 220.0 mm (8.66 inches)
         Limit .... 215.6 mm (8.49 inches)
      1996 on
         Standard.. 190.0 mm (7.5 inches)
         Limit .... 186.2 mm (7.33 inches)
   XR400R
      Standard .... 217.3 mm (8.56 inches)
      Limit .... 213.0 mm (8.39 inches)

Drive chain

Drive chain slider (on top of swingarm) minimum thickness
   1986 through 1995 XR250R .... Not specified
   XR250L, 1996 and later XR250R, all XR400R.................... 4.0 mm (5/32 inch)
Drive chain slipper (on frame) minimum thickness
   XR250L .... 8 mm (5/16 inch)
   1986 through 1995 XR250R .... 15 mm (19/32 inch)
Drive chain length
   XR250L .... Not specified
   XR250R
      1986 through 1995 (107 pins)
         Standard.. 1699 mm (66-29/32 inches)
         Limit .... 1716 mm (67-19/32 inches)
      1996 on (104 pins)
         Standard.. Not specified
         Limit .... 1659 mm (65-5/16 inches)
   XR400R
      Standard .... Not specified
      Limit (41 pins)... 638 mm (25-7/64 inches)

Torque specifications

Handlebar bracket bolts
   XR250L... 24 Nm (17 ft-lbs)
   XR250R .... 27 Nm (20 ft-lbs)
   XR400R .... Not specified
Front axle nut... See Chapter 6
Upper triple clamp bolts
   XR250L... 24 Nm (17 ft-lbs)
   XR250R
      1986 through 1995 .... 25 to 30 Nm (18 to 22 ft-lbs)
      1996 on.. 33 Nm (24 ft-lbs)
   XR400R... Not specified
Lower triple clamp bolts
   XR250L... 33 Nm (24 ft-lbs)
   XR250R
      1986 through 1995.. 30 to 35 Nm (22 to 25 ft-lbs)
      1996 on.. 27 Nm (20 ft-lbs)
Damper rod bolt (XR250L).. 20 Nm (14 ft-lbs)*
Fork bottom bolt (XR250R)
   1986 through 1989 .... 60 to 84 Nm (43 to 61 ft-lbs)*
   1990 through 1995 .... 34 to 46 Nm (25 to 33 ft-lbs)*
   1996 on.. 20 Nm (14 ft-lbs)*
Fork center bolt (XR400R) .... 34 Nm (25 ft-lbs)*
Fork cap bolt
   XR250L... 24 Nm (17 ft-lbs)
   XR250R
      1986 through 1995.. 25 to 35 Nm (18 to 25 ft-lbs)
      1996 on.. 29 Nm (22 ft-lbs)
   XR400R .... 24 Nm (17 ft-lbs)

Fork cap locknut	
1990 through 1995 XR250R	15 Nm (11 ft-lbs)
1996 and later XR250R	24 Nm (17 ft-lbs)
XR400R	20 Nm (14 ft-lbs)
Steering stem bearing adjusting nut...	See Chapter 1
Steering stem nut	
XR250L	118 Nm (86 ft-lbs)
XR250R	
1986 through 1995	95 to 140 Nm (60 to 101 ft-lbs)
1996 on	98 Nm (72 ft-lbs)
XR400R	98 Nm (72 ft-lbs)
Rear shock absorber upper mounting bolt	
XR250L	45 Nm (33 ft-lbs)
XR250R	
1986 through 1995	40 to 50 Nm (29 to 36 ft-lbs)
1996 on..	44 Nm (33 ft-lbs)
XR400R	44 Nm (33 ft-lbs)
Rear shock absorber lower mounting bolt	
XR250L	35 Nm (25 ft-lbs)
XR250R	
1986 through 1995	30 to 40 Nm (22 to 29 ft-lbs)
1996 on..	44 Nm (33 ft-lbs)
XR400R	44 Nm (33 ft-lbs)
Shock arm to swingarm	
XR250L	70 Nm (51 ft-lbs)
XR250R	
1986 through 1995	60 to 80 Nm (43 to 57 ft-lbs)
1996 on..	70 Nm (51 ft-lbs)
XR400R	70 Nm (51 ft-lbs)
Shock arm to shock link	
XR250L	45 Nm (33 ft-lbs)
XR250R	
1986 through 1995	40 to 50 Nm (29 to 36 ft-lbs)
1996 on..	44 Nm (33 ft-lbs)
XR400R	44 Nm (33 ft-lbs)
Shock link to frame	
XR250L	44 Nm (33 ft-lbs)
XR250R	
1986 through 1995	40 to 50 Nm (29 to 36 ft-lbs)
1996 on..	49 Nm (36 ft-lbs)
XR400R	49 Nm (36 ft-lbs)
Swingarm pivot bolt...	90 Nm (65 ft-lbs)
Engine sprocket bolts..	Not specified
Rear sprocket bolts/nuts	
XR250L	37 Nm (27 ft-lbs)
XR250R	
1986 through 1995	27 to 33 Nm (20 to 24 ft-lbs)**
1996 on..	44 Nm (32 ft-lbs)
XR400R	32 Nm (24 ft-lbs)

*Apply non-permanent thread locking agent to the threads.
**Apply oil to the threads.

1   General information

The steering system on these models consists of a one-piece handlebar and a steering head attached to the front portion of the frame. XR250L models use ball bearings in the steering head; all other models use tapered roller bearings. The front suspension consists of damper rod forks (early models), or cartridge forks (later models). The rear suspension consists of a single shock absorber with concentric coil spring, a swingarm and Honda's Pro-Link suspension linkage. The suspension linkage produces a progressive rising rate effect, where the suspension stiffens as its travel increases. This allows a softer ride over small bumps in the terrain, together with firmer suspension control over large irregularities.

2   Handlebars - removal, inspection and installation

Refer to illustration 2.3

1   The handlebars rest in a bracket integral with the upper triple clamp. If the handlebars must be removed for access to other components, such as the steering head bearings, simply remove the bolts and slip the handlebars off the bracket. It's not necessary to disconnect the throttle, clutch, or decompressor cables, brake hose or the kill switch wire, but it is a good idea to support the assembly with a piece of wire or rope, to avoid unnecessary strain on the cables.

2   If the handlebars are to be removed completely, remove the clutch lever, then refer to Chapter 3 for the throttle housing removal procedure, Chapter 4 for the kill switch removal procedure and Chap-

2.3 Remove the bolts and lift off the upper brackets; on installation, the bracket punch marks face forward (upper arrow) and the punch mark in the handlebar (lower arrow) aligns with the edge of the lower bracket

3.3a On all except XR400R models, the fork cap bolt (upper arrow) is flush with the upper triple clamp; loosen the upper triple clamp bolts (lower arrows)

ter 6 for the brake master cylinder removal procedure.

3   Remove the upper bracket bolts, lift off the brackets and remove the handlebars **(see illustration)**.

4   Check the handlebars and brackets for cracks and distortion and replace them if any problems are found.

5   Place the handlebars in the lower brackets. Line up the punch mark on the handlebar with the parting line of the upper and lower brackets **(see illustration 2.3)**.

6   Install the upper brackets with their punch marks facing forward **(see illustration 2.3)**. Tighten the front bolts, then the rear bolts, to the torque listed in this Chapter's Specifications. **Caution:** *If there's a gap between the upper and lower brackets at the rear after tightening the bolts, don't try to close it by tightening beyond the recommended torque. You'll only crack the brackets.*

3   Front forks - removal and installation

Removal

Refer to illustrations 3.3a, 3.3b, 3.3c, 3.3d and 3.5

1   Support the bike securely upright with its front wheel off the ground so it can't fall over during this procedure. If you're working on a bike with fork air valve caps, use the valves to relieve any accumulated

fork air pressure.

2   Remove the front wheel, unbolt the brake caliper and detach the brake hose retainer from the left fork leg (see Chapter 6). If you're working on an XR250R or XR400R, remove the headlight assembly (see Chapter 4).

3   If you plan to disassemble the forks, loosen the fork cap bolts now **(see illustrations)**. This can be done later, but it will be easier while the forks are securely held in the triple clamps. If you're working on an XR250R equipped with cartridge forks or any XR400R, pry the bottom cover out of the fork tube **(see illustration)**. Loosen the fork bottom bolt or center bolt **(see illustration)**.

4   Detach the speedometer cable and withdraw it from the retainer on the right fork leg.

5   If you're working on an XR250R or XR400R, loosen the upper boot clamps. Loosen the upper and lower triple clamp bolts **(see illustration 3.3a and the accompanying illustration)**.

6   Lower the fork leg out of the triple clamps, twisting it if necessary.

Installation

7   Slide each fork leg into the lower triple clamp.

8   Slide the fork legs up, installing the tops of the tubes into the upper triple clamp. Position the upper end of each fork boot against the lower edge of the upper triple clamp. If you're working on an

3.3b On XR400R models, count the fork ridges exposed above the triple clamp (arrow); on installation, make sure they're the same for both forks

3.3c If you're planning to disassemble a cartridge fork, pry the plug out of the bottom of the fork . . .

3.3d . . . and loosen the bottom bolt or center bolt while the fork is still installed (XR400R center bolt shown)

Chapter 5 Steering, suspension and final drive

5-5

3.5 Loosen the lower triple clamp bolts (arrows) to remove the forks

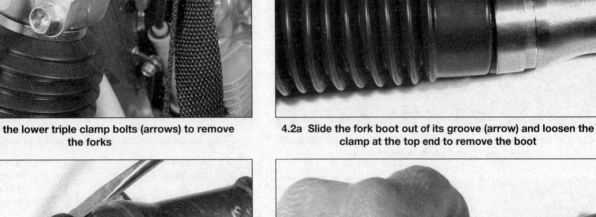

4.2a Slide the fork boot out of its groove (arrow) and loosen the clamp at the top end to remove the boot

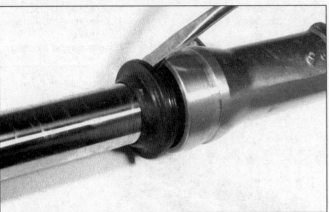

4.2b Pry the dust seal out of the outer fork tube

4.2c Pry the retaining ring out of its groove and slide it off the inner fork tube

4.2d Loosen the Allen bolt in the bottom of the outer fork tube - an air wrench is the easiest way to do this if you have one, but if not, unscrew the bolt with an Allen wrench while the fork cap is still installed; the spring pressure will keep the damper rod from turning inside the fork

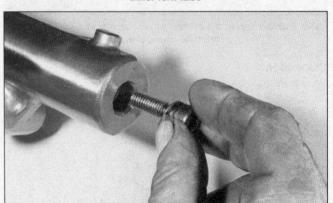

4.2e Remove the Allen bolt and its copper sealing washer; use a new washer on reassembly

---

4 Front forks - disassembly, inspection and reassembly

---

1   Remove the forks following the procedure in Section 3. Work on one fork at a time to prevent mixing up the parts.

Damper rod forks (XR250L and 1986 through 1989 XR250R)

Disassembly

Refer to illustrations 4.2a through 4.2l

2   To disassemble the forks, refer to the accompanying photo sequence **(see illustrations)**.

XR250L or XR250R, position the forks so the top of each tube is flush with the top surface of the upper triple clamp. If you're working on an XR400R, make sure the forks protrude an equal amount above each triple clamp **(see illustration 3.3b)**.
9   Tighten the triple clamp bolts to the torque listed in this Chapter's Specifications.
10   The remainder of installation is the reverse of the removal steps.

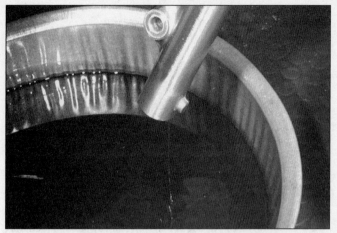

4.2f Let the oil drain from the bottom of the fork; pump the inner fork tube up and down to expel the oil

4.2h Pull the spring out of the fork; its narrow end faces into the fork tube on reassembly

Inspection

Refer to illustration 4.6
3   Clean all parts in solvent and blow them dry with compressed air, if available. Check the inner and outer fork tubes and the damper rod for score marks, scratches, flaking of the chrome and excessive or

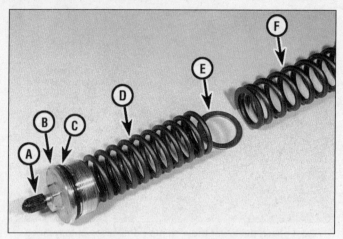

4.2g Unscrew the cap bolt - be careful of spring tension!

A	Air valve cap	D	Short spring (XR250L) -
B	Cap bolt		spacer on XR250R models
C	O-ring	E	Spring seat
		F	Long spring (all models)

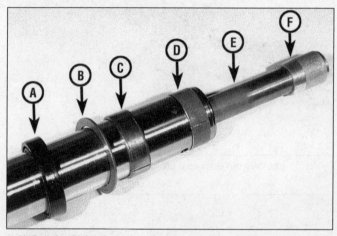

4.2i Pull the fork tubes sharply apart until they separate; the seal, back-up ring and bushings will come off with the inner tube

A	Oil seal	D	Fork tube bushing
B	Back-up ring	E	Damper rod
C	Fork slider bushing	F	Oil lock piece

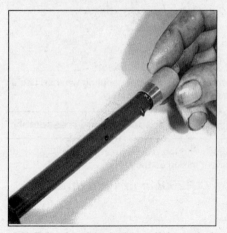

4.2j Take the oil lock piece off the end of the damper rod . . .

4.2k . . . and remove the damper rod from the inner fork tube

4.2l Pry the oil seal out of its bore; be careful not to scratch the seal's seating area in the fork tube

4.6 Replace the Teflon ring on the damper rod if it's worn or damaged

abnormal wear. Look for dents in the tubes and replace them if any are found. Check the fork seal seat for nicks, gouges and scratches. If damage is evident, leaks will occur around the seal-to-outer tube junction. Replace worn or defective parts with new ones.

4   Have the inner fork tube checked for runout at a dealer service department or other repair shop. **Warning:** *If the tube is bent, it should be replaced with a new one. Don't try to straighten it.*

5   Measure the overall length of the fork spring and check it for cracks or other damage. Compare the length to the minimum length listed in this Chapter's Specifications. If it's defective or sagged, replace both fork springs with new ones. Never replace only one spring.

6   Check the Teflon ring on the damper rod for wear or damage and replace it if problems are found **(see illustration)**. **Note:** *Don't remove the ring from the damper rod unless you plan to replace it.*

7   Check the fork tube bushing and fork slider bushing for wear **(see illustration 4.2i)** and replace them if their condition is in doubt.

Reassembly

Refer to illustrations 4.12a, 4.12b, 4.13, 4.14, 4.15a and 4.15b

8   Place the rebound spring over the damper rod and slide the rod assembly into the inner fork tube until it protrudes from the lower end **(see illustrations 4.6 and 4.2i)**.

9   Place the oil lock piece on the base of the damper rod **(see illustration 4.2i)**.

10   Insert the inner fork tube/damper rod assembly into the outer fork tube until the Allen-head bolt (with copper washer) can be threaded into the damper rod from the lower end of the outer tube **(see illustration 4.2e)**. **Note:** *Apply a non-permanent thread locking agent to the threads of the bolt.* Keep the two tubes fairly horizontal so the oil lock piece doesn't fall off the damper rod inside the outer fork tube. Temporarily install the fork spring and cap to place tension on the damper rod so it won't spin inside the fork tube while you tighten the Allen bolt.

11   Tighten the Allen bolt securely, then remove the fork cap and spring.

12   Lubricate the lips and outer diameter of the fork seal with the recommended fork oil (see this Chapter's Specifications). Slide the seal down the inner tube with the lips facing down. Drive the seal into position with a fork seal driver (Honda part no. 07747-0010100 and 07447-0010300 or 07947-1180001) **(see illustration)**. If you don't have access to one of these, it is recommended that you take the fork to a Honda dealer or other repair shop for seal installation. You can also make a substitute tool **(see illustration)**. If you're very careful, the seal can be driven in with a hammer and drift punch. Work around the circumference of the seal, tapping gently on the outer edge of the seal until it's seated **(see illustration 4.2l)**. Be careful - if you distort the seal, you'll have to disassemble the fork and end up taking it to a dealer anyway!

13   Install the retaining ring, making sure it's completely seated in its groove **(see illustration)**.

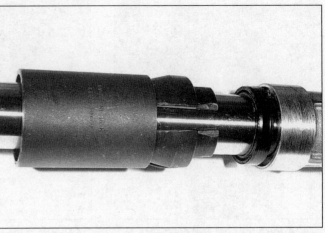

4.12a A seal driver like this one is the ideal way to seat outer tube bushings and install fork seals

4.12b If you don't have a seal driver, a section of pipe can be used the same way the seal driver would be used - as a slide hammer (be sure to tape the ends of the pipe so it doesn't scratch the fork tube)

4.13 Make sure the retaining ring seats in its groove

4.14 Push the dust seal down until it seats in the outer fork tube

4.15a Pour the specified amount of oil into the fork

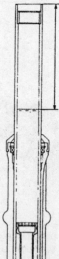

Oil Level

4.15b Measure the oil level in the fork with a stiff tape measure; add or drain oil to correct the level

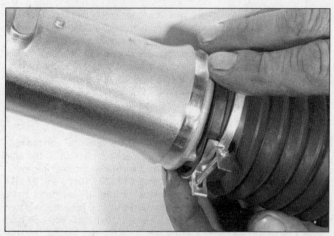

4.18a Loosen the clamps and detach the fork boot

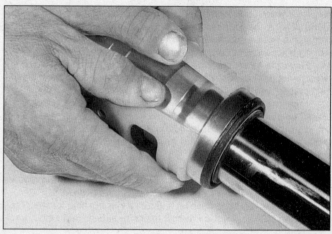

4.18b If there's a plastic guide for the boot, remove it

4.19 Unscrew the cap bolt from the fork (XR400R shown)

4.20a The XR400R spring seat has a slot that allows removal from the damper rod

14   Install the dust seal, making sure it seats completely **(see illustration)**. Pull the fork boot down into its groove on the outer fork tube and secure the upper end to the inner fork tube with the clamping band.

15   Compress the fork fully and add the recommended type and quantity of fork oil listed in this Chapter's Specifications **(see illustration)**. Measure the fork oil level from the top of the fork tube **(see illustration)**. If necessary, add or remove oil to bring it to the proper level.

16   Install the fork spring, with the tightly wound coils facing down (XR250L) or up (XR250R). Install the O-ring and fork cap.

17   Install the fork, following the procedure outlined in Steerion 3.

Tighten the cap bolt after installation to the torque listed in this Chapter's Specifications.

Cartridge forks (1990 and later XR250R, all XR400R)

Disassembly

Refer to illustrations 4.18a, 4.18b, 4.19, 4.20a, 4.20b, 4.20c, 4.20d, 4.23, 4.25, 4.26, 4.27, 4.28 and 4.29

Caution: *Before you start, set the rebound damping adjuster on*

4.20b On all except XR400R models, hold the fork cap with one wrench and loosen the locknut with another

4.20c On XR400R models, hold the damping adjuster flats with one wrench and loosen the locknut with another

4.20d Unscrew the cap bolt from the damper rod

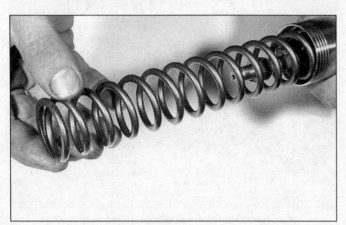

4.23 Pull the spring out of the fork tube

4.25 Pry the dust seal out of its bore

XR400R models to its softest setting to prevent damage to the adjuster needle.

18   Loosen the boot clamps and slide the boot off the fork **(see illustration)**. Remove the plastic guide (if equipped) **(see illustration)**.

19   Release all air pressure from the fork (1990 through 1995 XR250R) and unscrew the fork cap bolt **(see illustration)**. **Warning:** *Air and spring pressure in the fork may cause the cap bolt to shoot out when it's unscrewed. Make sure the cap bolt is not pointed at any yourself or anyone else.*

20   If necessary, squeeze the inner and outer fork tubes together to expose the spring. If you're working on an XR400R, remove the spring seat **(see illustration)**. Hold the cap nut (XR250R) or damping adjuster (XR400R) with one wrench and loosen the locknut away from the cap bolt with another wrench **(see illustrations)**. Unscrew the cap bolt, then the locknut from the damper rod.

21   If you're working on an early XR250R, remove the upper spring seat, the short spring, the lower spring seat and the long spring.

22   If you're working on a later XR250R, remove the spring seat and the fork spring.

23   If you're working on an XR400R, remove the fork spring **(see illustration)**.

24   Place the open (upper) end of the fork over a drain pan, then compress and extend the piston rod several times to pump out the oil.

25   Pry the dust seal out of its bore, taking care not to scratch the fork tube **(see illustration)**.

26   Pry the oil seal retainer out of its groove, again taking care not to scratch the fork tube **(see illustration)**.

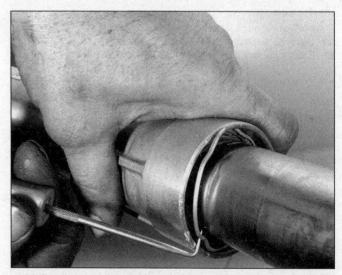

4.26 Pry the retaining ring out with a pointed tool; be careful not to scratch the seal bore

4.27 Unscrew the bottom bolt (XR250R) or center bolt (XR400R); use a new sealing washer on installation

4.28 Pull the piston and rod out of the fork tube

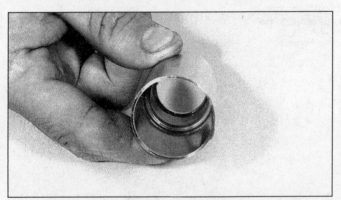

4.29 Remove the oil lock piece; note which way it fits

27   Unscrew the bottom or center bolt and remove the bolt with its sealing washer **(see illustration)**.
28   Pull the piston and rod out of the inner fork tube **(see illustration)**.
29   Hold one fork tube in each hand and pull the tubes apart sharply several times (like a slide hammer) to separate them. Once they're separated, remove the oil lock piece from the inner fork tube **(see illustration)**.

Inspection

Refer to illustrations 4.31a, 4.31b, 4.31c and 4.33
30   Refer to Steps 3 through 5 above to inspect the forks.
31   Check the fork tube bushings as well as the bushing on the fork

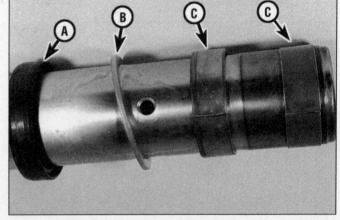

4.31a Don't remove the bushings unless they're worn

A   Oil seal   B   Back-up ring   C   Bushings

piston for wear **(see illustrations)**. If the Teflon coating has worn off 3/4 or more of the surface, exposing the copper, replace the bushings. Don't remove the bushings unless they need to be replaced.
32   Check the ring on the fork piston rod. If it's worn, replace it.
33   Check the bottom bolt or center bolt for wear or damage **(see illustration)**. Replace its O-ring(s) or sealing washer whenever the fork is disassembled.

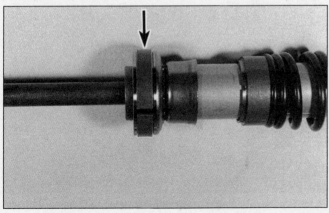

4.31b There's a bushing on the piston (arrow) . . .

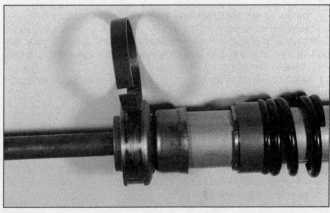

4.31c . . . to remove it, expand it at the slit and slip it off the fork

Chapter 5 Steering, suspension and final drive

5-11

4.33 Check the bottom bolt (XR250R) or center bolt (XR400R) for wear or damage (XR400R center bolt shown)

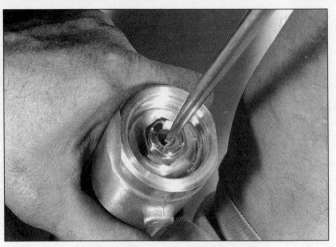

4.59 Turn the screw to adjust damping

Reassembly

1986 through 1995 XR250R

34 Place the rebound spring over the damper rod and slide the rod assembly into the inner fork tube until it protrudes from the lower end.

35 Place the oil lock piece on the base of the damper rod.

36 Insert the inner fork tube/damper rod assembly into the outer fork tube until the Allen-head bolt (with copper washer) can be threaded into the damper rod from the lower end of the outer tube. **Note:** *Apply a non-permanent thread locking agent to the threads of the bolt.* Keep the two tubes fairly horizontal so the oil lock piece doesn't fall off the damper rod inside the outer fork tube. Temporarily install the fork spring and cap to place tension on the damper rod so it won't spin inside the fork tube while you tighten the Allen bolt.

37 Tighten the Allen bolt securely, then remove the fork cap and spring.

38 Lubricate the lips and outer diameter of the fork seal with the recommended fork oil (see this Chapter's Specifications). Slide the seal down the inner tube with the lips facing down. Drive the seal into position with a fork seal driver (Honda part no. 07747-0010100 and 07447-0010300 or 07947-1180001) **(see illustration 4.12a)**. If you don't have access to one of these, it is recommended that you take the fork to a Honda dealer or other repair shop for seal installation. You can also make a substitute tool **(see illustration 4.12b)**. If you're very careful, the seal can be driven in with a hammer and drift punch. Work around the circumference of the seal, tapping gently on the outer edge of the seal until it's seated. Be careful - if you distort the seal, you'll have to disassemble the fork and end up taking it to a dealer anyway!

39 Install the retaining ring, making sure it's completely seated in its groove.

40 Install the dust seal, making sure it seats completely.

41 Compress the fork all the way. Pour half the amount of fork oil listed in this Chapter's Specifications into the inner fork tube. Pour the remaining fork oil slowly into the piston rod until it flows from the breather hole.

42 Slowly pump the piston rod up and down eight to ten times. Compress the fork all the way and leave it sitting upright for five minutes so the oil level can stabilize. Then measure the oil level and compare it to the values listed in this Chapter's Specifications. Add or drain oil as needed. **Warning:** *To prevent unstable handling, make sure the oil level is exactly the same in both forks.* **Note:** *When the air pressure in the fork is at the standard setting, a higher oil level (shorter distance from the top of the fork tube) will have the same effect as increasing the stiffness of the fork spring.*

43 Thread the fork cap locknut all the way onto the fork piston rod.

44 Install the long spring, spring seat, short spring and remaining spring seat.

Thread the fork cap bolt onto the piston rod against the locknut, then tighten the cap and nut against each other to the torque listed in this Chapter's Specifications. Threads the cap bolt into the fork tube (tighten it to the specified torque after installation, when the fork is held in the triple clamps).

45 Make sure the breather holes in the fork boot will face outward when the fork is installed on the bike. Pull the fork boot down into its groove on the outer fork tube and secure the upper end to the inner fork tube with the clamping band.

1996 and later XR250R

Refer to illustration 4.59

46 Wrap the end of the inner fork tube with electrical tape to protect the new oil seal on installation. Coat the lip of the new oil seal with the recommended fork oil. Install the bushings (if removed), back-up ring and oil seal on the inner fork tube **(see illustration 4.31a)**.

47 Install the inner tube in the outer tube. Seat the outer tube bushing in the tube with a seal driver **(see illustration 4.12a)**. Use the same tool to seat the oil seal just below the retainer ring groove.

48 Install the retainer ring and make sure it seats securely in its groove.

49 If the piston rod and its spring were removed from the fork damper, install them.

50 Install the oil lock piece on the bottom of the fork damper, then install the damper in the outer fork tube.

51 Place the outer fork tube in a padded vise, tightening it just enough to keep the fork tube from rotating but not tight enough to distort the fork tube. Place a new sealing washer on the bottom bolt. Coat the threads of the bottom bolt with a non-permanent thread locking agent, then tighten it to the torque listed in this Chapter's Specifications.

52 Look up the amount of fork oil recommended in this Chapter's Specifications. Pour half that amount into a container and place it nearby.

53 Compress the piston rod all the way, then slowly pour fork oil (from the main container, not the container you set aside) into the piston rod until it starts to flow out the end of the damper rod. Once this happens, pour the fluid you set aside into the fork leg.

54 Slowly pump the piston rod up and down eight to ten times. Compress the fork all the way and leave it sitting upright for five minutes so the oil level can stabilize. Then measure the oil level and compare it to the values listed in this Chapter's Specifications. Add or drain oil as needed.

55 Thread the locknut all the way onto the piston rod, then attach a two-foot length of mechanic's wire to the locknut.

56 Pass the fork spring over the length of wire, then use the wire to hold the piston rod up while you position the spring in the fork tube. Pass the spring seat over the wire and position it on the spring.

57 Hold onto the locknut so the piston rod won't drop and remove the wire. Thread the cap bolt onto the rod, then tighten the cap bolt and locknut against each other to the torque listed in this Chapter's Specifications.

58 Thread the cap bolt into the fork tube and tighten it to the torque listed in this Chapter's Specifications.

5.6a Loosen the steering stem nut with a socket . . .

5.6b . . . and unscrew it from the steering stem

5.6c Lift off the washer . . .

59   Install the fork boot over the plastic guide, with its row of breather holes to the outside of the fork. Return the damper screw to its original setting **(see illustration)**.

XR400R

60   If the piston rod was removed from the damper, insert it from the bottom, then thread the locknut all the way onto the top end of the piston rod.
61   Install the damper from the top of the fork tube, then install the oil lock piece from the bottom.
62   Install the fork tube in the fork slider (outer fork tube) and push it all the way down.
63   Place a new sealing washer on the center bolt. Apply non-permanent thread locking agent to the threads of the center bolt, then place it in the bottom of the outer fork tube and thread it into the damper.
64   Seat the outer fork tube bushing with a seal driver **(see illustration 4.12a)**. Place the old bushing (or an equivalent spacer if you're reusing the old bushing) on top of the bushing to protect it.
65   Wrap the upper end of the inner fork tube with electrical tape to protect the oil seal. Coat the seal with fork oil, then slide it onto the fork tube with its marked side upward. Seat the oil seal in its bore with a seal driver **(see illustration 4.12a)**. Install the retaining ring in its groove, then seat the dust seal with the same tool used for the oil seal. Remove the tape from the end of the fork tube.
66   Install the fork spring in the fork tube.
67   Dip a new fork cap O-ring in fork oil and place it on the fork cap. Install the washer on top of the spring, Install the fork cap on the damper rod and thread it down against the locknut. Compress the spring and install the spring seat. Hold the fork cap with one wrench, then tighten the locknut against the fork cap to the torque listed in this Chapter's Specifications.
68   Temporarily thread the fork cap into the fork tube, then compress the fork two to four inches. This is necessary to place pressure on the damper so it won't spin while the center bolt is being tightened. One way to compress the fork is to reinstall both forks in the motorcycle, tighten the upper and lower triple clamp bolts and install the axle (without the wheel). Loop a tie-down strap between the axle and the lower triple clamp and pull it tight to compress the forks. **Caution:** *Don't loop the strap over the oil cooler.*
69   With the fork compressed, tighten the center bolt to the torque listed in this Chapter's Specifications. Unscrew the cap from the fork.
70   Compress the fork all the way. Pour half the amount of fork oil listed in this Chapter's Specifications into the inner fork tube.
71   Slowly pump the piston rod up and down eight to ten times, then slowly push it all the way down.
72   Pour fork oil into the end of the piston rod until it starts to flow out the end of the piston rod, then slowly pump the rod eight to ten times again.
73   Pour the remaining amount of fork oil into the fork tube, then

pump the rod again.
74   Compress the fork all the way and leave it sitting upright for five minutes so the oil level can stabilize. Then measure the oil level and compare it to the values listed in this Chapter's Specifications. **Warning:** *To prevent unstable handling, make sure the oil level is exactly the same in both forks.*
75   Thread the locknut all the way onto the piston rod, then attach a two-foot length of mechanic's wire to the locknut.
76   Pass the fork spring over the length of wire, then use the wire to hold the piston rod up while you position the spring in the fork tube. Position the spring seat on the spring.
77   Hold onto the locknut so the piston rod won't drop and remove the wire. Thread the cap bolt onto the rod, then tighten the cap bolt and locknut against each other to the torque listed in this Chapter's Specifications.
78   Thread the cap bolt into the fork tube. After installing the fork on the motorcycle, tighten it to the torque listed in this Chapter's Specifications.
79   Install the plastic guide for the fork boot so its tab fits into the notch in the outer fork tube. Install the fork boot over the plastic guide, with its clamp screw heads toward the outside.

5   Steering head bearings - replacement

Refer to illustrations 5.6a through 5.6e, 5.7a, 5.7b, 5.8a, 5.8b, 5.9a, 5.9b, 5.10, 5.12a, 5.12b, 5.12c, 5.14, 5.17 and 5.18

1   If the steering head bearing check/adjustment (see Chapter 1) does not remedy excessive play or roughness in the steering head bearings, the entire front end must be disassembled and the bearings and races replaced with new ones.
2   Remove the headlight assembly (see Chapter 4).
3   Remove the speedometer or trip odometer (see Chapter 4). Remove any brake hose or cable retainers from the triple clamp.
4   If you're working on an XR250L, remove the clutch cable bracket and reflectors from the triple clamps.
5   Remove the handlebars (see Section 2), the front wheel and brake caliper (see Chapter 6), the front fender (see Chapter 7) and the forks (see Section 3).
6   Loosen the steering stem nut with a socket **(see illustration)**. Remove the nut, washer, upper triple clamp and lockwasher (if equipped) **(see illustrations)**.
7   Using a spanner wrench of the type described in Chapter 1, remove the stem locknut and bearing cover **(see illustrations)** while supporting the steering head from the bottom.
8   Remove the steering stem and lower triple clamp assembly **(see illustrations)**. If it's stuck, gently tap on the top of the steering stem with a plastic mallet or a hammer and a wood block.
9   Remove the upper bearing **(see illustrations)**.

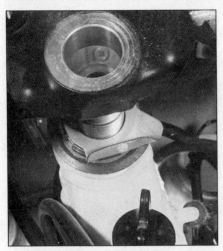

5.6d . . . the upper triple clamp . . .

5.6e . . . and the lockwasher (1986 through 1995 XR250R only)

5.7a Remove the bearing adjusting nut . . .

5.7b . . . and lift off the bearing cover

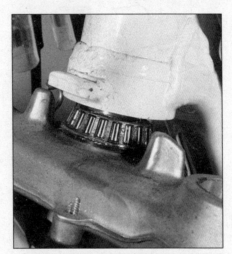

5.8a Lower the steering stem out of the steering head - this is the tapered roller bearing used on XR250R and XR400R models . . .

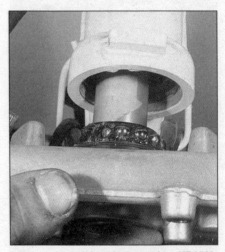

5.8b . . . the ball bearings used on XR250L models can easily pop out of their cages, so be careful not to lose them

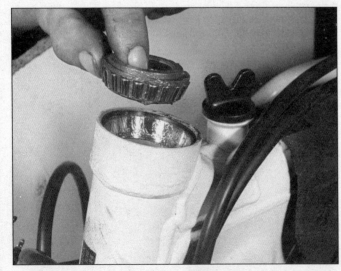

5.9a If the bike has roller bearings, lift the upper bearing out of the steering head . . .

5.9b . . . with ball bearings, lift out the top race and the ball cage

5.10 Steering stem and bearing details (tapered roller bearings)

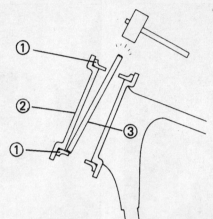

5.12a Drive out the bearing races with a hammer and brass drift

1 Outer races
2 Steering head
3 Brass drift

5.12b Place the drift against the edge of the lower bearing race (arrow) and tap evenly around it to drive the bearing out

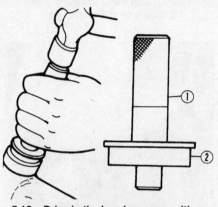

5.12c Drive in the bearing races with a bearing driver or socket the same diameter as the bearing race

1 Bearing driver handle
2 Bearing driver

5.14 Leave the lower bearing and grease seal (arrow) on the steering stem unless you plan to replace them

10   Clean all the parts with solvent and dry them thoroughly, using compressed air, if available **(see illustration)**. If you do use compressed air, don't let the bearings spin as they're dried - it could ruin them. Wipe the old grease out of the frame steering head and bearing races.

11   Examine the races in the steering head for cracks, dents, and pits. If even the slightest amount of wear or damage is evident, the races should be replaced with new ones.

12   To remove the races, drive them out of the steering head with Honda tool no. 07953-MJ10000 or a hammer and drift punch **(see illustrations)**. A slide hammer with the proper internal-jaw puller will also work. Since the races are an interference fit in the frame, installation will be easier if the new races are left overnight in a refrigerator. This will cause them to contract and slip into place in the frame with very little effort. When installing the races, use a bearing driver the same diameter as the outer race **(see illustration)**, or tap them gently into place with a hammer and punch or a large socket. Do not strike the bearing surface or the race will be damaged.

13   Check the bearings for wear. Look for cracks, dents, and pits in the races and flat spots on the bearings. Replace any defective parts with new ones. If a new bearing is required, replace both of them as a set.

14   Check the grease seal under the lower bearing and replace it with a new one if necessary **(see illustration)**.

15   To remove the lower bearing and grease seal from the steering stem, you may need to use a bearing puller, which can be rented. Don't remove this bearing unless it, or the grease seal underneath,

must be replaced. Removal will damage the grease seal, so replace it whenever the bearing is removed.

16   Inspect the steering stem/lower triple clamp for cracks and other damage. Do not attempt to repair any steering components. Replace them with new parts if defects are found.

17   Pack the bearings with high-quality grease (preferably a moly-based grease) **(see illustration)**. Coat the outer races with grease also.

5.17 Work the grease completely into the rollers or balls

18   Install the grease seal and lower bearing onto the steering stem. Drive the lower bearing onto the steering stem using a pipe the same diameter as the bearing inner race **(see illustration)**. Drive the bearing on until it's fully seated.

19   Insert the steering stem/lower triple clamp into the frame head. Install the upper bearing, bearing cover, and adjusting nut. Refer to the adjustment procedure in Chapter 1 and tighten the adjusting nut to the torque listed in the Chapter 1 Specifications.

20   Make sure the steering head turns smoothly and that there's no play in the bearings.

21   Install a new lockwasher (if equipped) and the upper triple clamp. Bend the lockwasher (if equipped) against the upper triple clamp **(see illustration 5.6e)**, then install the washer and nut, but don't tighten it yet.

22   Install the fork tubes and tighten the lower triple clamp bolts to the torque listed in this Chapter's Specifications.

23   Tighten the steering stem nut to the torque listed in this Chapter's Specifications.

24   Tighten the upper triple clamp bolts to the torque listed in this Chapter's Secifications.

25   The remainder of installation is the reverse of removal.

26   Check the alignment of the handlebars and the front wheel. If necessary, loosen the triple clamp bolts, have an assistant hold the front wheel, then turn the handlebars as to align them with the front wheel. Tighten the triple clamp bolts to the torque listed in this Chapters Specifications.

6   Rear shock absorber and suspension linkage - removal, inspection and installation

Removal

Refer to illustrations 6.4, 6.5, and 6.6

1   Support the bike securely so it can't be knocked over during this procedure. Support the swingarm with a jack so the suspension can be raised or lowered as needed for access.

2   Remove the seat, both side covers and the air cleaner case (see Chapters 7 and 3). Cover the carburetor inlet with a rag to keep out dirt. If you're working on an XR400R, remove the sub-frame (see Chapter 7).

3   If you're working on an XR250L or a 1986 through 1995 XR250R, remove the shock reservoir's retaining bands and detach the reservoir from the bike.

4   Remove the upper mounting bolt **(see illustration)**.

5   Unbolt the shock arm from the swingarm **(see illustration)**.

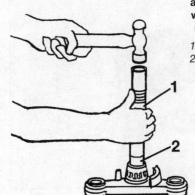

5.18 Drive the grease seal and bearing lower race on with a hollow driver (or an equivalent piece of pipe)

1   *Driver*
2   *Bearing and grease seal*

6   Unbolt the shock link from shock arm and frame **(see illustration)**.

7   Remove the shock from the bike together with the shock arm. On 1996 and later XR250R and all XR400R models, the shock reservoir is solidly attached to the shock, rather than being connected by a hose.

Inspection

Refer to illustrations 6.10a, 6.10b, 6.11a, 6.11b, 6.11c and 6.11d

8   The shock absorber can be overhauled, but it's a complicated procedure that requires special tools not readily available to the typical owner. If inspection reveals problems, have the shock rebuilt by a dealer or motorcycle repair shop.

9   Check the shock absorber for damage and oil leaks. If these can be seen, have the shock overhauled.

10   Check the bearings at the upper end of the shock and in the shock linkage for leaking grease, looseness or signs of damage **(see illustrations)**. If any of these problems can be seen, have the bearing pressed out and a new one pressed in by a dealer or motorcycle repair shop.

11   The pivots at the ends of the shock link and the shock arm consist of needle bearings, sleeves and grease seals **(see illustrations)**.

12   Clean all parts thoroughly with solvent and dry them with compressed air, if available. Check all parts for scoring, damage or heavy corrosion and replace them as necessary. Needle bearing replacement requires a press and a shouldered drift the same diameter as the inside of the bearings. If you don't have these, have the bearings replaced by a Honda dealer or other motorcycle repair shop.

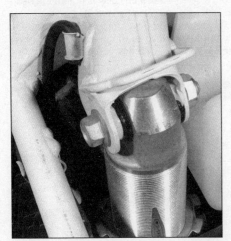

6.4 Remove the bolt and nut from the upper end of the shock absorber (XR250L shown)

6.5 Remove the nut (arrow) and the Allen bolt that secure the shock arm to the swingarm

6.6 Unbolt the shock link from the frame (left arrow) and the shock arm (right arrow); note the directions of the bolt heads

6.10a Check the bearing in the shock absorber
(1997 and earlier shown) . . .

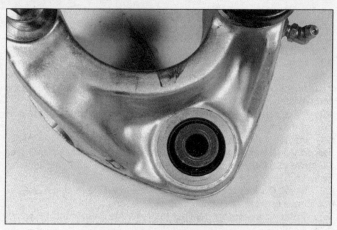

6.10b . . . and in the shock arm
(1997 and earlier shown)

6.11a Pull the covers off the shock arm end pivots . . .

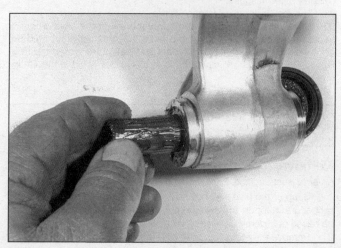

6.11b . . . withdraw the pivot collars . . .

Installation

13   Apply a thin coat of moly-based grease to the sleeves and install them in the needle bearings.

14   The remainder of installation is the reverse of the removal steps. Tighten the bolts to the torques listed in this Chapter's Specifications.

7   Swingarm bearings - check

1   Refer to Chapter 6 and remove the rear wheel, then refer to Sec-

tion 6 and remove the rear shock absorber.

2   Grasp the rear of the swingarm with one hand and place your other hand at the junction of the swingarm and frame. Try to move the rear of the swingarm from side-to-side. Any wear (play) in the bushings should be felt as movement between the swingarm and the frame at the front. The swingarm will actually be felt to move forward and backward at the front (not from side-to-side). If any play is noted, the bearings should be replaced with new ones (see Section 9).

3   Next, move the swingarm up and down through its full travel. It should move freely, without any binding or rough spots. If it doesn't move freely, refer to Section 9 for servicing procedures.

6.11c . . . and inspect the needle bearings

6.11d Shock link details (grease fittings not used on all models)

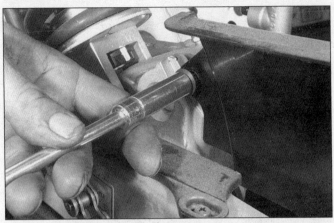

8.4a Unbolt the upper chain slider from the swingarm . . .

8.4b . . . and slip it off its post (if equipped)

8.4c Unbolt the chain guide

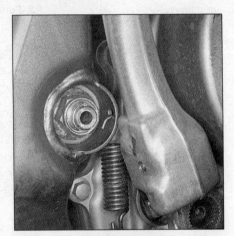

8.5a Unscrew the locknut (1996 and later XR250R shown) . . .

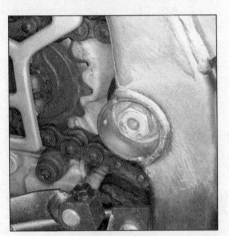

8.5b . . . support the swingarm and pull the pivot bolt out

8   Swingarm - removal and installation

Refer to illustrations 8.4a, 8.4b, 8.4c, 8.5a, 8.5b, 8.5c, 8.6a and 8.6b

1   Refer to Section 10 and disconnect the drive chain.
2   Remove the rear wheel and, on early 250 models, unhook the brake pedal return spring from the swingarm (see Chapter 6). If you're working on a bike with a rear disc brake, detach the brake hose from the retainers on the swingarm and support the caliper so it doesn't hang by the hose.

3   Unbolt the shock linkage from the swingarm (Section 6).
4   Check the chain slider and guide on the swingarm for wear or damage and replace them if necessary **(see illustrations)**.
5   Support the swingarm from below, then unscrew its pivot bolt nut and pull the bolt out **(see illustrations)**.
6   Check the chain slider, chain adjuster plates and brake disc guard

8.5c On later XR250R and all XR400R models, the center section of the swingarm bolt (arrow) passes through the rear of the engine crankcase, rather than through the frame

8.6a Remove the chain slider if it's worn

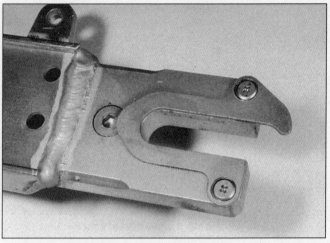

8.6b Check the adjuster plates for wear or damage

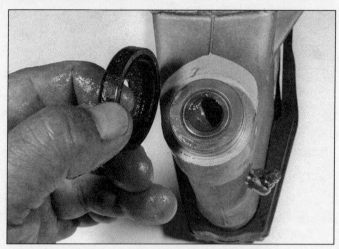

9.2 Pull the dust covers off the swingarm

9.3 Slide the pivot collar out

9.4 Have the needle bearings pressed out and new ones pressed in if they're worn

10.1 Remove the clip from the master link; its open end (arrow) faces rearward when the chain is on the top run; don't forget to reinstall the master link O-rings

for wear or damage **(see illustrations)**. Replace them as necessary.

7   Installation is the reverse of the removal steps, with the following additions:

a) *Tighten the swingarm pivot bolt and nut to the torque listed in this Chapter's Specifications.*
b) *Refer to Chapter 1 and adjust the drive chain and rear brake pedal (drum brake models).*
c) *Lubricate the swingarm bearings through the grease fittings* (see Chapter 1).

9   Swingarm bearings - replacement

Refer to illustrations 9.2, 9.3 and 9.4

1   Refer to Section 8 and remove the swingarm.
2   Pull the dust covers off the swingarm **(see illustration)**.
3   Pull the pivot collar out of the swingarm **(see illustration)**.
4   Check the needle bearings for wear or damage **(see illustration)**. Needle bearing replacement requires a special puller, a press and a shouldered drift the same diameter as the inside of the bearings. If you don't have these, have the bearings replaced by a Honda dealer or other motorcycle repair shop.
5   Coat the bearings and pivot collar with moly-based grease and slip the collar into the swingarm. Install the dust covers.

10   Drive chain - removal, cleaning, inspection and installation

Removal

Refer to illustrations 10.1, 10.3a, 10.3b and 10.3c

1   Turn the rear wheel to place the drive chain master link where it's easily accessible **(see illustration)**.
2   Remove the clip and pull the master link out of the chain.
3   Remove the engine sprocket cover **(see illustrations)**.
4   Lift the chain off the sprockets and remove it from the bike.
5   Check the chain guards on the swingarm and frame for wear or damage and replace them as necessary (see Section 8).

Cleaning and inspection

6   Soak the chain in a high flash point solvent for approximately five or six minutes. Use a brush to work the solvent into the spaces between the links and plates.
7   Wipe the chain dry, then check it carefully for worn or damaged links. Replace the chain if wear or damage is found at any point.
8   Stretch the chain taut and measure its length between the number of pins listed in this Chapter's Specifications. Compare the measured length to the specified value and replace the chain if it's beyond the limit. If the chain needs to be replaced, refer to Section 11 and

10.3a Remove the bolts from the sprocket cover (arrows) (this is an XR250L) . . .

10.3b . . . and this is an XR400R (XR250R similar)

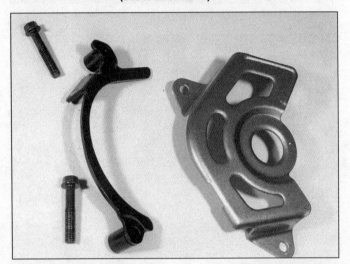

10.3c Sprocket cover and spacer details (XR250R, XR400R)

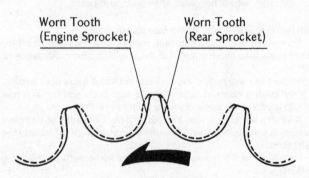

Worn Tooth (Engine Sprocket)   Worn Tooth (Rear Sprocket)

Direction of rotation

11.3 Check the sprockets in the areas indicated to see if they're worn excessively

check the sprockets. If they're worn, replace them also. If a new chain is installed on worn sprockets, it will wear out quickly.

9   Lubricate the chain with spray chain lube compatible with O-ring chains.

Installation

10   Installation is the reverse of the removal steps, with the following additions:

a) Install the master link clip so its opening faces the back of the motorcycle when the master link is in the upper chain run **(see illustration 10.1)**. Be sure to reinstall the O-rings in the master link.

b) Refer to Chapter 1 and adjust the chain.

11 Sprockets - check and replacement

Refer to illustrations 11.3, 11.5a, 11.5b, 11.6 and 11.8

1   Support the bike securely so it can't be knocked over during this procedure.

2   Whenever the sprockets are inspected, the chain should be inspected also and replaced if it's worn. Installing a worn chain on new sprockets will cause them to wear quickly.

3   If you're working on an XR250L, remove the engine sprocket cover **(see illustration 10.3a)**. The sprocket is visible through the

11.5a The XR250L driven sprocket is attached to the damper hub with self-locking nuts

cover slots on XR250R and XR400R models. Check the teeth on the engine sprocket and rear sprocket for wear **(see illustration)**.

4   If the sprockets are worn, remove the chain (Section 10) and the rear wheel (see Chapter 6).

5   Remove the sprocket from the damper hub (XR250L) or rear

11.5b The XR250R and XR400R driven sprocket is attached to the wheel hub with Allen bolts and nuts

11.6 The engine sprocket is secured by a plate and two bolts; the Out mark on the plate faces away from the engine

wheel hub (XR250R and XR400R) **(see illustrations)**.

6   To remove the engine sprocket, remove two bolts and lift off the retainer plate **(see illustration)**. Lift the sprocket off the transmission shaft.

7   Inspect the seal behind the engine sprocket. If it has been leaking, pry it out (taking care not to scratch the seal bore) and tap in a new seal with a socket the same diameter as the seal.

8   If you're working on an XR250L, inspect the rubber dampers (cush drive) and replace them if they're damaged or deteriorated **(see illustration)**.

9   Installation is the reverse of the removal steps, with the following additions:

 a) *Tighten the driven sprocket bolts and nuts to the torque listed in this Chapter's Specifications. Tighten the engine sprocket bolts securely, but don't overtighten them and strip the threads*

 b) *Install the master link clip so its opening faces the back of the motorcycle when the master link is in the upper chain run* **(see illustration 10.1)**.

 c) *Refer to Chapter 1 and adjust the chain.*

11.8 Replace the XR250L rubber dampers if they're damaged or deteriorated

Chapter 6
Brakes, wheels and tires

Contents

Specifications

Disc brakes

Brake fluid type	See Chapter 1
Brake pad minimum thickness	See Chapter 1
Front disc thickness	
XR250L	
Standard	3.5 mm (0.14 inch)
Limit	3.0 mm (0.12 inch)*
XR250R, XR400R	
Standard	3.0 mm (0.12 inch)
Limit	2.5 mm (0.10 inch)*
Rear disc thickness	
Standard	4.5 mm (0.18 inch)
Limit	4.0 mm (0.16 inch)*
Disc runout limit	
XR250L, 1996 and later XR250R, XR400R	0.25 mm (0.010 inch)
1990 through 1995 XR250R	0.15 mm (0.006 inch)

* Refer to marks stamped into the disc (they supersede information printed here)

Drum brakes

Brake lining minimum thickness	See Chapter 1
Brake pedal height	See Chapter 1
Drum diameter (1986 through 1989 XR250R)	
Standard	110 mm (4.33 inches)
Wear limit	111 mm (4.37 inches)*

* Refer to marks cast into the drum (they supersede information printed here)

Wheels and tires

Tire pressures	See Chapter 1
Tire tread depth	See Chapter 1
Axle runout limit	0.2 mm (0.008 inch)
Wheel out-of-round and lateral runout limit (front and rear)..................	2.0 mm (0.08 inch)

Torque specifications

Front axle	
XR250L	65 Nm (47 ft-lbs)
XR250R	
1986 through 1995...	50 to 80 Nm (36 to 58 ft-lbs)
1996 on..	74 Nm (54 ft-lbs)
XR400R	88 Nm (65 ft-lbs)
Front axle holder nuts...	13 Nm (108 in-lbs)
Rear axle nut	
XR250L	95 Nm (69 ft-lbs)
XR250R	
1986 through 1995...	80 to 110 Nm (58 to 80 ft-lbs)
1996 on..	93 Nm (69 ft-lbs)
XR400R	88 Nm (65 ft-lbs)
Front caliper	
XR250L	
Caliper bracket bolts	
1991 and 1992..	25 Nm (18 ft-lbs)
1993 on...	30 Nm (22 ft-lbs)
Caliper pad pin..	18 Nm (13 ft-lbs)
Pad pin plug...	2.5 Nm (22 inch-lbs)
Slider pin to bracket...	13 Nm (108 in-lbs) (1)
Slider pin to caliper..	23 Nm (17 ft-lbs) (1)
XR250R (1986 through 1995)	
Caliper bracket bolts	Not specified
Pad pin(s)...	15 to 20 Nm (7 to 14 ft-lbs)
Pad pin plug(s)..	2 to 3 Nm (17 to 26 inch-lbs)
Upper slider pin	20 to 25 Nm (14 to 18 ft-lbs) (1)
Lower slider pin to bracket...	15 to 20 Nm (7 to 14 ft-lbs) (1)
XR250R (1996 on)	
Caliper bracket bolts..	30 Nm (22 ft-lbs) (1)
Slider pin to caliper	13 Nm (108 in-lbs) (1)
Slider pin to caliper bracket...	23 Nm (17 ft-lbs)
Pad pins...	18 Nm (13 ft-lbs)
Pad pin plugs..	2.5 Nm (30 inch-lbs)
XR400R	
Caliper bracket bolts..	30 Nm (22 ft-lbs) (2)
Slider pin to caliper	23 Nm (17 ft-lbs) (1)
Slider pin to caliper bracket...	23 Nm (17ft-lbs) (1)
Pad pins...	18 Nm (13 ft-lbs)
Pad pin plugs..	2.5 Nm (30 inch-lbs)
Rear caliper	
Allen head slider pin to caliper	28 Nm (20 ft-lbs) (1)
Slider pin to bracket	13 Nm (108 in-lbs) (1)
Pad pins...	18 Nm (13 ft-lbs)
Pad pin plugs...	2.5 Nm (30 inch-lbs)
Brake line banjo fitting bolts	35 Nm (25 ft-lbs)
Brake disc-to-wheel bolts	
XR250L	
Front..	20 Nm (14 ft-lbs) (2)
Rear	43 Nm (31 ft-lbs) (2)
XR250R	
Front	
1986 through 1989......................................	14 to 16 Nm (10 to 12 ft-lbs)
1990 through 1995......................................	18 to 22 Nm (13 to 16 ft-lbs)
1996 on...	20 Nm (14 ft-lbs) (2)
Rear	
1989 through 1995......................................	40 to 45 Nm (29 to 33 ft-lbs)
1996 on...	42 Nm (31 ft-lbs) (2)
XR400R	
Front..	20 Nm (14 ft-lbs) (2)
Rear	42 Nm (31 ft-lbs) (2)
Rear drum brake arm pinch bolt...	8 to 12 Nm (72 to 108 inch-lbs)

Front master cylinder
  Mounting bolts
    XR250L .... 10 Nm (84 inch-lbs)
    XR250R
      1986 through 1995 .... Not specified
      1996 on .... 9 Nm (78 inch-lbs)
    XR400R .... Not specified
  Brake lever pivot bolt
    XR250L .... Not specified
    XR250R, XR400R .... 6 Nm (51 inch-lbs)
  Brake lever pivot bolt locknut
    XR250L .... Not specified
    XR250R, XR400R .... 6 Nm (51 inch-lbs)
Rear master cylinder mounting bolts
  XR250L, 1986 through 1995 XR250R .... Not specified
  1996 and later XR250R .... 14 Nm (120 in-lbs) (1)
  XR400R .... 14 Nm (120 in-lbs) (2)
Pedal pinch bolt (XR250L) .... Not specified

1. *Apply non-permanent thread locking agent to the threads.*
2. *Replace the bolts with new ones whenever they're removed.*

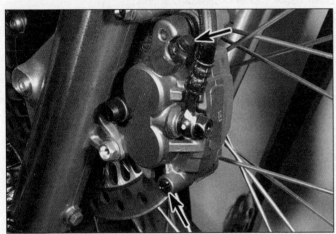

2.3a The front caliper's pad pin plug is at the bottom (lower arrow) and the bleed valve is at the top (upper arrow)

2.3b The rear caliper's pad pin plug is at the rear (A); the caliper mounting bolts (B) also secure a shield on XR250R and XR400R models

1 General information

The front wheel on all motorcycles covered by this manual is equipped with a hydraulic disc using a dual-piston pin slider caliper. The rear wheel on 1986 through 1989 XR250R models is equipped with a drum brake. The rear wheel on all other models is equipped with a hydraulic disc brake using a single-piston pin slider caliper.

All models are equipped with spoked steel wheels. **Caution:** *Disc brake components rarely require disassembly. Do not disassemble components unless absolutely necessary. If any hydraulic brake line connection in the system is loosened, the entire system should be disassembled, drained, cleaned and then properly filled and bled upon reassembly. Do not use solvents on internal brake components. Solvents will cause seals to swell and distort. Use only clean brake fluid, brake system cleaner or alcohol for cleaning. Use care when working with brake fluid as it can injure your eyes and it will damage painted surfaces and plastic parts.*

2 Brake pads - replacement

Refer to illustrations 2.3a, 2.3b, 2.4a, 2.4b, 2.5a, 2.5b, 2.6a and 2.6b
Warning: *The dust created by the brake system may contain asbestos, which is harmful to your health. Honda hasn't used asbestos in brake parts for a number of years, but aftermarket parts may contain it. Never blow it out with compressed air and don't inhale any of it. An approved filtering mask should be worn when working on the brakes.*

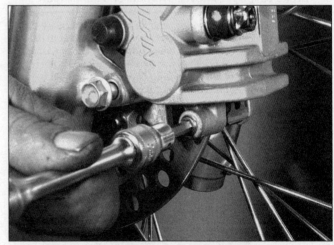

2.4a Unscrew the pad retaining pin; this is a front caliper . . .

1   Support the bike securely upright.
2   The caliper doesn't need to be removed for pad replacement.
3   Unscrew the plug that covers the pad retaining pin (two pins on 1986 through 1988 XR250R models) **(see illustrations)**.
4   Unscrew the pad retaining pin(s) with an Allen wrench **(see illustrations)**.

2.4b ... and this is a rear caliper

2.5a Pull out the pad retaining pin (arrow) and lift out the brake pad farthest from the piston ...

2.5b ... then pull the pin out the rest of the way and remove the remaining pad (caliper removed for clarity)

5   Pull the pads out of the caliper (**see illustrations**).
6   Inspect the pad spring (**see illustrations**) and replace it if it's rusted or damaged.
7   Refer to Chapter 1 and inspect the pads.
8   Check the condition of the brake disc (see Section 4). If it's in need of machining or replacement, follow the procedure in that Section to remove it. If it's okay, deglaze it with sandpaper or emery cloth, using a swirling motion.
9   Remove the cover from the master cylinder reservoir and siphon out some fluid. Push the pistons into the caliper as far as possible, while checking the master cylinder reservoir to make sure it doesn't overflow. If you can't depress the pistons with thumb pressure, try using a C-clamp. If the pistons stick, remove the caliper and overhaul it as described in Section 3.
10   Install the spring (if removed), new pads and the retaining pin. Tighten the retaining pin to the torque listed in this Chapter's Specifications. Install the plug over the retaining pin and tighten it to the torque listed in this Chapter's Specifications.
11   Operate the brake lever or pedal several times to bring the pads into contact with the disc. Check the operation of the brakes carefully before riding the motorcycle.

---

3   Brake caliper - removal, overhaul and installation

Warning: *If a caliper indicates the need for an overhaul (usually due to leaking fluid or sticky operation), all old brake fluid flushed from the system. Also, the dust created by the brake system may contain asbestos, which is harmful to your health. Never blow it out with compressed air and don't inhale any of it. An approved filtering mask should be worn when working on the brakes. Do not, under any circumstances, use*

petroleum-based solvents to clean brake parts. Use clean brake fluid, brake system cleaner or denatured alcohol only!
Note: *If you are removing the caliper only to remove the front forks or swingarm, don't disconnect the hose from the caliper.*

Removal

1   Support the bike securely upright. **Note:** *If you're planning to disassemble the caliper, read through the overhaul procedure, paying particular attention to the steps involved in removing the pistons with compressed air. If you don't have access to an air compressor, you can use the bike's hydraulic system to force the pistons out instead. To do this, remove the pads and pump the brake lever or pedal. If one front caliper piston comes out before the other, push it back into its bore and hold it in with a C-clamp while pumping the brake lever to remove the remaining piston.*

Front caliper
Refer to illustration 3.2

2   **Note:** *Remember, if you're just removing the caliper to remove the forks, ignore this step.* Disconnect the brake hose from the caliper. Remove the brake hose banjo fitting bolt and separate the hose from the caliper (**see illustration**). Discard the sealing washers. Plug the end of the hose or wrap a plastic bag tightly around it to prevent excessive fluid loss and contamination.
3   Unscrew the caliper mounting bolts and lift it off the fork leg, being careful not to strain or twist the brake hose if it's still connected.

Rear caliper
Refer to illustrations 3.6a and 3.6b

4   Loosen the rear axle nut and disengage the drive chain from the sprocket (see Chapters 1 and 5). If you're working on an XR250R or

2.6a The front caliper's pad spring fits under the pad pin like this ...

2.6b ... and the rear caliper's pad spring fits like this

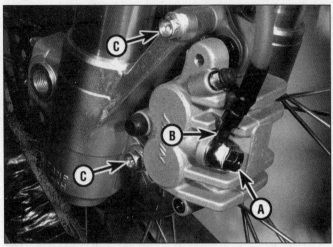

3.2 Unscrew the banjo fitting bolt if you're planning to remove the caliper for overhaul; remove the mounting bolts to detach the caliper from the fork leg - on installation, be sure the brake hose fits in the alignment notch

a) Brake hose banjo bolt
b) Brake hose alignment notch
c) Caliper mounting bolts

XR400R, remove the caliper shield **(see illustration 2.3b)**.

5　**Note:** *If you're only removing the caliper to remove the swingarm, ignore this step.* Disconnect the brake hose from the caliper. Remove the brake hose banjo fitting bolt and separate the hose from the caliper. Discard the sealing washers. Plug the end of the hose or wrap a plastic bag tightly around it to prevent excessive fluid loss and contamination.

6　Unscrew the caliper mounting Allen bolt and slide the caliper off the bracket pin **(see illustrations)**. Lower the caliper, being careful not to strain or twist the brake hose if it's still connected.

Overhaul

Refer to illustrations 3.8, 3.9a, 3.9b, 3.13, 3.16a, 3.16b and 3.16c

7　Remove the brake pads and anti-rattle spring from the caliper (see Section 2, if necessary). Clean the exterior of the caliper with denatured alcohol or brake system cleaner.

8　If you're working on a front caliper, separate it from the bracket **(see illustration)**.

9　Pack a shop rag into the space that holds the brake pads. Use compressed air, directed into the caliper fluid inlet, to remove the piston(s) **(see illustrations)**. Use only enough air pressure to ease the piston(s) out of the bore. If a piston is blown out forcefully, even with the rag in place, it may be damaged. **Warning:** *Never place your fingers in front of the piston in an attempt to catch or protect it when applying compressed air, as serious injury could occur.*

10　Using a wood or plastic tool, remove the piston seals. Metal tools may cause bore damage.

3.6a Unscrew the Allen-head caliper pin . . .

3.6b . . . then pivot the caliper up off the disc and slide it clear of the bracket

3.8 Slide the front caliper off the bracket

3.9a Front caliper piston and seal details (one of two pistons shown); the metal cap on the end of the piston (arrow) faces out of the bore

3.9b Rear caliper details

1　Pin boot　　3　Pad spring　　5　Piston seal
2　Caliper body　4　Dust seal　　6　Piston

3.13 Fit the seals all the way into their grooves

3.16a Install the boot in the front caliper with its wide end facing the same direction as the pistons (arrow)

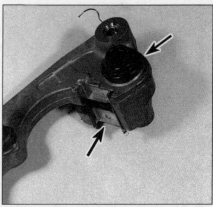

3.16b Install the boot in the front caliper bracket with its wide end facing the same direction as the pin (right arrow) and install the spring in the bracket notch (left arrow)

11   Clean the pistons and the bores with denatured alcohol, clean brake fluid or brake system cleaner and blow dry them with filtered, unlubricated compressed air. Inspect the surfaces of the pistons for nicks and burrs and loss of plating. Check the caliper bores, too. If surface defects are present, the caliper must be replaced. If the caliper is in

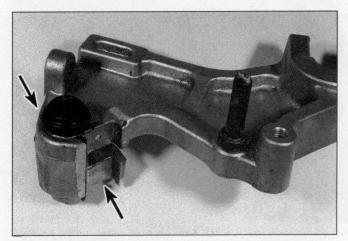

3.16c Install the boot in the rear caliper bracket with its wide end facing the same direction as the pin (left arrow) and install the spring in the bracket notch (right arrow)

3.18 Be sure the brake hose fits against the stopper (XR250L) or in the caliper bracket notch (XR250R and XR400R) when the banjo bolt is tightened

bad shape, the master cylinder should also be checked.
12   If you have precision measuring equipment, measure the diameter of the piston(s) and bore(s) and compare the measurements to the values listed in this Chapter's Specifications.
13   Lubricate the piston seals with clean brake fluid and install them in their grooves in the caliper bore **(see illustration)**. Make sure they seat completely and aren't twisted.
14   Lubricate the dust seals with clean brake fluid and install them in their grooves, making sure they seat correctly.
15   Lubricate the piston (both pistons on front calipers) with clean brake fluid and install it into the caliper bore. Using your thumbs, push each piston all the way in, making sure it doesn't get cocked in the bore.
16   Pull the old pin boots out of the caliper and bracket. Coat new ones with silicone grease and install them, making sure they seat completely **(see illustration 3.9b and the accompanying illustrations)**.
17   Make sure the pad springs are in position on the caliper brackets **(see illustrations 3.16b and 3.16c)**.

Installation

Refer to illustration 3.18
18   Installation is the reverse of the removal steps, with the following additions:

a) *Apply silicone grease to the slider pins on the caliper bracket and caliper.*
b) *Space the pads apart so the disc will fit between them.*
c) *Use new sealing washers on the brake hose fitting. If you're working on a front caliper, position the brake hose fitting in the caliper notches (see illustration 3.2). If you're working on a rear caliper, position the brake hose against the stop on the swingarm* **(see illustration)**.
d) *Tighten the caliper mounting bolt(s) and brake line banjo bolt to the torque listed in this Chapter's Specifications.*
e) *If you're working on a rear caliper, engage the drive chain with the sprocket and adjust chain slack (see Chapter 1).*

19   Fill the master cylinder with the recommended brake fluid (see Chapter 1) and bleed the system (see Section 10). Check for leaks.
20   Check the operation of the brakes carefully before riding the motorcycle.

---

4   Brake disc(s) - inspection, removal and installation

Inspection

Refer to illustrations 4.3 and 4.4
1   Support the bike securely upright. Place a jack beneath the bike and raise the wheel being checked off the ground. Be sure the bike is securely supported so it can't be knocked over.

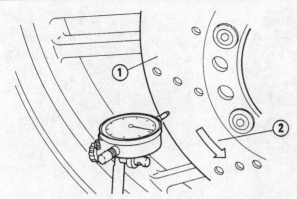

4.3 Set up a dial indicator against the brake disc (1) and turn the disc in its normal direction of rotation (2) to measure runout

2   Visually inspect the surface of the disc(s) for score marks and other damage. Light scratches are normal after use and won't affect brake operation, but deep grooves and heavy score marks will reduce braking efficiency and accelerate pad wear. If the discs are badly grooved they must be machined or replaced.
3   To check disc runout, mount a dial indicator to a fork leg or the swingarm, with the plunger on the indicator touching the surface of the disc **(see illustration)**. Slowly turn the wheel and watch the indicator needle, comparing your reading with the limit listed in this Chapter's Specifications. If the runout is greater than allowed, check the hub bearings for play (see Chapter 1). If the bearings are worn, replace them and repeat this check. If the disc runout is still excessive, the disc will have to be replaced.
4   The disc must not be machined or allowed to wear down to a thickness less than the minimum allowable thickness, listed in this Chapter's Specifications. The thickness of the disc can be checked with a micrometer. If the thickness of the disc is less than the minimum allowable, it must be replaced. The minimum thickness is also stamped into the disc **(see illustration)**.

Removal

5   Remove the wheel (see Section 11). **Caution:** *Don't lay the wheel down and allow it to rest on the disc - the disc could become warped. Set the wheel on wood blocks so the disc doesn't support the weight of the wheel.*
6   Mark the relationship of the disc to the wheel, so it can be installed in the same position. Remove the nuts or Allen head bolts that retain the disc to the wheel **(see illustration 4.4)**. Loosen the bolts a little at a time, in a criss-cross pattern, to avoid distorting the disc. **Note:** *Allen head bolts must be replaced with new ones on installation.*

Installation

7   Position the disc on the wheel, aligning the previously applied matchmarks (if you're reinstalling the original disc). On models so equipped, make sure the arrow (stamped on the disc) marking the direction of rotation is pointing in the proper direction **(see illustration 4.4)**.
8   If the brake disc is secured by Allen head bolts, use new ones. Apply a non-hardening thread locking compound to the threads of the nuts or bolts. Install the nuts or bolts, tightening them a little at a time in a criss-cross pattern, until the torque listed in this Chapter's Specifications is reached. Clean off all grease from the brake disc using acetone or brake system cleaner.
9   Install the wheel.
10   Operate the brake lever or pedal several times to bring the pads into contact with the disc. Check the operation of the brakes carefully before riding the motorcycle.

5   Brake drum and shoes - removal, inspection and installation

Warning: *The dust created by the brake system may contain asbestos, which is harmful to your health (Honda hasn't used asbestos in brake parts for a number of years, but aftermarket parts may contain it). Never blow it out with compressed air and don't inhale any of it. An approved filtering mask should be worn when working on the brakes.*

Removal

Refer to illustration 5.2
1   Remove the wheel (see Section 11).
2   Lift the brake panel out of the wheel **(see illustration)**.

Inspection

Refer to illustrations 5.3, 5.6, 5.9, 5.10, 5.11, 5.12a and 5.12b
3   Check the brake drum for wear or damage. Measure the diameter at several points with a drum micrometer (or have this done by a Honda dealer). If the measurements are uneven (indicating that the drum is out-of-round) or if there are scratches deep enough to snag a fingernail, replace the drum. The drum must also be replaced if the diameter is greater than that cast inside the drum **(see illustration)**. Honda recommends against resurfacing brake drums.
4   Check the linings for wear, damage and signs of contamination from road dirt or water. If the linings are visibly defective, replace them.
5   Measure the thickness of the lining material (just the lining material, not the metal backing) and compare with the value listed in the Chapter 1 Specifications. Replace the shoes if the material is worn to the minimum or less.

4.4 Marks on the disc indicate the minimum thickness (left arrow) and direction of rotation (right arrow)

5.2 Lift the brake panel out of the drum

5.3 The maximum diameter is cast inside the brake drum

5.6 Spread the shoes and fold them into a V to release the spring tension

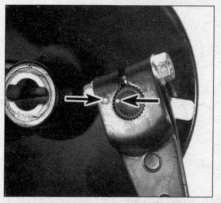

5.9 Look for alignment marks on the brake arm and cam (arrows); make your own marks if you can't see any

5.10 Remove the pinch bolt and nut and take the brake arm off the cam

5.11 Remove the wear indicator; the wide spline on the wear indicator fits into a wide groove in the brake cam

5.12a Replace the brake cam seal if it's worn or damaged

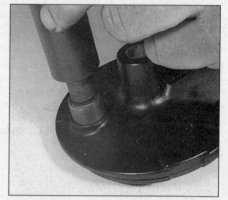

5.12b Pry out the old seal, then press a new one in with a socket the same diameter as the seal

6   To remove the shoes, fold them toward each other to release the spring tension and lift them off the brake panel **(see illustration)**.

7   Check the ends of the shoes where they contact the brake cam and anchor pin. Replace the shoes if there's visible wear.

8   Check the brake cam and anchor pin for wear and damage. The brake cam can be replaced separately; the brake panel must be replaced if the anchor pin is unserviceable.

9   Look for alignment marks on the brake arm and anchor pin **(see illustration)**. Make your own if they aren't visible.

10   Remove the pinch bolt and nut and pull the brake arm off the cam **(see illustration)**.

11   Lift off the wear indicator **(see illustration)**. Pull the brake cam out of the brake panel.

12   Check the brake cam dust seal for wear and damage **(see illustration)**. To replace it, pry it out of the brake panel and tap in a new one using a socket or seal driver the same diameter as the seal **(see illustration)**.

Installation

Refer to illustrations 5.16 and 5.17

13   Apply high-temperature brake grease to the brake cam, the anchor pin and the ends of the springs.

14   Install the cam through the dust seal. Install the wear indicator **(see illustration 5.11)**. Align its wide groove with the wide spline in the cam.

15   Install the brake arm on the cam, aligning the punch marks. Tighten the nut and bolt to the torque listed in this Chapter's Specifications.

16   Hook the ends of the springs to the shoes. Position the shoes in a V on the brake panel, then fold them down into position **(see illustration)**. Make sure the ends of the shoes fit correctly on the cam and the anchor pin.

17   The remainder of installation is the reverse of the removal steps. Make sure the notch in the brake panel aligns with the boss on the swingarm **(see illustration)**.

6   Front brake master cylinder - removal, overhaul and installation

1   If the master cylinder is leaking fluid, or if the lever doesn't produce a firm feel when the brake is applied, and bleeding the brakes doesn't help, master cylinder overhaul is recommended. Before disassembling the master cylinder, read through the entire procedure and

5.16 The assembled brakes should look like this

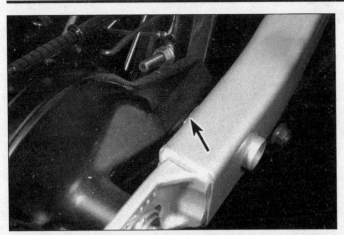

5.17 Be sure the protrusion on the swingarm fits into the notch in the brake panel (arrow)

6.5a Remove the banjo bolt (right arrow) and disconnect the brake line from the master cylinder; on installation, use new sealing washers, position the neck of the brake hose within the stoppers (left arrow) and be sure the UP mark on the clamp is upright

Removal

Refer to illustrations 6.5a and 6.5b

3   Place rags beneath the master cylinder to protect the paint in case of brake fluid spills.

4   If you're working on an XR250L, disconnect the wires from the brake light switch. If you're planning to unscrew the rearview mirror from the master cylinder, do it now while the master cylinder is still attached to the handlebar.

5   Brake fluid will run out of the upper brake hose during this step, so either have a container handy to place the end of the hose in, or have a plastic bag and rubber band handy to cover the end of the hose. The objective is to prevent excess loss of brake fluid, fluid spills and system contamination. Remove the banjo fitting bolt **(see illustrations)** and separate the brake hose from the master cylinder.

6   Remove the master cylinder mounting bolts. Take the master cylinder off the handlebar.

7   Remove the master cylinder mounting bolts and separate the master cylinder from the handlebar together with the hand shield.

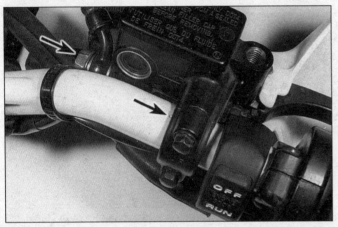

6.5b On XR250L models, the banjo fitting bolt is at the end of the master cylinder (left arrow); on all models, align the split in the clamp with the punch mark on the handlebar (right arrow)

make sure that you have the correct rebuild kit. Also, you will need some new, clean brake fluid of the recommended type, some clean rags and internal snap-ring pliers. **Caution:** *To prevent damage to the paint from spilled brake fluid, always cover the gas tank when working on the master cylinder. Immediately rinse off any spilled brake fluid with plenty of clean water.*

2   **Caution:** *Disassembly, overhaul and reassembly of the brake master cylinder must be done in a spotlessly clean work area to avoid contamination and possible failure of the brake hydraulic system components.*

Overhaul

Refer to illustrations 6.9a, 6.9b, 6.10, 6.11a, 6.11b and 6.13

8   Remove the master cylinder cover, retainer (if equipped) and diaphragm (see Chapter 1).

9   Remove the locknut (and bushing on XR250R and XR400R) from the underside of the lever pivot bolt, then unscrew the bolt **(see illustrations)**. Remove the hand protector (it's held on by the pivot bolt).

10   The lever on XR250R and XR400R models is equipped with a spring **(see illustration)**. This doesn't have to be removed to remove

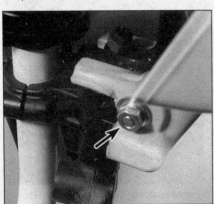

6.9a Remove the locknut (arrow) and the bushing (if equipped) . . .

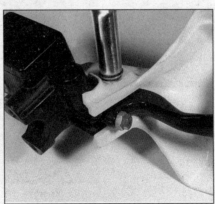

6.9b . . . and unscrew the pivot bolt to detach the lever

6.10 Remove the lever and spring from the master cylinder

6.11a Remove the snap-ring from the master cylinder bore

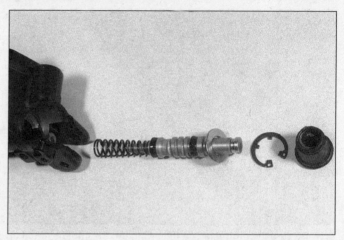

6.11b Remove the piston assembly from the bore

6.13 Make sure the baffle plate is
securely retained in the bottom
of the reservoir

7.4a On XR250L models, remove the
cotter pin and clevis pin (right arrow) to
detach the master cylinder from the pedal;
the pedal is secured to its pivot shaft
by a pinch bolt (left arrow)

7.4b On XR250R and XR400R models,
remove the cotter pin and clevis pin (right
arrow) to detach the master cylinder from
the pedal; the pedal itself is secured by a
cotter pin and washer (left arrow)

the hydraulic components, but make sure it doesn't get lost.

11   Using snap-ring pliers, remove the snap-ring and slide out the piston assembly and the spring (see illustrations). Lay the parts out in the proper order to prevent confusion during reassembly.

12   Clean all of the parts with brake system cleaner (available at auto parts stores), isopropyl alcohol or clean brake fluid. **Warning:** *Do not, under any circumstances, use a petroleum-based solvent to clean brake parts. If compressed air is available, use it to dry the parts thoroughly (make sure it's filtered and unlubricated).* Check the master cylinder bore and piston for corrosion, scratches, nicks and score marks. If damage or wear can be seen, the master cylinder must be replaced with a new one. If the master cylinder is in poor condition, then the caliper should be checked as well.

13   Check the baffle plate in the bottom of the reservoir to make sure it's securely held by its retainer (see illustration).

14   Honda supplies a new piston in its rebuild kits. If the cup seals are not installed on the new piston, install them, making sure the lips face away from the lever end of the piston (see illustration 6.11b). Use the new piston regardless of the condition of the old one.

15   Before reassembling the master cylinder, soak the piston and the rubber cup seals in clean brake fluid for ten or fifteen minutes. Lubricate the master cylinder bore with clean brake fluid, then carefully insert the piston and related parts in the reverse order of disassembly. Make sure the lips on the cup seals do not turn inside out when they are slipped into the bore.

16   Depress the piston, then install the snap-ring (make sure the snap-ring is properly seated in the groove with the sharp edge facing

out) (see illustration 6.11a). Install the rubber dust boot (make sure the lip is seated properly in the piston groove).

17   Install the brake lever, hand shield and pivot bolt bushing (if equipped). Tighten the pivot bolt locknut.

7.6a Remove the mounting bolts (lower arrows) to detach the
master cylinder from the frame; on installation, use new sealing
washers on the banjo bolt and be sure the neck of the
fluid hose fits between the stoppers (upper arrow)

7.6b The fluid reservoir is secured by a single bolt

7.7a Remove the snap-ring . . .

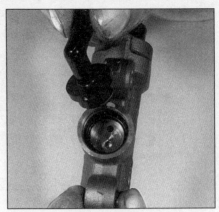

7.7b . . . then work the fluid feed fitting free of its bore and remove the O-ring

Installation

18   Installation is the reverse of the removal steps, with the following additions:

a) *Attach the master cylinder to the handlebar. Align the upper gap between the master cylinder and clamp with the punch mark on the handlebar* **(see illustration 6.5b)**.

b) *Make sure the arrow and the word UP on the master cylinder clamp are pointing up, then tighten the bolts to the torque listed in this Chapter's Specifications* **(see illustration 6.5b)**.

c) *Use new sealing washers at the brake hose banjo fitting. Tighten the banjo fitting bolt to the torque listed in this Chapter's Specifications.*

19   Refer to Section 10 and bleed the air from the system.

7 Rear brake master cylinder - removal, overhaul and installation

1   If the master cylinder is leaking fluid, or if the pedal does not produce a firm feel when the brake is applied, and bleeding the brake does not help, master cylinder overhaul is recommended. Before disassembling the master cylinder, read through the entire procedure and make sure that you have the correct rebuild kit. Also, you will need some new, clean brake fluid of the recommended type, some clean rags and internal snap-ring pliers.

2   **Caution:** *Disassembly, overhaul and reassembly of the brake master cylinder must be done in a spotlessly clean work area to avoid contamination and possible failure of the brake hydraulic system components.*

Removal

Refer to illustrations 7.4a, 7.4b, 7.6a and 7.6b

3   Support the bike securely upright.

4   Remove the cotter pin from the clevis pin on the master cylinder pushrod **(see illustrations)**. Remove the clevis pin.

5   Have a container and some rags ready to catch spilling brake fluid. Using a six-point box wrench, unscrew the banjo fitting bolt from the top of the master cylinder. Discard the sealing washers on either side of the fitting.

6   Remove the two master cylinder mounting bolts and detach the cylinder from the bracket **(see illustration)**. Pull the master cylinder out from behind the bracket, squeeze the fluid feed hose clamp with pliers and slide the clamp up the hose. Disconnect the hose from the fitting and take the master cylinder out. If necessary, remove the reservoir mounting bolt and detach it from the frame **(see illustration)**.

Overhaul

Refer to illustrations 7.7a, 7.7b, 7.8, 7.9, 7.10a, 7.10b and 7.14

7   Using a pair of snap-ring pliers, remove the snap-ring from the fluid inlet fitting and detach the fitting from the master cylinder. Remove the O-ring from the bore **(see illustrations)**.

8   Count the number of exposed threads on the end of the pushrod inside the clevis **(see illustration)**. Write this number down for use on assembly. Hold the clevis with a pair of pliers and loosen the locknut, then unscrew the clevis and locknut from the pushrod.

9   Carefully remove the rubber dust boot from the pushrod **(see illustration)**.

10   Depress the pushrod and, using snap-ring pliers, remove the snap-ring **(see illustration)**. Slide out the piston, the cup seal and

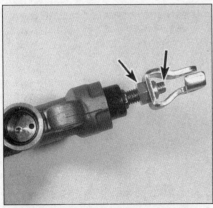

7.8 Write down the number of exposed threads in the clevis (right arrow), then loosen the locknut (left arrow) and unscrew the locknut and clevis from the pushrod

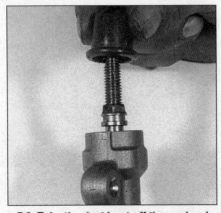

7.9 Take the dust boot off the pushrod

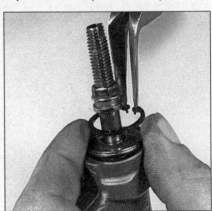

7.10a Remove the snap-ring from the master cylinder bore and withdraw the piston assembly and spring

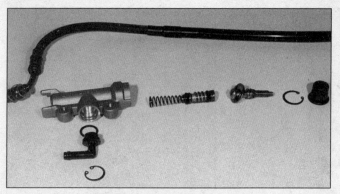

7.10b Rear master cylinder details

spring. Lay the parts out in the proper order to prevent confusion during reassembly **(see illustration)**.

11   Clean all of the parts with brake system cleaner (available at motorcycle dealerships and auto parts stores), isopropyl alcohol or clean brake fluid. **Warning:** *Do not, under any circumstances, use a petroleum-based solvent to clean brake parts. If compressed air is available, use it to dry the parts thoroughly (make sure it's filtered and unlubricated).* Check the master cylinder bore for corrosion, scratches, nicks and score marks. If damage is evident, the master cylinder must be replaced with a new one. If the master cylinder is in poor condition, then the caliper should be checked as well.

12   Honda supplies a new piston in its rebuild kits. If the cup seals are not installed on the new piston, install them, making sure the lips face away from the lever end of the piston **(see illustration 7.10b)**. Use the new piston regardless of the condition of the old one.

13   Before reassembling the master cylinder, soak the piston and the rubber cup seals in clean brake fluid for ten or fifteen minutes. Lubricate the master cylinder bore with clean brake fluid, then carefully insert the parts in the reverse order of disassembly. Make sure the lips on the cup seals do not turn inside out when they are slipped into the bore.

14   Lubricate the end of the pushrod with PBC (poly butyl cuprysil) grease, or silicone grease designed for brake applications, and install the pushrod and stop washer into the cylinder bore. Depress the pushrod, then install the snap-ring (make sure the snap-ring is properly seated in the groove with the sharp edge facing out) **(see illustration)**. Install the rubber dust boot (make sure the lip is seated properly in the groove in the piston stop nut).

15   Install the locknut and clevis to the end of the pushrod, leaving the same number of exposed threads inside the clevis as was written down during removal. Tighten the locknut. This will ensure the brake pedal will be positioned correctly.

16   Install the feed hose fitting, using a new O-ring. Install the snap-ring, making sure it seats properly in its groove.

Installation

17   Install the fluid reservoir if it was removed. Connect the fluid feed hose to the fitting on the master cylinder and secure it with the clamp.

18   Position the master cylinder on the frame and install the bolts, tightening them securely.

19   Connect the banjo fitting to the top of the master cylinder, using new sealing washers on each side of the fitting. Tighten the banjo fitting bolt to the torque listed in this Chapter's Specifications.

20   Connect the clevis to the brake pedal and secure the clevis pin with a new cotter pin.

21   Fill the fluid reservoir with the specified fluid (see Chapter 1) and bleed the system following the procedure in Section 10.

22   Check the position of the brake pedal (see Chapter 1) and adjust it if necessary. Check the operation of the brakes carefully before riding the motorcycle.

8   Brake pedal - removal and installation

1   Support the bike securely upright so it can't be knocked over during this procedure.

XR250L

Refer to illustration 8.2

2   Unhook the pedal return spring from the swingarm **(see illustration)**.

3   If you're working on a drum brake model, refer to Chapter 1 and unscrew the brake adjuster wingnut from the rod. Pull the rod forward and detach it from the brake arm.

4   Remove the pedal pinch bolt **(see illustration 7.4a)**. Detach the pedal from the pivot arm and remove the pivot arm from the frame.

XR250R, XR400R

Refer to illustration 8.5

5   Unhook the pedal return spring from the frame **(see illustration)**.

6   Remove the cotter pin and master cylinder pushrod clevis **(see illustration 7.4b)**. Remove the cotter pin and washer from the brake pedal shaft and slide the brake pedal out of the frame.

7   Inspect the pedal pivot arm or shaft seals. If they're worn, damaged or appear to have been leaking, pry them out and press in new ones.

8   Installation is the reverse of the removal steps, with the following additions:

   a) Lubricate the pedal shaft or pivot arm seal lips and the pivot hole with multi-purpose grease.
   b) If you're working on an XR250L, tighten the pedal pinch bolt to the torque listed in this Chapter's Specifications.
   c) Use new cotter pins.
   d) Refer to Chapter 1 and adjust brake pedal freeplay (drum brake models) and height (all models).

7.14   Make sure the snap-ring is securely seated in its groove

8.2   The XR250L and 1986 through 1995 XR250R brake pedal return spring is hooked to the swingarm (disc brake model shown; drum brake model similar)

8.5   The brake pedal spring on later XR250R and all XR400R models is hooked to the frame

9.4a The front brake hose is secured to the fork leg by a clamp; XR400R models use this plastic reinforcement bracket

9.4b The rear brake hose is secured to the swingarm by clips; use non-permanent thread locking agent on the threads of the clip screws

9 Brake hoses and lines - inspection and replacement

Inspection

1   Once a week, or if the motorcycle is used less frequently, before every ride, check the condition of the brake hoses.
2   Twist and flex the rubber hoses while looking for cracks, bulges and seeping fluid. Check extra carefully around the areas where the hoses connect with the metal fittings, as these are common areas for hose failure.

Replacement

Refer to illustrations 9.4a and 9.4b
3   The high-pressure brake hoses have banjo fittings on each end of the hose. The fluid feed hose that connects the rear master cylinder reservoir to the master cylinder is secured by spring clamps.
4   Cover the surrounding area with plenty of rags and unscrew the banjo bolt on either end of the hose. Detach the hose or line from any clips that may be present and remove the hose **(see illustrations)**.
5   Position the new hose or line, making sure it isn't twisted or otherwise strained. On hoses equipped with banjo fittings, make sure the metal tube portion of the banjo fitting is located against the stop on the component it's connected to, if equipped. Install the banjo bolts, using new sealing washers on both sides of the fittings, and tighten them to the torque listed in this Chapter's Specifications.
6   Flush the old brake fluid from the system, refill the system with the recommended fluid (see Chapter 1) and bleed the air from the system (see Section 10). Check the operation of the brakes carefully before riding the motorcycle.

10 Brake system bleeding

Refer to illustrations 10.5a and 10.5b
1   Bleeding the brakes is simply the process of removing all the air bubbles from the brake fluid reservoir, the lines and the brake caliper. Bleeding is necessary whenever a brake system hydraulic connection is loosened, when a component or hose is replaced, or when the master cylinder or caliper is overhauled. Leaks in the system may also allow air to enter, but leaking brake fluid will reveal their presence and warn you of the need for repair.
2   To bleed the brake, you will need some new, clean brake fluid of the recommended type (see Chapter 1), a length of clear vinyl or plastic tubing, a small container partially filled with clean brake fluid, some rags and a wrench to fit the brake caliper bleeder valve.
3   Cover the fuel tank and other painted components to prevent damage in the event that brake fluid is spilled.
4   Remove the reservoir cover or cap and slowly pump the brake lever or pedal a few times, until no air bubbles can be seen floating up from the holes at the bottom of the reservoir. Doing this bleeds the air from the master cylinder end of the line. Reinstall the reservoir cover or cap.
5   Attach one end of the clear vinyl or plastic tubing to the brake caliper bleeder valve and submerge the other end in the brake fluid in the container **(see illustrations)**. **Note:** *Some models have a bleeder valve at the front master cylinder. In this case, start the bleeding procedure at the master cylinder bleeder valve, then move to the caliper bleeder valve.*
6   Check the fluid level in the reservoir. Do not allow the fluid level to drop below the lower mark during the bleeding process.

10.5a Pull the rubber cap off the bleed valve (front caliper shown) . . .

10.5b . . . and connect a clear plastic hose to the valve (rear caliper shown)

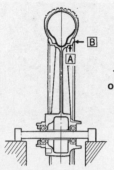

11.2 Check the wheel for out-of-round (A) and lateral movement (B)

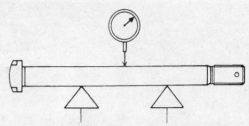

11.5 Check the axle for runout using a dial indicator and V-blocks -divide the total indicator reading by one-half to obtain the actual runout

7   Carefully pump the brake lever or pedal three or four times and hold it while opening the caliper bleeder valve. When the valve is opened, brake fluid will flow out of the caliper into the clear tubing and the lever will move toward the handlebar or the pedal will move down.

8   Retighten the bleeder valve, then release the brake lever or pedal gradually. Repeat the process until no air bubbles are visible in the brake fluid leaving the caliper and the lever or pedal is firm when applied. Remember to add fluid to the reservoir as the level drops. Use only new, clean brake fluid of the recommended type. Never reuse the fluid lost during bleeding.

9   Be sure to check the fluid level in the master cylinder reservoir frequently.

10   Replace the reservoir cover or cap, wipe up any spilled brake fluid and check the entire system for leaks. **Note:** *If bleeding is difficult, it may be necessary to let the brake fluid in the system stabilize for a few hours (it may be aerated). Repeat the bleeding procedure when the tiny bubbles in the system have settled out.*

---

11   Wheels - inspection, removal and installation

Inspection

Refer to illustrations 11.2 and 11.5

1   Clean the wheels thoroughly to remove mud and dirt that may interfere with the inspection procedure or mask defects. Make a general check of the wheels and tires as described in Chapter 1.

2   Support the motorcycle securely upright with the wheel to be checked in the air, then attach a dial indicator to the fork slider or the swingarm and position the stem against the side of the rim **(see illustration)**. Spin the wheel slowly and check the side-to-side (axial) runout of the rim, then compare your readings with the value listed in this Chapter's Specifications. In order to accurately check radial runout

with the dial indicator, the wheel would have to be removed from the machine and the tire removed from the wheel. With the axle clamped in a vise, the wheel can be rotated to check the runout.

3   An easier, though slightly less accurate, method is to attach a stiff wire pointer to the outer fork tube or the swingarm and position the end a fraction of an inch from the wheel (where the wheel and tire join). If the wheel is true, the distance from the pointer to the rim will be constant as the wheel is rotated. Repeat the procedure to check the runout of the rear wheel. **Note:** *If wheel runout is excessive, refer to the appropriate Section in this Chapter and check the wheel bearings very carefully before replacing the wheel.*

4   The wheels should also be visually inspected for cracks, flat spots on the rim and other damage. Individual spokes can be replaced. If other damage is evident, the wheel will have to be replaced with a new one. Never attempt to repair a damaged wheel.

5   Before installing the wheel, check the axle for straightness. If the axle is corroded, first remove the corrosion with fine emery cloth. Set the axle on V-blocks and check it for runout with a dial indicator **(see illustration)**. If the axle exceeds the maximum allowable runout limit listed in this Chapter's Specifications, it must be replaced.

Removal

Front wheel

Refer to illustrations 11.8, 11.9 and 11.10

6   Support the bike from below with a jack beneath the engine. Securely prop the bike upright so it can't fall over when the wheel is removed.

7   Refer to Chapter 4 and disconnect the speedometer cable.

8   If you're working on an XR400R, remove the axle holder from the left fork leg **(see illustration)**.

9   On all models, unscrew the nuts from the axle holder and lift it off the right fork leg **(see illustration)**.

11.8 On XR400R models only, remove the left axle holder nuts; the UP mark must be upright and the arrow must point upward on installation . . .

11.9 . . . all models have an axle holder on the right fork leg

11.10 Unscrew the axle (it threads into the opposite fork leg)

10   Unscrew the axle from the left fork (see illustration). Support the wheel and pull the axle out. Lower the wheel away from the motorcycle, sliding the brake disc out from between the pads.

Rear wheel

Refer to illustrations 11.14a, 11.14b and 11.14c
11   Support the bike from below with a jack beneath the swingarm. Securely prop the bike upright so it can't fall over when the wheel is removed.
12   If you're working on a drum brake model, remove the rear brake adjuster wingnut from the brake rod (see Chapter 1). Pull the rod out of its pivot and remove the pivot from the brake arm.
13   Loosen the rear axle nut and back off the chain adjusters all the way (see Chapter 1). Disengage the drive chain from the rear sprocket.
14   Hold the axle with a wrench and remove the axle nut, washer, chain adjuster and stopper plate (see illustrations).
15   Support the wheel and slide it back until the axle clears the swingarm, then lower the wheel away from the motorcycle. Pull the axle out.

Installation

16   Installation is the reverse of the removal steps, with the following additions:
a)   *If you're installing a front wheel, make sure the speedometer gear protrusion fits into the notch in the fork leg (see illustration 11.2 in Chapter 4). Lubricate the end of the speedometer cable with multi-purpose grease.*

11.14a Remove the axle nut and washer . . .

b)   *If you're installing a rear wheel, make sure the stopper fits over the pin on the swingarm (see illustration 11.14c). On drum brake models, make sure the boss on the swingarm fits into the brake panel notch (see illustration 5.17).*
c   *If you're working on a front wheel, tighten the axle to the torque listed in this Chapter's Specifications, then install the holder with its UP mark upright and tighten the holder nuts to the torque listed in this Chapter's Specifications. Install both holders on XR400R models.*
d)   *If you're working on a rear wheel, tighten the axle nut to the torque listed in this Chapter's Specifications.*
e)   *Refer to Chapter 1 and adjust the rear brake (drum brake models) and drive chain slack.*

12   Wheels - alignment check

1   Misalignment of the wheels, which may be due to a cocked rear wheel or a bent frame or triple clamps, can cause strange and possibly serious handling problems. If the frame or triple clamps are at fault, repair by a frame specialist or replacement with new parts are the only alternatives.
2   To check the alignment you will need an assistant, a length of string or a perfectly straight piece of wood and a ruler graduated in 1/64 inch increments. A plumb bob or other suitable weight will also be required.
3   Support the motorcycle securely upright, then measure the width

11.14b . . . slide off the chain adjuster . . .

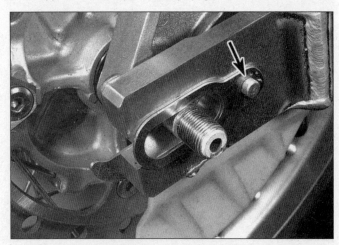

11.14c . . . and slide the stopper plate off the pin (arrow)

13.3 Lift the speedometer drive out of the wheel; on installation, align the drive lugs with the gear notches (arrows)

13.4a Pry the grease seal out of the right side . . .

of both tires at their widest points. Subtract the smaller measurement from the larger measurement, then divide the difference by two. The result is the amount of offset that should exist between the front and rear tires on both sides.

4   If a string is used, have your assistant hold one end of it about half way between the floor and the rear axle, touching the rear sidewall of the tire.

5   Run the other end of the string forward and pull it tight so that it is roughly parallel to the floor. Slowly bring the string into contact with the front sidewall of the rear tire, then turn the front wheel until it is parallel with the string. Measure the distance from the front tire sidewall to the string.

6   Repeat the procedure on the other side of the motorcycle. The distance from the front tire sidewall to the string should be equal on both sides.

7   As was previously pointed out, a perfectly straight length of wood may be substituted for the string. The procedure is the same.

8   If the distance between the string and tire is greater on one side, or if the rear wheel appears to be cocked, refer to Chapter 6, *Swingarm bearings - check*, and make sure the swingarm is tight.

9   If the front-to-back alignment is correct, the wheels still may be out of alignment vertically.

10   Using the plumb bob, or other suitable weight, and a length of string, check the rear wheel to make sure it is vertical. To do this, hold the string against the tire upper sidewall and allow the weight to settle just off the floor. When the string touches both the upper and lower tire sidewalls and is perfectly straight, the wheel is vertical. If it is not, place thin spacers under one leg of the centerstand.

11   Once the rear wheel is vertical, check the front wheel in the same manner. If both wheels are not perfectly vertical, the frame and/or major suspension components are bent.

13   Wheel and rear coupling bearings - inspection and maintenance

Front wheel bearings

Refer to illustrations 13.3, 13.4a, 13.4b, 13.6a and 13.6b

1   Support the bike securely and remove the front wheel (see Section 11).

2   Set the wheel on blocks so as not to allow the weight of the wheel rest on the brake disc.

3   From the right side of the wheel, remove the speedometer drive unit **(see illustration)**.

4   Pry out the grease seal from the right side of the wheel **(see illustration)**. Remove the speedometer gear from beneath the grease seal **(see illustration)**.

5   Turn the wheel over. Remove the cover and pry the grease seal out of the left side.

6   The usual method of removing front wheel bearings is to insert a metal rod (preferably a brass drift punch) through the center of one hub bearing and tap evenly around the inner race of the opposite bearing to drive it from the hub **(see illustration)**. The bearing spacer will also come out. On these motorcycles, it's generally not possible to tilt the rod enough to catch the edge of the opposite bearing's inner race. In

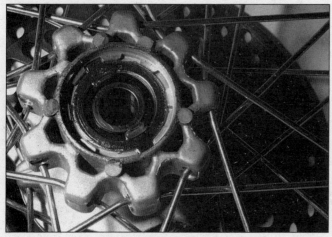

13.4b . . . and remove the speedometer gear

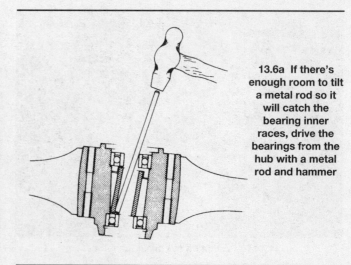

13.6a If there's enough room to tilt a metal rod so it will catch the bearing inner races, drive the bearings from the hub with a metal rod and hammer

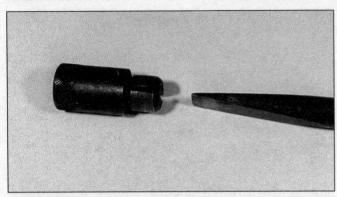

13.6b If you can't position a metal rod against the bearings, this tool can be used instead - place the split portion inside the bearing and pass the wedge through the hub into the split; tapping on the end of the rod will spread the split portion, locking it to the bearing, so the split portion and bearing can be driven out together

13.16 On XR250L models, remove the collar from the outer side of the sprocket hub . . .

this case, use a bearing remover tool consisting of a shaft and remover head **(see illustration)**. The head fits inside the bearing, then the wedge end of the shaft is tapped into the groove in the head to expand the head and lock it inside the bearing. Tapping on the shaft from this point will force the bearing out of the hub.

7   Lay the wheel on its other side and remove the remaining bearing using the same technique. **Note:** *The bearings must be replaced with new ones whenever they're removed, as they're almost certain to be damaged during removal.*

8   If you're installing bearings that aren't sealed on both sides, pack the new bearings with grease from the open side. Rotate the bearing to work the grease in between the bearing balls.

9   Thoroughly clean the hub area of the wheel. Install the bearing into the recess in the right side of the hub, with the sealed side facing out. Using a bearing driver or a socket large enough to contact the outer race of the bearing, drive it in until it seats.

10   Turn the wheel over and install the bearing spacer and bearing, driving the bearing into place as described in Step 9.

11   Coat the lip of a new grease seal with grease.

12   Install the grease seal on the right side of the wheel; it should go in with thumb pressure but if not, use a seal driver, large socket or a flat piece of wood to drive it into place.

13   Clean off all grease from the brake disc using acetone or brake system cleaner. Install the wheel.

Rear coupling bearing (XR250L)

Refer to illustrations 13.16 and 13.17

14   Refer to Section 11 and remove the rear wheel. Lay the wheel on

its brake side. If the bike has a rear disc brake, support the wheel on blocks so its weight doesn't rest on the brake disc.

15   Lift the final driven flange (sprocket hub) out of the rear wheel (see Chapter 5).

16   Pull out the collar and pry the grease seal from the sprocket side of the coupling **(see illustration)**.

17   Remove the coupling collar from the other side of the coupling **(see illustration)**.

18   Drive the bearing out of the coupling with a bearing driver or drift punch.

19   Clean the bearing with a high flash-point solvent (one which won't leave any residue) and blow it dry with compressed air (don't let the bearing spin as you dry it).

20   Apply a few drops of oil to the bearing. Hold the outer race of the bearing and rotate the inner race - if the bearing doesn't turn smoothly, has rough spots or is noisy, replace it with a new one.

21   If the bearing checks out okay and will be reused, wash it in solvent once again and dry it, then pack the bearing from the open side with high-quality bearing grease.

22   Drive the bearing into the coupling with a bearing driver or socket that bears against the outer race of the bearing.

23   Coat the lip of a new grease seal with grease and install it. It may go in with thumb pressure, but if not, tap it in with a hammer and socket, bearing driver or flat piece of wood.

Rear wheel bearings

Refer to illustrations 13.24, 13.26 and 13.27

24   The left rear wheel bearing on 1986 through 1995 XR250R models

13.17 . . . and the coupling spacer from the inner side

13.24 The bearing retainer is staked in place (arrow); this makes it impractical to remove it with makeshift tools

13.26 Remove the collar from the disc side of the wheel

13.27 Turn the wheel over and remove the collar from the sprocket side

13.28a These tools are used to remove the bearing retainer; pass the shaft through the hub and fit the pins on the disc into the holes in the bearing retainer

13.28b Thread the nut portion of the tool onto the shaft and tighten it to lock the pins on the disc securely into the holes in the bearing retainer

13.28c Turn the shaft with a socket or wrench to unscrew the retainer from the hub

is held in place by a threaded retainer that is staked in position **(see illustration)**. Removal requires special tools for which there are no good substitutes. Before you try to replace the bearings, read through the procedure. It may be more practical to take the wheel to a Honda dealer and have the bearings replaced. The threaded retainer is not used on 1996 and later XR250R models or any XR400R models.

25   Refer to Section 11 and remove the rear wheel.

26   If you're working on a 1990 or later model, remove the collar from the grease seal on the right side of the wheel, then pry the grease seal out **(see illustration)**.

27   On the other side of the wheel, remove the collar from the bearing retainer and grease seal **(see illustration)**. You may need to pry it out with a pair of screwdrivers. If it's really stuck, use a bearing remover tool **(see illustration 13.6b)**.

1986 through 1995 XR250R

Refer to illustrations 13.28a, 13.28b and 13.28c

28   Insert the shaft of the retainer wrench into the hub from the retainer side. Engage the pins of the wrench with the holes in the retainer, then thread the retainer wingnut onto the shaft **(see illustrations)**. Turn the retainer wrench with a socket to unscrew the retainer **(see illustration)**.

13.30 Drive in the bearing on the sprocket side, using a bearing driver that contacts the outer race (the sealed side of the bearing faces out)

13.31 Insert the spacer into the hub; on 1986 through 1995 XR250R models, make sure its LH mark is toward the left side of the hub

All models

Refer to illustrations 13.30, 13.31 and 13.32

29   Remove the bearings with the special tools used for front wheel bearings (see Step 6).

30   Thoroughly clean the hub area of the wheel. Install the left bearing into the recess in the hub, with the sealed side facing out. Using a bearing driver or a socket large enough to contact the outer race of the bearing, drive it in until it seats **(see illustration)**.

31   Turn the wheel over. Apply a coat of multi-purpose grease to the inside of the spacer and install it in the hub **(see illustration)**. If you're working on a 1986 through 1995 XR250R, be sure the LH mark on the spacer is toward the left side of the wheel.

32   Pack the remaining bearing from the open side with grease, then install it in the hub, driving the bearing in with a socket or bearing driver large enough to contact the outer race of the bearing **(see illustration)**. Drive the bearing in until it seats.

1986 through 1995 XR250R models

33   Pry the grease seal out of the bearing retainer. Place a new one on the retainer, positioned so its lip will face into the hub when the retainer is installed. Tap the seal in, using a bearing driver or socket the same diameter as the seal.

34   Thread the retainer partway into the hub, then install it with the same tools used for removal **(see illustrations 13.28a, 13.28b and 13.28c)**.

All models

35   Install a new grease seal in the right side of the hub **(see illustration 13.26)**. It may go in with thumb pressure, but if not, use a seal driver, large socket or a flat piece of wood to drive it into place.

36   If you're working on a 1991 or later model, install the collar in the right side of the hub. On all models, install the grease seal and collar in the left side of the hub.

37   If you're working on an XR250L, press a little grease into the bearing in the rear wheel coupling. Install the coupling to the wheel, making sure the coupling spacer is located in the inside of the inner race (between the wheel and the coupling). **Caution:** *If the coupling spacer is left out, the wheel bearings will be ruined when the axle is tightened.*

38   Clean off all grease from the brake disc using acetone or brake system cleaner. Install the wheel.

14   Tires - removal and installation

1   To properly remove and install tires, you will need at least two motorcycle tire irons, some water and a tire pressure gauge.

13.32 Drive in the bearing on the brake disc side, using a driver that contacts the outer race

2   Begin by removing the wheel from the motorcycle. If the tire is going to be re-used, mark it next to the valve stem, wheel balance weight or rim lock.

3   Deflate the tire by removing the valve stem core. When it is fully deflated, push the bead of the tire away from the rim on both sides. In some extreme cases, this can only be accomplished with a bead breaking tool, but most often it can be carried out with tire irons. Riding on a deflated tire to break the bead is not recommended, as damage to the rim and tire will occur.

4   Dismounting a tire is easier when the tire is warm, so an indoor tire change is recommended in cold climates. The rubber gets very stiff and is difficult to manipulate when cold.

5   Place the wheel on a thick pad or old blanket. This will help keep the wheel and tire from slipping around.

6   Once the bead is completely free of the rim, lubricate the inside edge of the rim and the tire bead with water only. Honda recommends against the use of soap or other tire mounting lubricants, as the tire may shift on the rim. Remove the locknut and push the tire valve through the hole.

7   Insert one of the tire irons under the bead of the tire at the valve stem and lift the bead up over the rim. This should be fairly easy. Take care not to pinch the tube as this is done. If it is difficult to pry the bead up, make sure that the rest of the bead opposite the valve stem is in

the dropped center section of the rim.

8   Hold the tire iron down with the bead over the rim, then move about 1 or 2 inches to either side and insert the second tire iron. Be careful not to cut or slice the bead or the tire may split when inflated. Also, take care not to catch or pinch the inner tube as the second tire iron is levered over. For this reason, tire irons are recommended over screwdrivers or other implements.

9   With a small section of the bead up over the rim, one of the levers can be removed and reinserted 1 or 2 inches farther around the rim until about 1/4 of the tire bead is above the rim edge. Make sure that the rest of the bead is in the dropped center of the rim. At this point, the bead can usually be pulled up over the rim by hand.

10   Once all of the first bead is over the rim, the inner tube can be withdrawn from the tire and rim. Push in on the valve stem, lift up on the tire next to the stem, reach inside the tire and carefully pull out the tube. It is usually not necessary to completely remove the tire from the rim to repair the inner tube. It is sometimes recommended though, because checking for foreign objects in the tire is difficult while it is still mounted on the rim.

11   To remove the tire completely, make sure the bead is broken all the way around on the remaining edge, then stand the tire and wheel up on the tread and grab the wheel with one hand. Push the tire down over the same edge of the rim while pulling the rim away from the tire. If the bead is correctly positioned in the dropped center of the rim, the tire should roll off and separate from the rim very easily. If tire irons are used to work this last bead over the rim, the outer edge of the rim may be marred. If a tire iron is necessary, be sure to pad the rim as described earlier.

12   Refer to Section 15 for inner tube repair procedures.

13   Mounting a tire is basically the reverse of removal. Some tires have a balance mark and/or directional arrows molded into the tire sidewall. Look for these marks so that the tire can be installed properly. The dot should be aligned with the valve stem.

14   If the tire was not removed completely to repair or replace the inner tube, the tube should be inflated just enough to make it round. Sprinkle it with talcum powder, which acts as a dry lubricant, then carefully lift up the tire edge and install the tube with the valve stem next to the hole in the rim. Once the tube is in place, push the valve stem through the rim and start the locknut on the stem.

15   Lubricate the tire bead, then push it over the rim edge and into the dropped center section opposite the inner tube valve stem. Work around each side of the rim, carefully pushing the bead over the rim. The last section may have to be levered on with tire irons. If so, take care not to pinch the inner tube as this is done.

16   Once the bead is over the rim edge, check to see that the inner tube valve stem and the rim lock are pointing to the center of the hub. If they're angled slightly in either direction, rotate the tire on the rim to straighten it out. Run the locknut the rest of the way onto the stem and rim lock but don't tighten them completely.

17   Inflate the tube to approximately 1-1/2 times the pressure listed in the Chapter 1 Specifications and check to make sure the guidelines on the tire sidewalls are the same distance from the rim around the circumference of the tire. **Warning:** *Do not over inflate the tube or the tire may burst, causing serious injury.*

18   After the tire bead is correctly seated on the rim, allow the tire to deflate. Replace the valve core and inflate the tube to the recommended pressure, then tighten the valve stem locknut securely and tighten the cap. Tighten the locknut on the rim lock to the torque listed in the Chapter 1 Specifications.

15 Tubes - repair

1   Tire tube repair requires a patching kit that's usually available from motorcycle dealers, accessory stores or auto parts stores. Be sure to follow the directions supplied with the kit to ensure a safe repair. Patching should be done only when a new tube is unavailable. Replace the tube as soon as possible. Sudden deflation can cause loss of control and an accident.

2   To repair a tube, remove it from the tire, inflate and immerse it in a sink or tub full of water to pinpoint the leak. Mark the position of the leak, then deflate the tube. Dry it off and thoroughly clean the area around the puncture.

3   Most tire patching kits have a buffer to rough up the area around the hole for proper adhesion of the patch. Roughen an area slightly larger than the patch, then apply a thin coat of the patching cement to the roughened area. Allow the cement to dry until tacky, then apply the patch.

4   It may be necessary to remove a protective covering from the top surface of the patch after it has been attached to the tube. Keep in mind that tubes made from synthetic rubber may require a special patch and adhesive if a satisfactory bond is to be achieved.

5   Before replacing the tube, check the inside of the tire to make sure the object that caused the puncture is not still inside. Also check the outside of the tire, particularly the tread area, to make sure nothing is projecting through the tire that may cause another puncture. Check the rim for sharp edges or damage. Make sure the rubber trim band is in good condition and properly installed before inserting the tube.

TIRE CHANGING SEQUENCE - TUBED TIRES

1 Deflate tire. After pushing tire beads away from rim flanges push tire bead into well of rim at point opposite valve. Insert tire lever adjacent to valve and work bead over edge of rim.

2 Use two levers to work bead over edge of rim. Note use of rim protectors.

3 Remove inner tube from tire.

4 When first bead is clear, remove tire as shown.

5 When fitting, partially inflate inner tube and insert in tire.

6 Work first bead over rim and feed valve through hole in rim. Partially screw on retaining nut to hold valve in place.

7 Check that inner tube is positioned correctly and work second bead over rim using tire levers. Start at a point opposite valve.

8 Work final area of bead over rim while pushing valve inwards to ensure that inner tube is not trapped.

Notes

Chapter 7
Frame and bodywork

Contents

Specifications

Torque specifications

Rider's right-side footpeg bracket
XR250L, 1986 through 1995 XR250R
Rear bolt .... 90 Nm (65 ft-lbs)*
Front bolt .... 55 Nm (40 ft-lbs)*
1996 and later XR250R, XR400R .... 43 Nm (31 ft-lbs)
Skid plate (XR250L, 1986 through 1995 XR250R)
Front through-bolt and nut .... 27 Nm (20 ft-lbs)
Rear bolts .... Not specified
Skid bars (1996 and later XR250R, XR400R) .... Not specified
Sub-frame
Upper bolt and nut .... 26 Nm (20 ft-lbs)
Lower bolts .... 42 Nm (31 ft-lbs)

2.2 On XR250L models, remove the seat strap nut on each side and pull the strap off the studs . . .

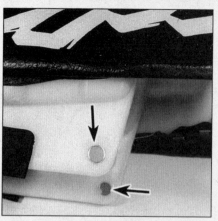

2.3 . . . remove the bolt from the hole on each side of the seat . . .

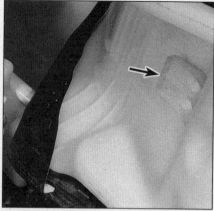

2.4 . . . and detach the tab under the front of the seat from the hook on the frame

1   General information

This Chapter covers the procedures necessary to remove and install the fenders and other body parts. Since many service and repair operations on these motorcycles require removal of the fenders and/or other body parts, the procedures are grouped here and referred to from other Chapters.

In the case of damage to plastic body parts, it is usually necessary to remove the broken component and replace it with a new (or used) one. The material that the fenders and other plastic body parts are composed of doesn't lend itself to conventional repair techniques. There are, however, some shops that specialize in "plastic welding", so it would be advantageous to check around before throwing the damaged part away. **Note:** *When attempting to remove any body panel, first study the panel closely, noting any fasteners and associated fittings, to be sure of returning everything to its correct place on installation. In some cases, the aid of an assistant will be required when removing panels, to help avoid damaging the paint. Once the visible fasteners have been removed, try to lift off the panel as described but DO NOT FORCE the panel - if it will not release, check that all fasteners have been removed and try again. Where a panel engages another by means of lugs and grommets, be careful not to break the lugs or damage the bodywork. Remember that a few moments of patience at this stage will save you a lot of money in replacing broken panels!*

2   Seat - removal and installation

XR250L

Refer to illustrations 2.2, 2.3 and 2.4

1   Remove the side covers (see Section 5).
2   Remove the nut and detach the strap from each side of the seat **(see illustration)**.
3   Remove the mounting bolt on each side of the seat **(see illustration)**.
4   Lift the back end of the seat. Pull it back and down to disengage the front end from the hook on the fuel tank and lift it off **(see illustration)**.
5   Installation is the reverse of removal.

XR250R, XR400R

Refer to illustrations 2.6 and 2.7

6   Remove the mounting bolt on each side of the seat **(see illustration)**.
7   Lift the back end of the seat. Pull it back and down to disengage the front tab from the button on the fuel tank and the side tabs from the hooks on the frame **(see illustration)**. Lift the seat off.
8   Installation is the reverse of removal.

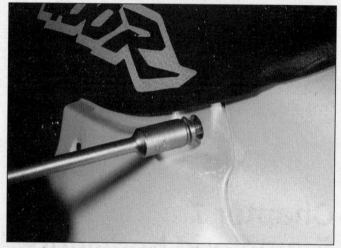

2.6 On all except XR250L models, remove the bolt from each side of the seat . . .

3   Footpegs - removal and installation

Refer to illustrations 3.2 and 3.4
1   Support the bike securely so it can't be knocked over during this procedure.

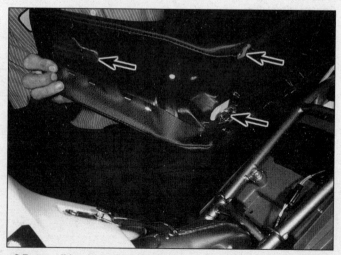

2.7 . . . pull back the seat to disengage the wire loop (left arrow) and the two tabs (right arrows)

3.2 Remove the cotter pin (arrow), washer and pivot pin to detach the footpeg from the bracket

3.4 On XR250L models, the passenger footpeg brackets are bolted to the frame

4.1 Unhook the sidestand spring from the posts on the sidestand and frame, then remove the mounting bolt and locknut

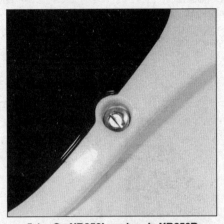

5.1a On XR250L and early XR250R models, remove the left side cover mounting bolt . . .

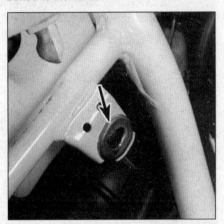

5.1b . . . and carefully pull the lugs free of the grommets (arrow)

2   To detach the footpeg from the bracket, remove the cotter pin, washer and footpeg pivot pin **(see illustration)**. Separate the footpeg from the motorcycle.

3   On the right side only, the rider's footpeg bracket can be detached from the motorcycle if necessary. Remove the bolts, then detach the bracket from the frame.

4   To remove the passenger footpeg brackets on XR250L models, unbolt them from the frame **(see illustration)**.

5   Installation is the reverse of removal, with the following additions:

a) *Tighten the bracket fasteners securely if they were removed.*

b) *Use a new cotter pin and wrap its ends around the pivot pin.*

4   Sidestand - removal and installation

Refer to illustration 4.1

1   Unhook the sidestand spring from its posts **(see illustration)**.

2   Remove the self-locking nut and pivot bolt and separate the sidestand from the motorcycle.

3   Installation is the reverse of the removal steps.

5   Side covers - removal and installation

XR250L, 1986 through 1995 XR250R

Refer to illustrations 5.1a, 5.1b and 5.2

1   On the right side, remove the side cover bolt **(see illustration)**. Pull the cover free of the grommets and take it off the motorcycle **(see illustration)**.

2   On the left side, twist the three quick-release fasteners to disengage them, then lift the cover off **(see illustration)**.

3   Installation is the reverse of removal. Tighten the bolt or fasteners securely, but don't overtighten them.

5.2 On the right side of XR250L and early XR250R models, twist the quick-release fasteners to detach the side cover

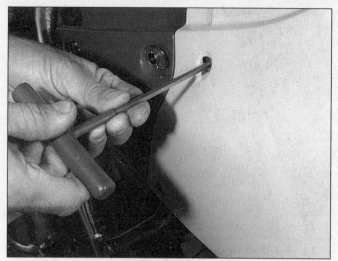

5.5a   On later XR250R and all XR400R models, unscrew the two Allen bolts . . .

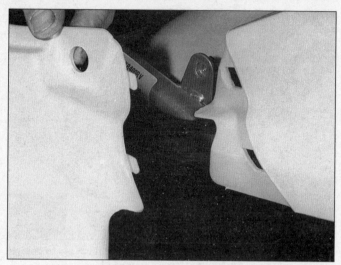

5.5b   . . . and detach the tabs to remove the side covers

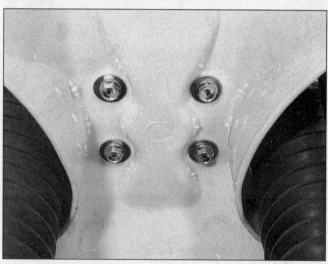

6.1a   The front fender bolts are accessible from below

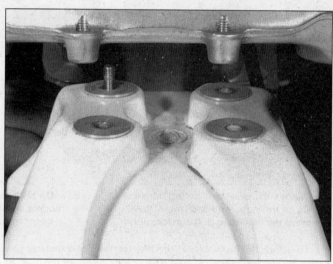

6.1b   Don't forget the washers on top of the fender

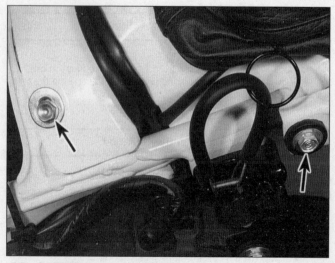

7.2a   On XR250L and early XR250R models, remove two bolts on each side (arrows) to detach the rear fender

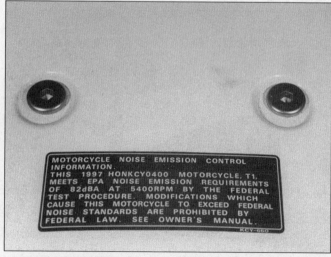

7.2b   On later XR250R and all XR400R models, remove two Allen bolts from the top of the fender . . .

7.2c . . . and one bolt on each side at the front of the fender . . .

7.2d . . . then lift the fender off and remove the mounting collars

1996 and later XR250R, all XR400R

Refer to illustrations 5.5a and 5.5b

4   Remove the seat (see Section 2).
5   Remove the side cover Allen bolts, then unhook the tabs to detach the side cover from the motorcycle **(see illustrations)**.
6   Installation is the reverse of removal. Tighten the bolts securely, but don't overtighten them.

6   Front fender - removal and installation

Refer to illustrations 6.1a and 6.1b

1   Remove the fender bolts **(see illustration)**. Lower the fender clear of the lower triple clamp and remove the washers **(see illustration)**.
2   Installation is the reverse of removal. Be sure to reinstall the grommets in their correct locations. Tighten the bolts securely, but don't overtighten them and strip the threads.

7   Rear fender - removal and installation

Refer to illustrations 7.2a, 7.2b, 7.2c, 7.2d and 7.3

1   Remove the seat and both side covers (see Sections 2 and 5).
2   Remove the fender mounting bolts (and grommets if equipped) and take the fender off **(see illustrations)**.

3   If necessary, unbolt the inner fender and lift it off **(see illustration)**.
4   Installation is the reverse of removal. Tighten the bolts securely, but don't overtighten them and strip the threads.

8   Skid plate/bars - removal and installation

Refer to illustration 8.3

1   Support the bike securely so it can't be knocked over during this procedure.
2   If you're working on an XR250L or a 1986 through 1995 XR250R, remove one nut at the front of the skid plate and two bolts from underneath, then lower the skid plate away from the motorcycle.
3   If you're working on a 1996 or later XR250R or an XR400R, remove the bolts at the front and rear of the bars **(see illustration)**. Lower the bars away from the motorcycle.
4   Installation is the reverse of removal. Tighten the bolts securely, but don't overtighten them and strip the threads.

9   Sub-frame (1996 and later XR250R, all XR400R) - removal and installation

Refer to illustration 9.5

1   Before you start, obtain a tie wrap to replace the one on the frame. You'll need to cut the old one to remove it.

7.3 Remove two bolts to detach the inner fender

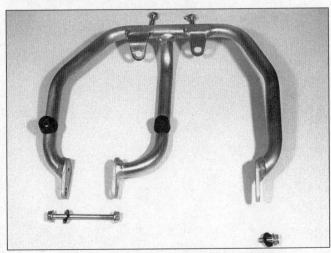

8.3 Skid bar details (later XR250R, all XR400R)

2   Remove the seat (see Section 2) and the muffler (see Chapter 3).
3   Cut the tie wrap on the upper left sub-frame member to release the breather and carburetor vent tubes and the tail light wiring harness. Disconnect the tail light wiring connector.
4   Loosen the clamping band that secures the carburetor to the air cleaner housing (see Chapter 3).
5   Unbolt the sub-frame from the main frame and lift it off, together with the air box and rear fender **(see illustration)**.
6   Installation is the reverse of the removal steps. Tighten the sub-frame bolts to the torques listed in this Chapter's Specifications.

10 Frame - general information, inspection and repair

1   All models use a semi-double cradle frame made of round-section steel tubing. A detachable sub-frame is used on 1996 and later XR250R models, as well as all XR400R models (see Section 9).
2   The frame shouldn't require attention unless accident damage has occurred. In most cases, frame replacement is the only satisfactory remedy for such damage. A few frame specialists have the jigs and other equipment necessary for straightening the frame to the required standard of accuracy, but even then there is no simple way of assessing to what extent the frame may have been overstressed.
3   After the motorcycle has accumulated a lot of miles, the frame should be examined closely for signs of cracking or splitting at the welded joints. Corrosion can also cause weakness at these joints. Loose engine mount bolts can cause ovaling or fracturing to the mounting bolt holes. Minor damage can often be repaired by welding,

9.5 The sub-frame on later XR250R and all XR400R models is secured by a lower bolt on each side of the bike and an upper through-bolt (arrows)

depending on the nature and extent of the damage.
4   Remember that a frame that is out of alignment will cause handling problems. If misalignment is suspected as the result of an accident, it will be necessary to strip the machine completely so the frame can be thoroughly checked.

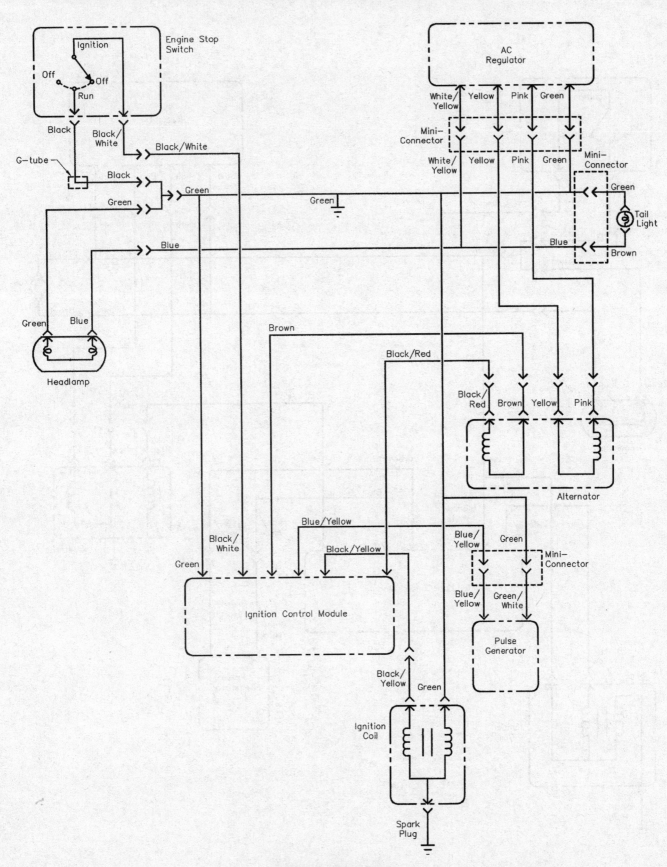

XR400R wiring diagram

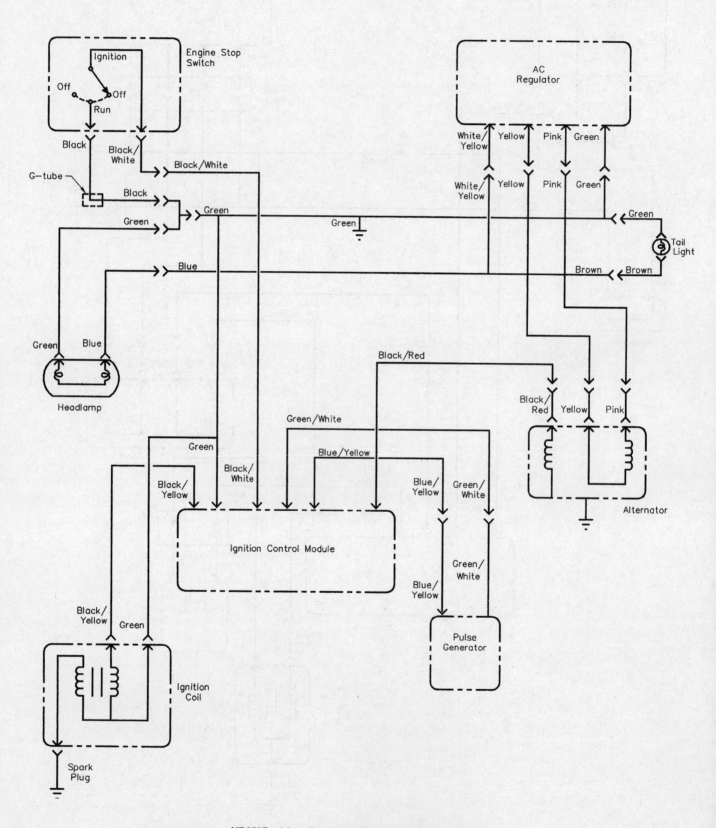

XR250R wiring diagram (1986 through 1995 models)

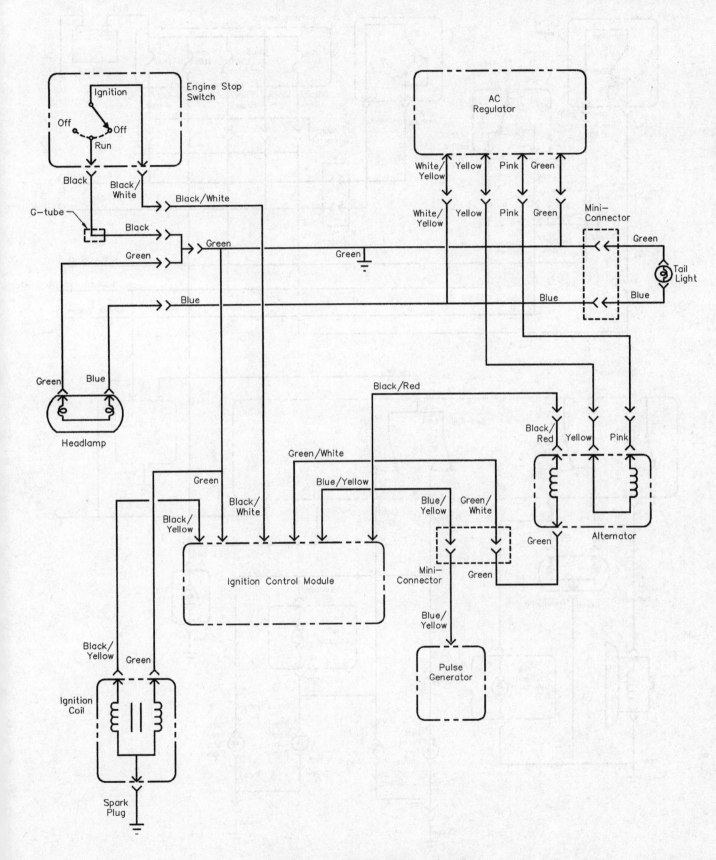

XR250R wiring diagram (1996-on models)

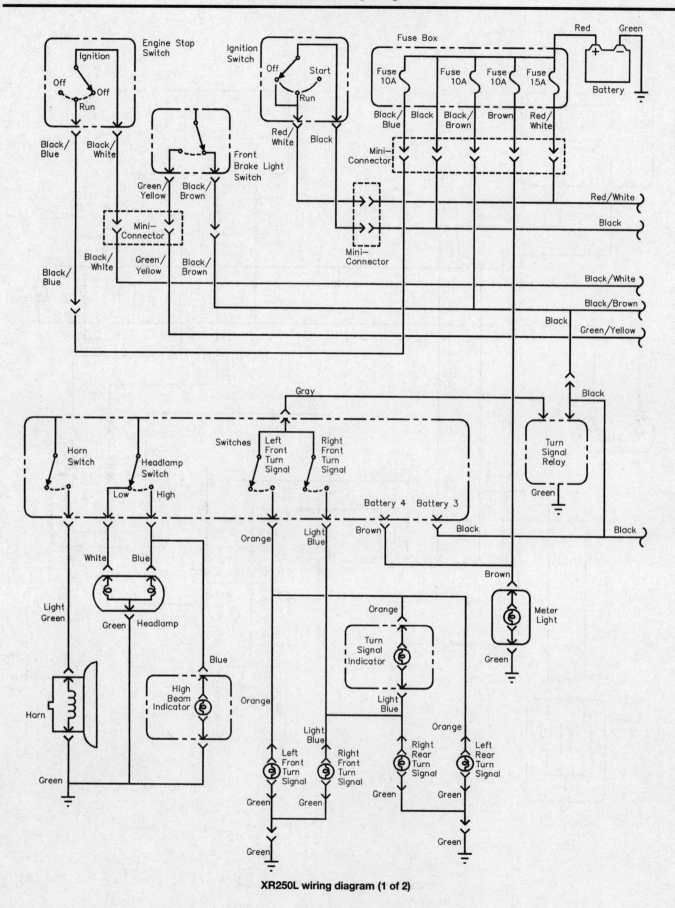

XR250L wiring diagram (1 of 2)

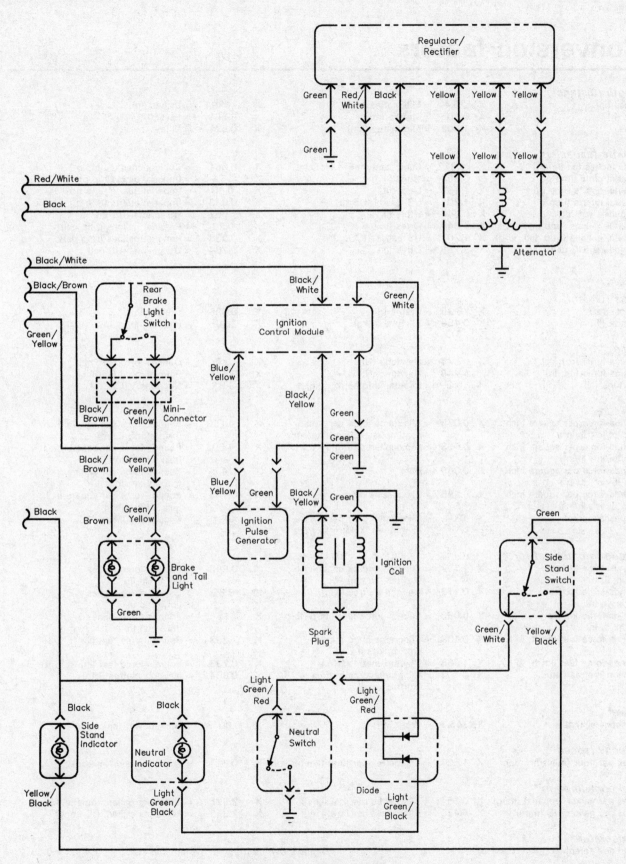

XR250L wiring diagram (2 of 2)

Conversion factors

Length (distance)

Inches (in)	X	25.4	= Millimetres (mm)	X 0.0394	= Inches (in)
Feet (ft)	X	0.305	= Metres (m)	X 3.281	= Feet (ft)
Miles	X	1.609	= Kilometres (km)	X 0.621	= Miles

Volume (capacity)

Cubic inches (cu in; in^3)	X	16.387	= Cubic centimetres (cc; cm^3)	X 0.061	= Cubic inches (cu in; in^3)
Imperial pints (Imp pt)	X	0.568	= Litres (l)	X 1.76	= Imperial pints (Imp pt)
Imperial quarts (Imp qt)	X	1.137	= Litres (l)	X 0.88	= Imperial quarts (Imp qt)
Imperial quarts (Imp qt)	X	1.201	= US quarts (US qt)	X 0.833	= Imperial quarts (Imp qt)
US quarts (US qt)	X	0.946	= Litres (l)	X 1.057	= US quarts (US qt)
Imperial gallons (Imp gal)	X	4.546	= Litres (l)	X 0.22	= Imperial gallons (Imp gal)
Imperial gallons (Imp gal)	X	1.201	= US gallons (US gal)	X 0.833	= Imperial gallons (Imp gal)
US gallons (US gal)	X	3.785	= Litres (l)	X 0.264	= US gallons (US gal)

Mass (weight)

Ounces (oz)	X	28.35	= Grams (g)	X 0.035	Ounces (oz)
Pounds (lb)	X	0.454	= Kilograms (kg)	X 2.205	= Pounds (lb)

Force

Ounces-force (ozf; oz)	X	0.278	= Newtons (N)	X 3.6	= Ounces-force (ozf; oz)
Pounds-force (lbf; lb)	X	4.448	= Newtons (N)	X 0.225	= Pounds-force (lbf; lb)
Newtons (N)	X	0.1	= Kilograms-force (kgf; kg)	X 9.81	= Newtons (N)

Pressure

Pounds-force per square inch (psi; lbf/in^2; lb/in^2)	X	0.070	= Kilograms-force per square centimetre (kgf/cm^2; kg/cm^2)	X 14.223	= Pounds-force per square inch (psi; lbf/in^2; lb/in^2)
Pounds-force per square inch (psi; lbf/in^2; lb/in^2)	X	0.068	= Atmospheres (atm)	X 14.696	= Pounds-force per square inch (psi; lbf/in^2; lb/in^2)
Pounds-force per square inch (psi; lbf/in^2; lb/in^2)	X	0.069	= Bars	X 14.5	= Pounds-force per square inch (psi; lbf/in^2; lb/in^2)
Pounds-force per square inch (psi; lbf/in^2; lb/in^2)	X	6.895	= Kilopascals (kPa)	X 0.145	= Pounds-force per square inch (psi; lbf/in^2; lb/in^2)
Kilopascals (kPa)	X	0.01	= Kilograms-force per square centimetre (kgf/cm^2; kg/cm^2)	X 98.1	= Kilopascals (kPa)

Torque (moment of force)

Pounds-force inches (lbf in; lb in)	X	1.152	= Kilograms-force centimetre (kgf cm; kg cm)	X 0.868	= Pounds-force inches (lbf in; lb in)
Pounds-force inches (lbf in; lb in)	X	0.113	= Newton metres (Nm)	X 8.85	= Pounds-force inches (lbf in; lb in)
Pounds-force inches (lbf in; lb in)	X	0.083	= Pounds-force feet (lbf ft; lb ft)	X 12	= Pounds-force inches (lbf in; lb in)
Pounds-force feet (lbf ft; lb ft)	X	0.138	= Kilograms-force metres (kgf m; kg m)	X 7.233	= Pounds-force feet (lbf ft; lb ft)
Pounds-force feet (lbf ft; lb ft)	X	1.356	= Newton metres (Nm)	X 0.738	= Pounds-force feet (lbf ft; lb ft)
Newton metres (Nm)	X	0.102	= Kilograms-force metres (kgf m; kg m)	X 9.804	= Newton metres (Nm)

Power

Horsepower (hp)	X	745.7	= Watts (W)	X 0.0013	= Horsepower (hp)

Velocity (speed)

Miles per hour (miles/hr; mph)	X	1.609	= Kilometres per hour (km/hr; kph)	X 0.621	= Miles per hour (miles/hr; mph)

Fuel consumption*

Miles per gallon, Imperial (mpg)	X	0.354	= Kilometres per litre (km/l)	X 2.825	= Miles per gallon, Imperial (mpg)
Miles per gallon, US (mpg)	X	0.425	= Kilometres per litre (km/l)	X 2.352	= Miles per gallon, US (mpg)

Temperature

Degrees Fahrenheit = (°C x 1.8) + 32   Degrees Celsius (Degrees Centigrade; °C) = (°F - 32) x 0.56

It is common practice to convert from miles per gallon (mpg) to litres/100 kilometres (l/100km), where mpg (Imperial) x l/100 km = 282 and mpg (US) x l/100 km = 235

Index

Notes